Landmark

Intermediate Teacher's Book

Simon Haines & Barbara Stewart

OXFORD

UNIVERSITY PRESS

OXFORD
UNIVERSITY PRESS

Great Clarendon Street, Oxford OX2 6DP

Oxford University Press is a department of the University
of Oxford.

It furthers the University's objective of excellence in
research, scholarship, and education by publishing
worldwide in

Oxford New York

Athens Auckland Bangkok Bogotá Buenos Aires Calcutta
Cape Town Chennai Dar es Salaam Delhi Florence
Hong Kong Istanbul Karachi Kuala Lumpur Madrid
Melbourne Mexico City Mumbai Nairobi Paris
São Paulo Singapore Taipei Tokyo Toronto Warsaw

with associated companies in Berlin Ibadan

Oxford and Oxford English are registered trade marks
of Oxford University Press in the UK and in certain
other countries

ISBN 0 19 433081 8

Printed in Hong Kong

Acknowledgements

Tests and photocopiable materials by Jane Hudson

Illustrations by: Roger Fereday: pp.151, 155, 156, 157, 164;
Steve Roberts p.173; David Semple p.159

Contents

Introduction

Landmark is a two-level general English course which recognizes that learners at intermediate levels already have a strong background in the language. The course builds on their existing knowledge and at the same time systematically helps them to develop their understanding and range of language abilities.

What's in the book?

There are twelve 10-page units each with seven clear lesson sequences. There are thematic and language links between the lessons, but they can be taught separately.

The seven sequences are:
- **Preview (Grammar Review)** An introduction to the unit theme and revision of an area of grammar.
- **Reading or Listening (Grammar 2)** Skills development followed by the exploration and exploitation of a further area of grammar related to the Review grammar.
- **Skills** Integrated development of reading, listening and speaking skills.
- **Grammar extra** Exploration and exploitation of an area of non-verb grammar.
- **Exploring words** A focus on topic vocabulary.
- **Writing** Development of writing skills with focus on styles.
- **Language in action** Listening and focus on functional language followed by oral practice, incorporating pronunciation.

Approach to Grammar

We recognize that much grammar at this level is not new to students, so the course clearly distinguishes between review grammar and the exploration and practice of what is new or less familiar. Grammar is contextualized in reading or listening texts, so its presentation is integrated with the development of these skills. In the non-verb grammar sections, there are varied styles of presentation. The course takes a guided discovery approach, based on concept checking tasks and making use of learners' existing knowledge.

The **Language commentary**, a separate grammar reference section, complements the guided discovery approach by allowing students to check their answers and consolidate their understanding.

Vocabulary

Vocabulary development features prominently in *Landmark*. Each unit has a lesson which deals with topic vocabulary related to the unit theme. In addition many reading and listening texts are followed by vocabulary tasks.

Approach to Skills

There is a systematic development of the four skills. An important feature of receptive skills work is that students are expected to be able to interpret the underlying meaning and implications of what they hear or read.

Speaking
Landmark provides frequent speaking activities throughout the unit to discuss topics, to practise grammar points and functional language, and to express personal opinions. There are also speaking tasks where students work together in groups then present their ideas to the rest of the class.

Listening
Listening material ranges from authentic to semi-scripted or scripted. Authentic recordings are usually short vox pops which give students the opportunity to hear real language at natural speed. Pre-, while- and post-listening tasks help students to develop their listening skills.

Reading
The reading material in this book is adapted from authentic sources and is suitable for adult learners. Pre-, while- and post-reading tasks help students get the most out of texts.

Writing
The course adopts a process-oriented approach to writing. Each unit devotes a full lesson to the development of writing skills, at the same time providing plenty of opportunity for discussion. Practice is given in writing in different styles, ranging from e-mails and faxes to reviews and short stories. There are some model text extracts on the page and also model texts in the **Writing models** in the Teacher's Book.

Approach to functional language

Landmark recognizes the importance of the appropriate use of language for interactive purposes and focuses on correct form, register and pronunciation. The approach takes into account the fact that some exponents are not new to students at this level.

Pronunciation

The main pronunciation section focuses on global aspects of pronunciation and is integrated with the practice of functional language. It is a separate section at the back of the book so that it can be used during the practice phase of the lesson or dealt with separately if teachers prefer.

Themes

Each unit of *Landmark* is based on a general theme: the different sections develop aspects of this theme. In Unit 8 for example, the overall theme is *Making contact*. The Preview topic is modern communications; Listening features someone talking about being shy; in Skills the topic is being bilingual.

These thematic links allow for the building of topic vocabulary and involve students in the subject matter. Where appropriate, topics are personalized; by contributing their knowledge, experience and opinions, students are actively involved in the learning process.

How to use the book

Preview — First sequence

This introduces the overall theme of the unit.

Your thoughts

Students' initial thoughts and responses to the theme are elicited through questions and discussion points. This can be done as a whole-class activity or in pairs or groups.

Read and listen

Short reading texts and listenings expand on the theme and offer opportunities for comprehension and vocabulary work, and discussion. Students work individually to read or listen and then work in pairs to answer the related questions.

Have your say

Students work in pairs or groups to give personal reactions to the theme. Here it is important to stress interest and involvement, rather than formal language content.

Grammar review

The review uses concept questions to check students' understanding of what is assumed to be familiar grammar. This approach also gives the teacher the opportunity to see how much students already know and is preparation for the grammar in the next section.

If you are confident of your students' knowledge, let them work independently through this section. They can work individually or in pairs, and should use the **Language commentary** at the back of their books to check their answers and consolidate their understanding.

Alternatively, you could work through each question step by step with the whole class, then read through the **Language commentary** with them.

Check

This consists of controlled and freer practice of the review language. Students work individually, in pairs or in groups through these practice exercises. Check answers to the controlled activity and clarify any points of difficulty before students move on to the freer practice.

There is extra controlled practice of the review grammar point in the Workbook.

Reading or Listening — Second sequence

Reading or Listening introduces a new topic and contextualizes the 'new' grammar point.

In your experience / In your view

Pairs or groups exchange opinions or personal information; this leads students into the topic.

Read or Listen

This section prepares students for the reading text or listening, provides them with a purpose for reading or listening and also gives a task to check their overall understanding.

Do not pre-teach all the difficult words which will come up; restrict yourself to items which are essential to students' understanding. The teacher's notes sometimes suggest a few items to pre-teach.

With reading texts, emphasize that students should read the text the first time for general understanding. To encourage this, set realistic time limits for this first reading, based on the type of text and the task. For listenings, decide how many times to play the recordings, but encourage students to try and make sense of what they hear on first listening.

Close up

In Reading sections this feature focuses on points of vocabulary in the text. There is no single 'correct' time to do *Close up*. It may be done immediately after the first reading or can be left until later if you don't want to interrupt the flow of the skills development work.

Understanding ideas

As well as understanding the literal meaning of texts, students are asked to interpret what they read or hear – to read or listen 'between the lines'. This means that a variety of interpretations may be equally valid.

Encourage students to suggest a range of interpretations. Where possible, they should give reasons or evidence for their ideas. They may need to re-read parts of the text or the whole text before answering the questions. Possible answers are suggested in the Teacher's Book.

Vocabulary

In some units there is an additional focus on vocabulary. This may look directly at the meaning of words from the reading text or listening, or may focus on word-building.

Have your say

This rounding-off activity gives students a chance to react personally to the theme of the reading or listening. This is a fluency activity, so monitor, but allow students to discuss the subject without interruption.

Grammar

The language here is a development of the Review grammar in *Preview*.

Exploring concepts

Concept questions and other tasks get students to analyse examples of the target language and help them to understand the key features of form and use.

Get students to work individually or in pairs through the tasks. Students should work out their own ideas before checking them in the **Language commentary**.

If you think your students will find the grammar questions difficult, you may prefer to do this section with the whole class, or stop pairs after each question and check answers yourself before they move on.

Exploitation

Each grammar section is followed by tasks which practise the form and use of the target language. Some activities develop accuracy, while others develop fluency. Many are personalized pair or group activities.

Where accuracy is the aim, start by giving an example, then correct errors as you monitor. Where fluency is the prime aim, as in *Free Speech* and *Role play*, let students work uninterrupted. If necessary, return to problem areas after the completion of the task.

Skills – Third sequence

The focus in this section is on integrating listening, reading and speaking skills.

Speak / Write and speak / Listen and speak

Pair or group activities introduce the new topic. Students are asked to:

• compare ideas
• discuss and reach a consensus
• answer quiz questions
• complete questionnaires.

Listen / Read

Activities in this section give students practice in listening and reading both for general comprehension and for detail.

Understanding ideas

As in the previous sequence, students have to interpret the underlying meaning of what they read and hear.

Have your say

Short pair or group discussions give students the opportunity to react to what they have read or heard.

Vocabulary / Guessing meanings

This is vocabulary extension work, or practice in guessing the meanings of words from their context. Students at any level will come across words in texts which they do not know. Development of this skill is crucial if they are to read and understand information quickly.

Speak / Speak and write

This is a group speaking task, which gives students the opportunity to work together on an activity where there is a clear and concrete goal. Tasks can be:

• discuss and reach consensus
• plan or design something
• role play.

As an integral part of this activity, students have to take notes and present their ideas to the class. This is a fluency activity, so don't interrupt or correct as you monitor.

Grammar extra – Fourth sequence

This section explores an area of 'non-verb' grammar and often begins with a short activity which introduces the new 'mini' topic and / or contextualizes the new language point. Depending on the task, students work individually, in pairs or small groups, or as a class. Students may do a questionnaire, read a short text or listen to a recording.

Exploring concepts

Students work on the questions independently or in pairs. Refer them to the **Language commentary** to check their ideas before doing a final teacher check. Alternatively, work through the questions with the class one by one.

Exploitation

This section contains controlled practice and freer practice activities. Follow procedures suggested earlier.

Exploring words – Fifth sequence

This focuses on topic vocabulary related to the unit theme, and on other important areas such as collocations, idioms, synonyms, phrasal verbs. The tasks are designed to check and expand students' existing vocabulary and provide practice in using the vocabulary.

Students can work individually or in pairs or groups. Monitor practice activities, listening for appropriate use and pronunciation of vocabulary. In controlled activities, correct where necessary and appropriate. Don't interrupt the flow of discussions in freer activities; save any feedback until after the exercise is over.

Writing – Sixth sequence

This focuses on different styles of writing – from personal letters and e-mails to factual and imaginative descriptions.

Read

A short text or texts usually provides the initial context and sets the scene for the later writing task. (In Unit 2 there is a listening.) Activities include comprehension, discussion and vocabulary extension, and focus on key stylistic features.

Brainstorm and notes

Students work in pairs or small groups to brainstorm ideas for the writing task. This is an important part of the lesson as it gets students used to thinking 'round' a topic before they start writing, it encourages cooperation between students and stimulates ideas. Monitor, helping with ideas. Set a time limit for this phase.

Write

Students work through a series of stages:
*   writing a first draft
*   exchanging work with a partner
*   reading and thinking of improvements to each other's writing
*   discussing suggested improvements in pairs
*   writing a final draft.

It is better if all the stages, except writing the final draft, are done in class, so set time limits. The first draft should be written fairly quickly.

Use the **Writing models** at what you think is the appropriate stage of the lesson.

If students are not used to working co-operatively, explain the advantage of a 'new pair of eyes' looking at their work. Reassure students that *you* will mark and assess their final draft.

Language in action – Seventh sequence

The focus here is on
*   functional language, for example *giving reasons*
*   pronunciation.

Introduction

In pairs students work through a series of tasks:
*   an introductory task
*   listening
*   making a note of functional language
*   exchanging information
*   compiling lists of functional expressions.

The recording contains examples of the target language.

Pronunciation

Work through this section briskly, correcting errors of form and pronunciation. The exercises are at the back of the book so that the functional language is not on the same page as the listening tasks. Ideally it should be done before Practice, but as it also covers a separate pronunciation syllabus you may prefer to deal with it separately. It focuses on a particular feature of pronunciation and practises the target language.

Practice

This provides freer practice of the target language. Activities which include role plays, language games, problem solving, and class surveys, are done in pairs or groups.

Check through the instructions with the class and, if appropriate, allocate roles. Once students are talking, monitor conversations, listening for the correct and appropriate use of the target language. Don't interrupt the flow of conversations but make a note of any points that need reviewing at a later stage.

Unit summary

This is a checklist for students to focus on the areas they have covered in the unit. Students could tick each item after studying it in class and then add a second tick once they are confident about the language point. Alternatively, use it at the end of the unit to check the areas they feel confident about and highlight the areas they feel they need to revise.

Language commentary

This provides unit-by-unit information on the grammar. Detailed notes on meaning and form and examples help students to answer the *Exploring concepts* tasks.

Teacher's Book

Unit-by-unit notes consist of:
*   step-by-step suggestions for exploiting the Student's Book
*   an answer key, including suggested or possible answers for exercises which do not have specific right or wrong answers, for example *Understanding ideas* questions in reading or listening sections
*   tapescripts
*   background notes on certain topics.

Writing models – these are examples of the different text types students are asked to write. Photocopy the section and use it at any stage of the writing process.

Six tests – one after every two units, testing the grammar, vocabulary and functional language areas covered.

Photocopiable material – a range of interactive activities for further practice, and notes on how to use them.

Workbook

The 12 units of the Workbook will help students to consolidate their grammar, increase their vocabulary and improve their reading skills.

1 It's a pleasure

Theme

The overall theme of this unit is enjoyment.
Preview Pleasure and feelings of guilt
Reading Pleasure and guilt: pros and cons of popular activities
Skills Ideal holidays
Grammar extra Food and enjoyment
Writing Leisure facilities

Grammar

- Review of the use of frequency adverbs with the Present simple
- Present perfect simple with adverbs
- Comparison of adjectives

Vocabulary

- Types of holidays
- Holiday activities and equipment
- Verbs which collocate with activities

Writing

- Describing leisure facilities (a personal letter)

Functional language

- Asking and answering personal questions

Pronunciation

- Stressed and unstressed words

Workbook

- Grammar and functional language as above
- Topic vocabulary: holidays; the senses; place idioms
- Extract from an article on writing poems; children's poems

Preview

This introduces the first theme of the unit – life's pleasures. The reading and listening texts also contextualize the language of habits: frequency adverbs with the Present simple.

■ Your thoughts ■■■■■■■■■■■■■■■■ p. 4 ■

1 • Allow students a few minutes to list some of the things they enjoy doing. Make sure students use all the suggested categories to provide 'full' lists. Use the illustrations to help students with ideas if necessary.

2 • Either in pairs or as a whole-class mingle, get students to compare lists and discuss their different interests.
   • Have brief whole-class feedback.

■ Read ■■■■■■■■■■■■■■■■■

1 • Work through this pre-reading vocabulary activity with the whole class or suggest that students work in pairs. These words are important for understanding the text. Ask students to pool their ideas before they check in a dictionary if necessary.
   • Check answers.

> **Answers**
> a *companion* someone you do something with, not necessarily a friend
>   *friend* someone you like or love
> b *enjoy* like
>   *love* like a lot
>   *adore* love a lot
> c *pleasure* something which gives enjoyment
>   *thrill* something which gives intense excitement
> d *intellectual* to do with the mind (*intellect*)
>   *emotional* to do with feelings (*emotions*)

2a–b Students read the text, looking for activities which they also enjoy. (This gives them a personal angle on the task.)
   • They then read the text again to find who feels guilty and why.
   • Check answers.

> **Answers**
> 2 Hervé Leger. He feels guilty if he eats cream-filled cakes (when he's overweight).
> 3 Ferruccio Amendola. He feels guilty if his pleasures prevent him from being with family or friends.
> 4 Sonia Rykiel. Eating too much, going to the cinema in the afternoon and having too much chocolate in her handbag all make her feel guilty.

3 • Students scan the texts for the information they need to answer the questions. Point out that each question has more than one answer.
   • Check answers.

Answers
a 3 / 5
b 2 / 4
c 1 / 5
d 1 / 3 / 4 / 5 (sports)

▦ Vocabulary ▦▦▦▦▦▦▦▦▦▦▦ p. 5 ▦

   • Students work individually or in pairs on this matching task.
   • Check answers.

Answers
a 3   b 5   c 4   d 1   e 2

   • You could check their understanding of the vocabulary by asking them to discuss the following questions in pairs.

   – How do you *escape from* yourself or from stressful situations?
   – Do you ever feel *guilty* about eating?
   – Why do so many people worry about being *overweight*?
   – Have you ever *performed* in public? What did you do?
   – What are your favourite *outdoor* activities?

▦ Listen ▦▦▦▦▦▦▦▦▦▦▦▦▦▦▦

1 a Give students time to think of ideas individually or in small groups before you elicit a few ideas about activities that people feel guilty about. You could list these on the board.
   b Play **1.1**. Students listen and check their predictions.

1.1

Speaker 1 Yeah – smoking. The thing is I gave up nearly a year ago, but I sometimes take cigarettes from other people instead of simply saying 'No thanks, I don't smoke any more.'
Speaker 2 Showers. I usually spend at least half an hour in the shower, just enjoying it. But I know it's a terrible waste of water – that's why I feel guilty.
Speaker 3 I occasionally go to sleep in front of the TV instead of doing more important things like helping the kids with their homework or tidying the house. The worst time is when you fall asleep and wake up at about three in the morning and you've completely wasted the whole evening.
Speaker 4 Yes – it's something I enjoy doing 'cos it makes my life easier – I always drive to work and I feel guilty about it, for obvious reasons, you know, because using a car in the city is generally a bad thing – it causes pollution. These days I never walk, not even on warm sunny days. I mean I feel guilty about driving, but I still do it.
Speaker 5 Buying expensive shoes – I've got funny feet and the only comfortable shoes I can find are really expensive. Well, you see, they last for ages – so I hardly ever buy new shoes. Well, that's my excuse, anyway.
Speaker 6 Surfing the Internet on my Dad's computer. I don't often do it and it's usually pretty cheap – but I feel guilty because Dad doesn't know I found out his password.
Speaker 7 Spending ages on the phone. The thing is, I ring my boyfriend two or three times a week when my parents are out, even though they're pretty hard up and can't afford high phone bills.

Speaker 8 That's easy – secretly buying chocolate. I buy a bar every day when I'm on my way home from college. I just feel so tired – I really need the sugar – then, when it's all gone, I feel terrible.

2 • Play **1.1** again. This time students make notes about the activities and the reasons for the speakers' guilt feelings. Pause after each speaker to give them time to note their answers if necessary.
   • Allow students a few minutes to compare answers with a partner.
   • Check answers.

Answers

	Enjoyable activity	Reason for feeling guilty
Speaker 1	Smoking	She takes cigarettes from other people.
Speaker 2	Showers	She uses a lot of water because she spends so long in the shower.
Speaker 3	Going to sleep watching TV	He gets out of doing important things – helping children with homework / tidying the house.
Speaker 4	Driving to work	Cars cause pollution.
Speaker 5	Buying expensive shoes	Reason implied: waste of money.
Speaker 6	Surfing the Internet on dad's computer	Father doesn't know son has password.
Speaker 7	Spending ages on the phone	Her parents pay the bill and they are not very well-off.
Speaker 8	Buying chocolate	She does it secretly.

▦ Have your say ▦▦▦▦▦▦▦▦▦▦

1–2 Students discuss the questions in pairs or groups.
   • Monitor, but do not interrupt.
   • You could develop the second question into a class discussion or have brief whole-class feedback.

— Grammar review – Frequency expressions with the Present simple

1 • Students listen to **1.1** again and fill the gaps. The missing words are all frequency adverbs or expressions, but do not tell students this before they listen.
   • Check answers.

Answers

a	sometimes	f	hardly ever
b	usually	g	often
c	occasionally	h	usually
d	always	i	two or three times a week
e	never	j	every day

2a–c Students could work through these questions individually or in pairs, referring to the **Language commentary** at the back of their books. Alternatively, you could elicit answers from the class. As this might be the first time that students have done this kind of discovery activity, check answers to **a** and **b** with them, then show them how they can use their own ideas and check their guesses in the **Language commentary** on p.124.

Answers

a **how frequently** the actions took place.
b **a–g** in order:
*always   usually   often   sometimes   occasionally
hardly ever   never*
c • **before** the main verb.
• **after** the verb. Frequency expressions come after the verb *to be*.
• at the end of the clause.

Note You could clarify the issue of word order by working through the **Language commentary** notes with the whole class.

Check

3 • Work through the example to check that students understand the task. Remind them that sometimes more than one answer is possible.
• Students work individually, then compare answers in pairs.
• Check answers.

Answers

a She *sometimes* plays tennis for the college team. / *Sometimes* she plays tennis for the college team.
b He *never* drinks when he's driving.
c We visit our relatives in America *every year*. / *Every year* we visit our relatives in America.
d She doesn't *usually* smoke in her friend's car. / *Usually* she doesn't smoke in her friend's car.
e I'm *always* busy in the evenings.
a and d could also both come in end position, but less commonly.

4 • Work through the example question and answer to check students understand the task, then let them continue in groups.
• Although students give personal responses to these questions, this exercise also provides accuracy practice, so monitor and correct if necessary.
• You could finish the activity by asking a few students to tell you about their partner, e.g.
T   *Maria, does Juan ever buy flowers for someone?*
M   *Yes, quite often.*
   Yes, he often buys flowers for his girlfriend.

▶ Photocopiable activity 1 p.152

—— p. 6 ——

Reading

There are two parts to this text. The first looks at the connection between pleasure and guilt. The second lists the pros and cons of some very common 'pleasures'.

In your experience

1–2 Give students a couple of minutes to think of ideas, then elicit a few suggestions from the class before asking students to compare ideas in pairs or groups.

• If students are having any problems you could suggest they think about what is popular or fashionable with children, young people, the middle-aged and the elderly.

Read

1 a The first task is a skimming exercise, intended to get the students to read quickly and decide on the subject of the text.
• Explain the aim to the students and ask them to read the three possible titles for the text.
• Set a time limit of two to three minutes for a first reading, then elicit students' ideas.

Answer
The best title is Eat, drink and don't be sorry.

b The questions which follow reading texts in this book are usually a mixture of two types:
– 'straight' comprehension questions, where the answers are in the text for students to find,
– questions which require students to use their imagination to 'interpret' the article, in other words to 'read between the lines'.
• Explain this to students, using question 1 as an example of the first type and question 4 as an example of the second type.
• Students now read the text and answer the questions.
• Check answers.

Answers

1 They can enjoy themselves without feeling guilty.
2 Guilt weakens the biological effects of enjoyment. The body produces fewer, or less effective, infection-fighting substances.
3 Recent studies have looked at the positive rather than the negative effects of substances like caffeine, alcohol, etc.
4 Possible answers:
The 'beneficial' smells could be introduced deliberately into certain situations or places, especially those where people would normally be rather stressed or anxious for example, in offices, busy shopping centres, airports. Doctors or dentists might make use of the smells to help patients relax. Supermarkets might hope to encourage people to buy more of a particular kind of product. (In some places this already happens.)

Close up

Close up sections focus on points of grammar or vocabulary used in reading texts. They are best worked on as post-reading activities, but they may be referred to while reading, if you feel that a detailed understanding of the text is important.

Answers
• Human instincts include:
survival – finding food, escaping from danger, looking after young
communication – speaking a language, living in social groups
reproduction – having children

- The verb related to *strong* is *strengthen*.
  Similar pairs of adjectives and verbs:
  black – blacken   broad – broaden   deep – deepen
  flat – flatten   high – heighten   long – lengthen
  red – redden   rough – roughen   sad – sadden
  sharp – sharpen   short – shorten   wide – widen
  The suffix *-en* means *to make* or *become*. It is not possible
  to add *-en* to all adjectives. For example, you cannot say
  thinnen or *narrowen*.

2 • Students now read **Part 2** of the article.
  • Ask them to note the information they find surprising as
    they read.
  • Elicit and discuss their ideas.

▨ Understanding ideas ▨

This task again requires students to interpret the article by
adding their own ideas.

1–3 Students discuss these questions in pairs and note down
    possible answers.
  • Elicit their ideas.

Possible answers

1 If the body burns food quickly, the person is unlikely to put on
  weight. Some teenagers smoke in order to stay slim.

2 In any situation when they need to concentrate, e.g. when
  driving at night, in long important meetings, when they have
  drunk too much alcohol and feel sleepy.

3 Answers here may vary from person to person, but from the
  information in the article *Relaxing* and *Drinking coffee and tea*
  appear to be more beneficial than harmful.

▨ Have your say ▨

This is a final opportunity for a discussion of this topic.
  • Encourage students to express opinions and to use their
    own knowledge and experience to inform their ideas. This
    activity can be done either in pairs, in small groups or as a
    whole-class discussion.

— Grammar — Present perfect simple —— p. 7 ——
                      and adverbs

In this unit the Present perfect simple follows the Present
simple (*Preview*). This is a deliberate attempt to move away
from the Present simple–Present continuous contrast with
which most students at this level are all too familiar. It is also
to encourage students to notice that the Present perfect is a
Present tense. In Unit 3, the Present continuous (*Preview*) is
followed by the Present perfect continuous.

▨ Exploring concepts ▨

1–3 Students may work through these questions and tasks
    individually or in pairs. You could check their ideas after
    each of the three sections or, if you are confident of your
    students' ability, check all three sections together. Remind
    students to refer to the **Language commentary** on p.124.

- In 2, make sure that students understand that the primary
  feature or reason for using the Present perfect is to point
  out a link of some kind between the past and the present.
  In this section, students are asked to think about the
  present results or effects of the past events.
- Allow sufficient time for students to work through
  the questions.
- Check their answers.

Answers

1 The present of the verb *to have* + the past participle of the verb.

2 a We do not know exactly when the events happened. We only
    know that it was some time before now – it could be five
    minutes or a hundred years ago.
  b **b1** is the result of **a2**; **b2** is the result of **a3**; **b3** is the result
    of **a1**.

3 a 1 already   4 So far / for a week
     2 just / so far   5 still
     3 since January / yet   6 never
  b *yet* and *still*
    so far is used with a negative verb in **a2** and with an
    affirmative verb in **a4**.
  c 1 *so far / yet*   come at the end.
     2 *still*   comes before the auxiliary verb.
     3 *so far*   can come at the beginning or the end.
     4 *already / just / never*   come after the auxiliary verb.
  d *since January* (**a3**) – January is a point in time.
    for a week (**a4**) – a week is a period of time.

▨ Exploitation ▨

1 • Students work individually through this practice exercise,
    then compare answers with a partner.
  • Check answers.

Answers

a yet / still   b already   c so far

Note the word *only* in the original sentence means that *so far* is the
only possible answer – *already* is not correct.

d just   e yet (*so far* is also possible)

2 a Students complete the questions, using a question word
    and one of the verbs. This is in preparation for a speaking
    activity. Draw attention to the example to make sure they
    understand the task.
  • Check answers before the pairwork begins.

Answers

1 Who is … met   4 What is … seen
2 What is … bought   5 Where (or What) is … been to
3 What is … slept in

  b Students ask their partners questions 1–5 and note down
    each other's answers.
  • Monitor, correcting if necessary.
  c Two pairs now compare answers and decide which are the
    most interesting experiences.
  • Monitor, but do not interrupt. Save any corrections for a
    later stage.

- Finish the activity by asking each group of four to tell the class some of the interesting experiences they heard about.

Free speech

3 • This is primarily a fluency activity which may allow students to use the Present perfect. Unless you want to turn it into another controlled practice exercise, do not ask students to use specific language forms.

a Elicit one or two examples for each of the categories mentioned.
   • Students discuss two of these topics for about two minutes each.
   • Monitor, but do not interrupt or correct.

b Groups make a list of events they have discussed and present them to the rest of the class as radio or TV news headlines.
   • You could point out that this use of the Present perfect is very common at the beginning of news broadcasts, stressing the link between past events and the present; the listener is brought up to date.

Example answers
- The American President has resigned.
- Scientists have discovered the gene which controls our sense of humour.

— p. 8 —

Skills

The theme now moves on to holidays.

Write and speak

1–2 Introduce the new theme and get students to think about their ideal holiday. Elicit a suggestion for each of the headings.
   • Students make individual lists then try to find someone else in the class with the same ideas as theirs. You could suggest they find a compatible holiday partner.
   • Have brief whole-class feedback.
   • You could finish this stage by taking a vote on the most popular type of holiday.

Listen

1 • Explain the listening task: students listen for any of their ideal holiday ideas that are mentioned by the four speakers.
   • Play **1.2**.
   • Check which speaker had the closest ideal.

1.2

Speaker 1 My ideal holiday erm, my ideal holiday would be one where I forget completely about work, I think, er and one where I had as much money to spend as I wanted – that would be really good. Erm, every time I've been on holiday so far erm I've always been restricted in what I can do, erm, because I haven't got enough, enough money, so yeah, I think I could go anywhere and be happy if I had enough money to spend when I was there. What kind of things would you do?

Erm, I dunno – I love the countryside so I think I'd do quite a lot of touring – erm, I'd like to eat in some nice restaurants and er I've never swum er in the sea because the sea in England, er the sea around England is so cold, so I'd love to go somewhere where I could swim in the sea – that would be great.

Speaker 2 A perfect holiday for me is is going to places of erm natural beauty – erm, I quite like the idea of – I would love to go to places like the Grand Canyon so, that would be my perfect holiday but not as a package tour – I would, I would sort of go ideally with friends and you know we would do things in our own time and sort of stay in in hotels just as they sort of come along but and the important thing is not to spend a massive amount of money either.

Speaker 3 My ideal holiday would be, erm, some kind of mixture of relaxing on a beach, doing some kind of strenuous activity like er, walking in the mountains or something a little bit adventurous, er I'd also, probably I'd also want some sort of culture, like er, galleries or ancient monuments or something similar and food – it would have to have good food, erm so I'd want to go somewhere where I could do something relaxing, er something cultural, something a bit strenuous and a bit challenging, and somewhere where I could experience erm the local food and drink and a little bit of the local culture.

Speaker 4 A perfect holiday, erm I think something where everything was organized for me, all my food was cooked, everything was planned and I didn't have to think about anything at all. Somewhere warm but not too hot, somewhere near the sea, near water of some kind – I don't want to bake in the sun, but I don't want to spend all the time lying on a beach either.
I would like to look at wildlife somewhere – go to somewhere different and look at the wildlife – Africa – that would be quite a good thing because it's all very different but somewhere near the coast as well – East Africa I think that would be rather nice.

2 • Play **1.2** again. This time students complete the table with information they hear. You could pause after each speaker, or play the recording straight through.
   • Allow students time to compare answers, then check.

Answers

Speaker	The most important aspect(s) of the ideal holiday	Specific activities
1	Holiday would make speaker forget work No limit on money	Touring in countryside Eating in nice restaurants Swimming in warm sea
2	Area of natural beauty	Sightseeing with friends in a leisurely way
3	Mixture of different activities	Relaxing on the beach Walking in mountains Cultural visits to galleries or ancient monuments Trying local food and drink
4	Everything organized for the speaker – e.g. food cooked, everything planned	Lying on beach Looking at wildlife

Read

1 • Explain that students are going to read an article about a *virtual* seaside resort. Ask what *virtual* means in this context. They may know other expressions with virtual (e.g. *virtual reality*), but if not, get them to look at the photograph of the obviously false seaside resort.

2 a As they read the article for the first time, students think about which of the speakers they have just heard would most enjoy a holiday at this resort. This is a skimming exercise, intended to get students to read quickly. You could set a time limit of about three minutes.

- Elicit ideas.

Answer
Probably Speaker 4 would enjoy the Ocean Dome most. Everything is organized.

b Students now have a chance to react personally to the article. Let them work in pairs, groups or as a class to discuss their ideas.

- Monitor, but do not interrupt conversations.

▓ Guessing meanings ▓▓▓▓▓▓▓▓▓▓▓▓▓ p. 9 ▓

Some key words are dealt with here before students read the text again. Discourage the use of dictionaries at this stage. It is important that students get used to guessing or working out the meanings of unknown words.

- Students work individually, guessing the meaning of the words with the help of the prompt questions, then compare answers in pairs.
- Check answers.

Answers
a fake not real / artificial / false
b shade darker and cooler area protected from the direct light and heat of the sun. *If it is very hot, it is sensible to sit in the* **shade** *not in the sun.*
c craze an activity which is very popular or fashionable, often for a very short time. *In the 1990s there was a* **craze** *for Karaoke singing.*
d powdery very fine and dry, like dust

▓ Understanding ideas ▓▓▓▓▓▓▓▓▓▓▓▓▓▓

1–5 Students find the answers to these questions individually, noting them down if necessary. They then compare them in pairs.

- Check answers.

Answers
1 The writer is comparing this artificial resort with other artificial or virtual things (pets and pop stars) which originated in Japan.

2 There is a beach, water, sunshine, crowds of people.

3 The sand, waves and sunshine are fake; the air and the water temperatures are artificially controlled; the palm trees are made of plastic.

4 The Ocean Dome and the ski-slope are both artificial indoor environments.

5 The article suggests that everyone at the resort is a Japanese office worker. The fact that they are described as being *overstressed* suggests that they come here to relax.

▓ Speak ▓▓▓▓▓▓▓▓▓▓▓▓▓▓▓▓▓▓▓▓▓▓▓▓

This is a group speaking activity which draws together information and ideas from the preceding activities.

1 • Introduce the activity and form groups of three to five students. You could bring in authentic materials of the kind students are going to produce for themselves: holiday posters and newspaper advertisements.

- You could set an overall time limit for the activity.

a–c Monitor students' discussions, prompting or helping where necessary.

d Check that each group has made all the necessary decisions before they start producing their publicity material.

- If groups are large, more than one of the suggested kinds of publicity could be produced.

2 • This final presentation stage is designed to round off the whole activity, and gives a focus for the previous discussions. The presentations need not be formal and should not be over-prepared; the aim is to give students a chance to share what they have done. You might like to give them a general framework for the presentation, e.g. *We decided on … because … We thought the features should be … because we wanted to attract …* The groups can either appoint a spokesperson to give their presentation or share the task.

- In turn, using their publicity material, each group presents their ideas and plans to the rest of the class.
- The posters, advertisements, etc. could be displayed in the classroom in preparation for the vote.

3 • The class votes for the best 'ideal' resort. (Students should be asked not to vote for their own plan.)

──────────────────────────── p. 10 ──

Grammar extra

Comparison of adjectives

The third grammar section in each unit of *Landmark Intermediate* highlights an area of non-verb grammar.

▓ Read ▓▓▓▓▓▓▓▓▓▓▓▓▓▓▓▓▓▓▓▓▓▓▓▓▓

1a–b Students read and complete the survey on eating and drinking, which contextualizes examples of comparative and superlative forms. At this stage the focus should be on subject matter not language form.

- Students compare answers and opinions in pairs.
- Have brief whole-class feedback.

▓ Exploring concepts ▓▓▓▓▓▓▓▓▓▓▓▓▓▓▓▓

Note We assume that the comparison of adjectives will be revision for most students at this level and, for this reason, the first part of **Exploring concepts** is a test.

1 • Students work individually through items **a–h** to complete the rules. Use this as a check of how much they know – but it's designed as a lighthearted test, so if students get bogged down, help them out or let them work in pairs.

- Students may compare their endings in pairs, or you could check their answers with them straight away.
- Remind students about the **Language commentary** on p.125.

Answers

a double the last letter and add *-er.* (e.g. *hot – hotter, thin – thinner*)

b change the last letter to *i* and add *-er.* (e.g. *healthy – healthier; pretty – prettier*)

c put *more* or *less* in front of the adjective. (e.g. *enjoyable – more enjoyable; interested – less interested*)

d add *-st.* (e.g. *safe – safest; large – largest*)

e put *the most* or *the least* in front of the adjective. (e.g. *uninteresting – the most / the least uninteresting; entertaining – the most / the least entertaining*)

f *better*

g *bad*

h *as* + adjective + *as* (e.g. *as friendly as*)

2a–b This section lists words and phrases which can be used to modify comparative adjectives.

• Work through the questions with the class.

• Check answers.

Answers

a *a lot / far / much* refer to big differences.
a bit / a little / slightly refer to small differences.

b *much* and *a little* are the most formal; *a lot* and *a bit* are the most informal.

▶ **Photocopiable activity 2 p.153**

■ Exploitation ■

1 • Check that students understand the adjectives in the list. They can use the picture to help them with ideas.

Note There are examples of all the different types of adjective here to give students practice in forming all the comparatives.

• Elicit a few example sentences from the class, then let students continue in pairs.

• Check answers.

Sample answers

Hamburgers are more fattening than cheese.
Vegetables are healthier than sweets.
Cheese is richer than fish.
Chocolate is more popular than potatoes.
Cakes are sweeter than vegetables.

2a–b Get students to think of a format for the menu they are going to design. It could begin like this:

Breakfast	*Fruit / Toast / Black coffee*
Lunch	
Evening meal	
Types of food to avoid / to eat more of	

• Students choose one of the types of people listed, then design their menu.

• They should exchange menus with a student who has chosen a different type of person and compare ideas.

• Monitor discussions, listening for comparative and superlative expressions, but do not interrupt or correct at this stage.

Additional activity

As a writing activity, students could compare themselves with another person they know well: a good friend, a brother or sister, etc. Before setting the task, have a class or group brainstorm about the kind of things they could compare about people (age, looks, behaviour, etc.).

Exploring words

Holidays and activities

1 a Check that students understand the three holiday types listed here.

• Write the three words on the board and elicit suggestions for each category, then let students continue individually or in pairs. Point out that some words can belong to more than one group.

• Check answers.

Answers

• **Activity** *canoeing cycling fishing riding rock-climbing sailing skiing snorkelling surfing walking water-skiing*

• **Beach** *canoeing fishing sailing sand sea seaside resort snorkelling sunbathing surfing water-skiing*

• **Cultural** *art gallery castle or palace historical ruins monument museum sightseeing theatre*

b Students match the verbs listed with the holiday words. Suggest a time limit to this exercise, or set it for homework. Stress the importance of learning words not just in isolation but also with the words they go with (collocates). To check, get students to ask each other simple questions, beginning *Have you ever …? When did you last …? Do you often …?*

• Check answers.

Answers

go	*canoeing cycling fishing riding rock-climbing sailing sightseeing skiing snorkelling sunbathing surfing walking water-skiing to the theatre*
go round	*an art gallery a castle or palace historical ruins a museum*
lie	*on the sand*
play	*on the sand in the sea*
swim	*in the sea*
visit	*an art gallery a castle or palace historical ruins a monument a museum a seaside resort*

2 a Students now find the illustrations to match the activities in their Activity holiday list.

Answers

canoeing 3   cycling 11   fishing 4   riding 9
rock-climbing 7   sailing 2   skiing 10   snorkelling 5
surfing 6   walking 8   water-skiing 1

b Again referring to the illustration and following the example, students make sentences to describe what items of equipment are used for the different activities. They should use their dictionaries to check any words they do not know.

* Check answers.

Answers
To go

canoeing you need	*a canoe, a paddle and a helmet.*
cycling	*a bike and a helmet.*
fishing	*a rod and some bait.*
riding	*a horse, a saddle and a helmet.*
rock-climbing	*ropes, a helmet and boots.*
sailing	*a boat and a life-jacket.*
skiing	*skis, boots and goggles.*
snorkelling	*a snorkel and a wet-suit.*
walking	*boots, a (walking) stick and a backpack.*
water-skiing	*a boat and water-skis.*

c Students mingle and find out how many of their classmates have done these activities. Set a time limit of four or five minutes.

* Practise the two question forms with a few students first: *Do you go …ing?* or *Have you ever been …ing?*
* Monitor conversations listening for correct grammar and vocabulary.

3a–b Check students understand the statements before giving them time to decide, individually, which one they agree and disagree with.

* You might like to elicit some controversial statements from the class before asking students to make up two of their own. Make sure the statements are about the activities mentioned in the lesson. Students could work in pairs for this activity if they like.
c Students mingle to find out who agrees or disagrees with their statements and keep a note of answers.
d Have a brief class feedback session.

— p. 12 —

Writing

Describing leisure facilities

In this section students write about leisure facilities in their town or city. As in all the writing sections of *Landmark Intermediate*, there is an emphasis on the process of writing and not just the end product. Students are expected to read and comment on each other's writing and also to work together to brainstorm ideas and examine features of writing before they write. The **Writing guidelines** give models, and some key features of the type of writing; the **Reminder** box on the page highlights important features for students to bear in mind as they write.

▇ Read ▇

1 • The letter extract sets the scene for the writing activity which follows.
* Ask students to read the extract quickly.
* Check the answer to: *When do they want to come?*

Answer
The people are probably coming in early July.

2 • Elicit answers to this question.

Suggested answer
Tourist brochures often exaggerate. The writers of the letter would prefer the honest suggestions of someone who knows the place well but has no ulterior motive. They expect their friend to mention the bad as well as the good things about the place.

▇ Brainstorm and notes ▇

Students work in pairs or groups.

1–3 Before students begin the task, read through the examples with them and elicit a couple of ideas about leisure facilities that visitors to their town or city would find interesting.
* The next steps form an important information-gathering stage, so monitor throughout, helping with ideas if necessary.
* Students work in pairs or groups to make lists.
* Ask them to choose the two or three places they know most about or think would be most interesting, then to write more detailed notes.
* Read through the example and suggest students organize their notes from 2 to answer the four main questions. *Where? / How to get there?*, etc.
* Monitor this important information-gathering stage thoroughly, providing ideas if necessary.

▇ Write ▇

1 • Referring to the notes they have made, individual students are now going to write their own first drafts of a reply to the friends' letter. If class time is short, this first draft could be set as homework. However, as it is a first draft it should be written fairly quickly, and you might find that it is better to do the next two stages of drafting and commenting in class, and set the final version for homework. Whether in class or as homework, stress that the first draft of a piece of writing should be done quickly – at this stage it is the general shape and content of the writing that is most important. There will be a later opportunity for students to improve on accuracy, choice of vocabulary, spelling, etc.
* Start by reminding students that they are writing a reply to their friends' letter. Elicit their ideas for how they should begin the letter, and for what style they should use.

- Work through the **Reminder** eliciting or giving examples of the three points listed. Link ideas – with conjunctions – *but, and, although,* etc. and with relative pronouns – *who, where,* etc. Use opinion adjectives – *beautiful / exciting,* etc. Don't repeat nouns – use pronouns – *he / she / them,* etc.

2a–b Students exchange first drafts with a student from a different group.
- They should read each other's work and suggest improvements. Elicit some questions students could ask themselves about their partner's piece of writing, for example: *Does the letter answer the question in the original letter? Is the style informal? Does the facility described sound attractive? Has the writer followed the Reminder guidelines?*

c Finally, students discuss their ideas for improvements before writing their final version.
- Be available to give help during this phase. Take account of everybody's ideas. Be an objective adviser.
- Stress that at this stage students should pay attention to grammar, vocabulary, spelling, punctuation, layout, etc.
- This final writing task is best done as homework.

▶ **Writing model 1 (photocopiable) TB p.130**

— p. 13 —

Language in action

Asking and answering personal questions

The *Language in action* sections of *Landmark Intermediate* are devoted to functional language. This unit provides students with the opportunity to revise and practise asking and answering personal questions.

▮ Introduction ▮

1a–b Students read the ten answers and write down the questions that prompted them.
- They compare questions with a partner.

2 • Play **1.3**. Students check their questions.

1.3

1 I When were you born?
   A On the 23rd of December 1976 – it was a Friday.
2 I How long have you worked here?
   A For nearly two years, now. Before that I worked for a Japanese computer company.
3 I Do you like your job?
   A Yes, I do. The pay is good and the people I work with are really friendly. It's like one big happy family here.
4 I How much do you earn?
   A I'm sorry, but that's my business, but it's certainly better than my last job, so I'm not complaining.
5 I Are you married?
   A No, not yet, but I will be this time next year. The wedding is fixed for June 21st.

6 I What does your girlfriend do?
   A She's an assistant editor on the local newspaper.
7 I What does she look like?
   A She's short and slim with dark hair and she sometimes wears glasses.
8 I Are you planning to have any children?
   A Sorry, I'd rather not answer that if you don't mind. It's too far in the future. Let's just say neither of us is quite ready yet.
9 I What do you do in your spare time?
   A I play the bass guitar in a rock band, I go to concerts, the cinema. I do all kinds of things, erm – I'm quite keen on sport.
10 I Do you do any sports yourself?
   A Yes, I do. Tennis in the summer and basketball all the year round.

Answers
See Tapescript **1.3**.

3 a Students discuss these questions in pairs or as a class.
- Elicit ideas.
- This subject might make an interesting class discussion if there are students of different nationalities in the class.

Possible answers
– The interviewee thinks these questions are too personal. The interviewer is talking about private matters that he does not want to discuss in public.
– Answers to the second and third questions will depend on students' personal or cultural background.

b Check answers.

Answers
Expressions used when refusing to answer a question
(I'm sorry, but) that's my business.
(Sorry,) I'd rather not answer that (if you don't mind).

Note You could also get students to add *Mind your own business* to this list, but point out the difference in register.

▮ Pronunciation ▮▮▮▮▮▮▮▮▮▮▮▮▮▮▮▮ p. 150 ▮

The pronunciation section in *Landmark Intermediate* has a two-fold purpose: first to focus on a particular aspect of pronunciation and secondly to give students practice in using the language they are studying in *Language in action* in a controlled way before they do the freer *Practice* activities. This section looks at stressed and unstressed words.

1 • Students work on their own or in pairs, read the questions and decide which words they think will be stressed. Monitor, but don't correct.

2 • Play **1.4**. Ask students to correct any wrong ideas then check answers.

1.4

a What's your name?
b Where were you born?
c What do you do?
d What does your father do?
e How many jobs have you had?
f How many languages can you speak?
g Do you like your boss?
h What are your plans?

Answers
See Tapescript **1.4**.

3 • Elicit what kind of words were stressed and which were not stressed. If students don't know the grammatical names, they can give examples and you can supply them.

Answers
- *Wh-* words, nouns, and main verbs were stressed.
- Auxiliary verbs (*do, does, have*), modal verbs, the verb *be*, pronouns and possessive adjectives were not stressed.

- Elicit why *Wh-* words, nouns, main verbs, adjectives and adverbs are always stressed. (Because they are important, they are words which 'carry' the meaning of the sentence.) You could point out that the words which were not stressed on the tape are stressed when they are important, but that they will study this in a later unit.

4 • Play **1.4** again. Pause after each speaker and drill either chorally or individually. Make sure that students are using weak forms /dəz/, /həv/.

Practice p. 13

Role play

1a–b Start by checking that students understand the context and the task. You could remind them of a well-known scandal in their country. (If all else fails, remind them of Bill Clinton and Monica Lewinsky!)
- Divide students into pairs, and let them decide who will take the part of the interviewer (Student B).
- Student A chooses one of the suggested roles, decides what their guilty secret is and passes this information on to Student B.
- Allow about five minutes for both students to prepare their roles in the interview. Make sure students understand the task: the famous personality should decide how much they are prepared to say about the secret and the interviewer should think of questions which the interviewee will find it difficult to deal with.
- Be available to prompt and to help with ideas at this stage.

c–d Monitor the interviews, but do not interrupt or correct.
- As each pair finishes they should change roles. This second interview could follow the same pattern but be done more spontaneously – with little or no preparation.

2a–b As a final practice, students write their own personal questions to ask other students. They should think of questions to which they really want to know the answers. Remind students that they can refuse to answer some of the questions.
- Set a time limit for this mingling activity. Students ask as many others as they can.
- As you monitor, listen out for correct question forms and make a note of any points that need further practice at a later stage. If there is time, you could have a brief feedback session on some of the information they found out about each other.

Language check

To round off the unit, encourage students to read through the final **Language check** which summarizes the points covered in the unit. Students could tick points they feel confident about and highlight points they want to return to and revise.

2 Traditions

Preview

This introduces the first theme of the unit – family customs. The recordings and reading text also contextualize the language used for talking about the past – Past simple and *used to*.

Theme

The overall theme of this unit is traditions.
Preview Family customs
Listening Birthdays and April Fool's Day
Skills Traditional views on men's and women's abilities
Grammar extra Traditional costumes
Writing Popular festivals

Grammar

- Review of *used to*
- Present perfect and Past simple
- Adjective order before nouns

Vocabulary

- Idiomatic use of *stiff*, *sick* and *dead*
- Character adjectives
- Food and cooking

Writing

- Describing a popular festival

Functional language

- Invitations: making, accepting and refusing invitations

Pronunciation

- Main sentence stress and sounding enthusiastic

Workbook

- Grammar and functional language as above
- Topic vocabulary: food and cooking; food idioms
- Description of Chinese New Year celebrations

▮ Your thoughts ▮▮▮▮▮▮▮▮▮▮▮▮▮▮▮▮▮▮▮ p. 14 ▮

1 • Allow students a few minutes to think about family customs they have and whether they like or dislike these activities. Use these questions if necessary. *Do you have all or some of your meals together? Do you have the same food on a particular day? Do you go on holiday together? Do you always go to the same place? Do you do any weekend activities together? For example, play or watch a sport? visit relatives? go on a trip?*

2 • Students compare ideas to see how many of their family customs are similar. You could elicit one or two examples from the class to round off this section.

▮ Listen ▮

1 • Tell students that they are going to hear two people talking about past family customs.
  • Play **2.1**. This first listening is to check general understanding.
  • Check answers.

Answers
Speaker 1 is talking about family outings / trips in the car.
Speaker 2 is talking about summer holidays with her family in Spain.

2.1

Interview 1
I   What do you remember about family outings when you were young?
M Well, my father was a keen photographer and because of that he used to drive all over the country looking for pretty views to photograph while my mum, my sister and I sat in the car, bored stiff.
I   I can imagine.
M The worst thing was that he only wanted to take photographs when the sun was out, which wasn't, unfortunately, most of the time. So the three of us used to sit there praying for the sun to come out from behind a cloud so that we could get on our way.
I   Right.
M The only problem was that we were on our way to the next photograph, the next cloud and the next wait in the car.
I   Oh dear!

Interview 2

I When you were younger, how did you use to spend the summer holiday?

F We always spent our summer holiday as a family and every year we went to the same place – a small seaside town on the north coast of Spain called Laredo. Do you know it?

I No, I don't.

F Well, everyone there could speak English so there wasn't really any need for us to speak Spanish, but my father insisted on speaking it at every opportunity. The awful thing was that no one could understand him because he used to invent words – add an 'a' or an 'o' to an English word and think that that made it Spanish. Anyway, when we were first there, it didn't use to bother me because I didn't speak Spanish myself at that time. But then I started learning it at school and I realized just how bad his Spanish was.

I A bit embarrassing, yeah?

F Yeah, it was. We used to eat out a lot and I hated that because I was sure that all the waiters and other people in the restaurant were laughing at him. And I remember on one occasion he said something extremely rude and he didn't even realize. It was so embarrassing.

I I can imagine.

2 • Play **2.1** again. This time students listen for detail.
 • Check answers.

Answers

Speaker 1 disliked having to wait in the car for such a long time while his father waited for the sun to come out before he took a photograph. He found it very boring.
Speaker 2 disliked it when her father spoke Spanish because he spoke it very badly. She was embarrassed by this.

▮ Read ▮

1 • Ask students to read the letter. Check that they understand that the writer is describing a past family custom. You could briefly elicit how they decided this (use of Past simple and *used to*).

2a–b If they can, students answer the questions without referring back to the letter.
 • Check answers.

Answers

a Liz is describing visits to her Uncle James when she was young. Her mother used to take her and her brother to see her uncle whenever he was in port.
b The story is supposed to be amusing.

▮ Understanding ideas ▮ ————— p. 15 ▮

1–3 Students can first work on their own then compare ideas, or work in pairs. Remind them that there is no 'correct' answer; they have to use their imagination and the information in the listening and reading texts.
 • Check answers.

Possible answers

1 Speaker 1's father was selfish – he didn't care that everyone else was bored. He was the dominant family member – he obviously decided what everybody else did. He was patient – he was prepared to wait a long time for perfect photographic conditions. He was obsessive – he only thought about his photographs.

2 Maybe he was the type of person who felt that he should try to speak the language of the country he was in. Maybe he was showing off in front of his family.

3 It is funny because you would have expected it to be the other way round. The brother, who is in the navy now, had been sea-sick when they visited the uncle on board his ship, even though the boat was hardly moving. The speaker, who had loved everything to do with the sea, would now absolutely hate the idea of going on a cruise.

▮ Have your say ▮

• Allow students a few moments to think of an occasion when someone in their family embarrassed them. If students don't seem to have many ideas, you could start the ball rolling by describing an incident of your own.
• Students can describe the occasion in pairs or small groups.
• Monitor, but don't interrupt.
• You could elicit one or two examples from the class to round off the activity.

▮ Vocabulary ▮

1 • Give students a few moments to work out the meanings of *stiff*, *sick* and *dead*. Ask them which of the words can go <u>before</u> the adjective they are describing and which go <u>after</u>. Point out that these words are only used in informal English and do not collocate with all adjectives.

Answers

• *stiff*, *sick* and *dead* mean *very* or *extremely*.
• *stiff* and *sick* come after the adjective; *dead* comes before the adjective.

• For extra practice, ask students to answer these questions using an expression with *stiff*, *sick* or *dead*, e.g. *Did you enjoy the party? No. It was dead boring.*
 Why did you go straight to bed? How did you feel when you heard the scream? Why did you leave in the middle of the film? What was the exam like? How would you feel if you thought you might lose your job?

2 • Students work through these personal questions in pairs or small groups.
 • Monitor conversations, but only correct inappropriate use of the idiomatic expressions.

—Grammar review – *used to* —————

1–4 Students could work through all these questions individually or in pairs, referring to the **Language commentary** on p.125 to check their answers. Alternatively, they could do the questions one by one and you could check answers as they complete each one.

Answers

1 a 1 R, 2 R, 3 1 (first clause) and R (second clause), 4 1, 5 R, 6 R
b *used to* and Past simple + frequency adverb (*always*) are used to refer to past actions or situations which happened regularly. The word and expression *first* and *on one occasion* + Past simple are used to refer to an event which happened once.

2 a 2   **b** 1

3 Question: *Did* you *use to wear* glasses?
Affirmative: I *used to smoke* a pipe.
Negative: He *didn't use to be* so unfriendly. / He *never used to be* so unfriendly.
• Point out that the question and negative forms of *used to* are the same as any other regular verb in the Past simple.
• Check correct pronunciation of *used to*:
/tə/ before words beginning with a consonant. (*I used to go out every night.*)
/tu/ before words beginning with a vowel. (*We used to eat dinner together.*)
Check that students know the short answers for *used to*: *Yes, I* (etc.) *did. No, I* (etc.) *didn't.*

4 We know the speaker went skiing regularly in sentence **b**. The use of *used to* makes this clear. In sentence **a** it is possible that the speaker went skiing only once.

Check

5 • Elicit a couple of ideas, for example one affirmative form and one negative form, to check that students understand the task.

Possible answers
She used to be happy. She didn't use to look after children.
He used to live in a big house. He didn't use to live in a prison cell. He used to drive a big car. He used to smoke cigars. He didn't use to eat prison food.
He used to play football. He didn't use to cook. He used to be young and carefree.

6 • Students may need to spend a few moments thinking about changes in their life before they begin. You could give some examples of your own to start off the activity.
• It is probably better if both students contribute their ideas to each topic as they go through the list. You could also ask students to make lists of things which they have in common, and then elicit two examples from each pair to round off the activity.
• Monitor, correcting any mistakes in the use and pronunciation of *used to*.

▶ **Photocopiable activity 3 p.155**

Listening

In your experience

This activity introduces the theme of special days and special occasions.

1 • Before students work on their own to make a list of special days and occasions they celebrate every year, elicit a couple of examples from the class using the pictures, e.g. anniversaries, birthdays, national festivals.

2 • Students compare their list with a partner, then add any other occasions which people celebrate regularly or only once. Elicit ideas, e.g. passing an exam / graduating from university / the birth of a baby / new job / winning something (e.g. a prize in a sports event; the lottery).

Listen

There are two parts in this listening activity. **2.2** is about birthdays; **2.3** is about April Fool's Day.

1 • Before you play **2.2**, ask students to take notes as they listen. Speaker 5 refers to a game called *twister*: you could tell students this before they listen, or ask them to guess what it is after listening.
• Play the tape twice if necessary. Students can compare ideas before the second listening.

Answers

	a	b
1	Her boyfriend	Went for a meal and watched TV at home.
2	His family	Celebrated it in France.
3	Friends	Had a few drinks and went to a *club.
4	The speaker's boyfriend will celebrate with her and friends	Have a big party with a live band.
5	Five friends	Went bowling, had a birthday tea, played ** twister, ate lots of popcorn.

* = a discotheque   ** a game

2.2

Speaker 1   On my last birthday I decided that I wasn't going to go out with loads of friends erm as I normally do. Erm, I think it was on a Friday and erm I went out with my boyfriend and I think we went for a quiet meal somewhere, and then probably just went home and watched television like we normally do.

Speaker 2   My last birthday was about two weeks ago and I celebrated it in France. It was very special because we were on holiday and my children brought me a cake and they brought me some presents … and well they all sat on the bed … and they sat around whilst I opened my presents.

Speaker 3   My last birthday? Erm, I've just had my last birthday. It was yesterday. My twenty-fifth. Oh, what did I do? Can't remember! No. I went out with some mates for a few drinks. We went on to a club. I got to bed late. I've got a bit of a hangover today so it must have been good.

Speaker 4   It's my boyfriend's birthday next week, actually. He's 30 on Saturday, which is a bit special, so I've organized a party for him. It's supposed to be a surprise party but I'm not sure if I'll be able to keep it a secret for much longer. I've hired a room above a pub and there's going to be a live band playing. Er, I'm not sure how many people will come. I sent out 30 or so invitations last week and er I've sent out the same number this week. I'm not sure if everyone'll be able to come, but it should be good anyway.

Speaker 5   My last birthday was my favourite birthday because I had five of my friends round and we went bowling and then we had a birthday tea afterwards and we played twister and and ate lots of popcorn.

2 · Give students a few moments to think before they talk in pairs about their own birthday celebrations. This free speaking activity will give you the opportunity to see how well students are using the Past simple. Monitor, but do not interrupt conversations.

3 · In the second recording the theme switches from personal celebrations to national celebrations.
· If students celebrate April Fool's Day in their country you could ask them to guess the answers to questions **a–c**. Then elicit ideas, but don't confirm if these are right or wrong.
· Play **2.3** through once, then check students' answers to questions **a–d**.

Answers

a April 1st.
b Britain and many other European countries. Holland is mentioned.
c Old.
d Yes, some people were fooled.

2.3

I As you all know tomorrow is April 1st – April Fool's Day. So we thought it would be a nice idea to invite someone along to tell us a bit more about this festival. And to do just that we have Professor Stephen Pennington from the University of Hull. Good afternoon, Professor Pennington, and thank you for coming.
P Not at all. Good afternoon.
I Can I start by asking you a personal question, professor?
P By all means.
I Will you yourself be playing a joke on anyone tomorrow?
P But of course. That's the whole point of April Fool's Day.
I But isn't April Fool's Day more for children? I remember when I was young I always played jokes on my parents and my teachers on April 1st. The plastic fried egg on the breakfast plate – that sort of thing. But isn't it something people grow out of?
P Yes and no. Some adults get just as involved as children, believe me. You see, it's the one day in the year when you're allowed and even expected to be silly. And in the workplace it gives people the ideal opportunity to play a trick on their boss which they'd probably get the sack for any other day of the year.
I I see. So tell me, is April Fool's Day only celebrated in Britain?
P No, not at all. It's celebrated in many other European countries apart from Britain, though not always on April 1st. People have celebrated the festival for hundreds of years. It's actually believed to be linked to the ancient Roman festival of Hilaria.
I I didn't know that.
P Oh yes, although some people think it might have some connection with the spring Holi festival in India.
I I see. Tell us some April Fool jokes.
P Well, one of the best in my opinion was in the early sixties in England. In 1962, I think it was, a television company showed a short documentary film about spaghetti farming in Italy.
I Spaghetti farming?
P Yes. They showed villagers climbing up ladders and picking strings of spaghetti off the trees.

I They didn't.
P Yes, and the best thing was that they received hundreds of letters from viewers the next day asking how to grow spaghetti. That still makes me laugh.
I Amazing.
P Another good one was in the 70s in Holland when a Dutch newspaper announced on its front page that they had printed the paper with perfumed ink. Apparently loads of people were seen secretly sniffing their newspapers that day.
I What will they think of next? Well, I'm afraid we'll have to stop there Professor Pennington. Thank you. That's been both amusing and interesting.
P My pleasure.

· You could play **2.3** a second time for more detailed comprehension. Write these questions on the board before students listen.
   1 What joke did the interviewer play on her parents when she was young?
   2 What was the joke about spaghetti farming?
   3 What joke did a Dutch newspaper play on its readers?

Answers

1 She put a plastic fried egg on her parents' plates at breakfast.
2 A TV company made a documentary film about spaghetti. They tried to convince people that spaghetti grew on trees.
3 They said they had printed the paper with perfumed ink.

▮ Vocabulary ▮

· Allow students a few minutes to do this activity on their own or in pairs and then check ideas.

Answers

a Of course.
b the essential (real) purpose
c behave in a way which is not sensible
d be dismissed from one's job

▮ Understanding ideas ▮

1–3 Students can discuss these questions in pairs and note down possible answers.
· Check ideas.

Possible answers

1 Frightening someone with a plastic spider or snake.
Putting a 'whoopee cushion' on someone's seat so that when they sit down it makes a rude noise.

2 It tells us that the interviewer finds it hard to believe that the TV company actually did this.

3 Many people *secretly* sniffed their papers because they wanted to see if it was true but they didn't want to be seen doing it in case it was a joke.

▮ Have your say ▮

1–2 This is an opportunity for students to talk about their own personal experiences. They can discuss both questions in pairs, groups, or as a whole class.
· Elicit some ideas for **2**, for example a *Left-handed Day*, when everyone has to do everything with their left hand; a *Take Your Pet to Work Day*.

Grammar — Present perfect and Past simple

In *Preview* we looked at *used to* to describe past habits, and touched on the difference with the Past simple for one-off events. This section goes on to look at the differences between the Past simple and the Present perfect simple (introduced in Unit 1).

■ Exploring concepts

1–2 Students can work through these questions and tasks individually or in pairs. You could check their ideas after each section or, if you are confident of your students' ability, check all sections together. Remind students they should refer to the **Language commentary** on p.126.
- Allow sufficient time for students to work through the questions.
- Check answers.

Answers

1 a 1 When I (was) young, I always (played) jokes on my parents and my teachers on April 1st.
  2 He's 30 on Saturday so I've organized a party for him.
  3 My last birthday (was) about two weeks ago and I (celebrated) it in France.
  4 I've sent out the same number (of invitations) this week.
  5 People have celebrated the festival for hundreds of years.
b A Sentence 3   B Sentence 4   C Sentence 1
   D Sentence 5   E Sentence 2

2 a The person is speaking this afternoon or this evening.
  b The person is speaking this morning.

■ Exploitation

1 • Students work individually through this practice exercise, then compare answers with a partner.
  • Check answers.

Answers

a cried
b did ... go
c have ordered
d worked
e haven't spoken
f Did ... meet
g didn't go
h Have ... finished
i has lived

2 a Check that students know the past participles of the verbs in the list.
  • Check the question for *go abroad*: *Have you ever **been** abroad?* and not *Have you ever gone abroad?* Remind students that *been* means go and return, and *gone* means on the way to a place or still there.
  • Demonstrate the activity by asking a pair of students to read the example dialogue. If necessary, give a further example with one of the other prompts.
  • Let students work in pairs and monitor. Correct any mistakes in the verb forms only.
  b Elicit one piece of information from each student. Correct any mistakes in tense.

▶ **Photocopiable activity 4 p.156**

■ Free speech

3 a Students work in pairs to draw up a list of what their party has done in the areas given. Each student should make their own list. Provide help with vocabulary and ideas where necessary, for example:
Crime: reduce crime (build more prisons, introduce tougher laws)
The environment: improve the environment (ban cars from city centres, introduce recycling schemes)
Public transport: improve public transport (reduce fares, improve services)
Education: improve standards (build more schools, introduce new tests)
The health service: improve the health service (build more hospitals, increase nurses' pay, reduce waiting times)
The elderly: build more homes for people who can't look after themselves, introduce free dental treatment for people over 70

  b Students add extra information to their lists in note form to say exactly what they have done.

c–d Give students time to plan their campaign speech, then divide the class into groups of three or four. Make sure that students who have worked together are in different groups.
  • Students present their campaign speeches to the rest of their group. Then each student votes for another of the candidates in their group. You could round the activity off by asking who was elected in each group.

p. 18

Skills

This section looks at traditional views of men's and women's abilities. The quiz and the listening examine why men are better at some activities than women and vice versa.

■ Write and speak

1 • Introduce the theme by getting each student to write down two activities they think men do better than women and vice-versa.

2 • Divide the class into groups of three or four (preferably mixed sex).
  a Students should tell the other group members their ideas.
  b Together, they make new lists.
  c One person from each group should present the group's ideas to the class.
  • If you like, you could write each group's ideas on the board and at the end ask the whole class to vote on whether they agree or disagree. You could also elicit reasons for their choices, e.g. *Men are better than women at fixing cars because they are more interested in how things work. Women are better at ironing than men because they are taught how to iron by their mothers.*

Read

- Read the introduction with the class and explain any new vocabulary. Check that students understand *brain*.
- You could let the class answer the quiz questions on their own and use a dictionary to look up any words they don't understand. Alternatively, you could go through the quiz with the class question by question explaining vocabulary as you go. Make sure that students choose one answer only for each question. (Students will fill in the score and the meaning of the score as they listen to **2.4** and **2.5** .)

Listen
p. 19

1 · Play **2.4** (the first part of the conversation). Students write in the missing scores. Check answers.

Answers

Men score		Women score	
a) 10 points		a) 15 points	
b) 5 points		b) 5 points	
c) minus 5 points		c) minus 5 points	

2.4

A Have you finished answering the questions yet?
J Er, just a minute.
N Just finishing. OK.
A Right 'How to score'. OK. The scores are different for men. Right Nick? You'd better make a note of it.
N Yep.
A 'Men score: a: ten points; b: five points; c: minus five points.'
N Minus five points?
A Yeah. Ten points for a; five points for b and minus five points for c. Got that?
N Yeah.
J What about mine?
A Right. 'Women score: a: fifteen points; b: five points; c: minus five points.'
J a: fifteen; b: five and c: minus five.
A Uh huh.
J Why are the men's and women's scores different?
A Don't know. It doesn't say. OK. Are you ready to find out what your score means?
N/J Just a minute.
    Hang on a minute.

- Give students a few moments to add up their scores. Explain that they will find out what their score means when they listen to **2.5** (the second part of the conversation).

2 · Students decide whether they think statements **a–e** are True or False and compare ideas with a partner. You could ask for a show of hands to see what the general opinion is, but do not confirm or deny at this stage.

3 · Play **2.5** (the second part of the conversation). Students first of all fill in the missing information on **What your score means** then check their ideas about the True / False statements.
- Play the recording again if necessary. Students can compare answers before the second listening.
- Check answers.

Answers
What your score means:
Most men will score between **0** and **60** points. Most women will score between **50** and **100** points. Men who score above **60** may show a **female** *bias. Women who score below **50** may show a **male** bias.
* bias= tendency. They may have brains which behave more like a female brain than a male brain.

True / False statements
a False (Men and women use their brains differently.)
b True (Both use the left side of the brain for speaking.)
c False (When a skill is spread over two areas of the brain we will find it more difficult.)
d False (Men are better than women at mathematics.)
e False (Women are better than men at languages.)

2.5

A Right. What did you get Nick?
N I'm not saying till you tell me what it means.
A OK. It says 'Most men will score between 0 and 60. Most women will score between 50 and 100.'
N What happens if you don't?
A It says that 'men who score above 60 may show a female bias and women scoring below 50 may show a male bias.'
J What does that mean?
A Well, according to the article, men's and women's brains work in different ways. What did you get anyway, Nick?
N 65.
A Well, it just means that for some things your brain works like a woman's brain. I got 45 so that means that for some things my brain works like a man's brain. What did you get, Jan?
J 50.
A So you're fairly typical.
N I'm not sure I really agree.
J Just because you got 65! I'm not sure I really understand.
A OK. Well, according to scientific research, men and women use their brains differently. Before, scientists thought that everyone's brain worked in the same sort of way; the right side of the brain controlled some things and the left side of the brain controlled other things. But apparently, that's not the case. It depends on whether the brain is totally male or totally female, or whether it has some male characteristics, like mine does, or some female characteristics like yours does, Nick.
N I'm still not clear.
A OK. Well, generally speaking men's and women's brains work differently. For example, men use the right side of their brain for working on an abstract problem like a mathematical equation, while women use both sides of their brain. For language, although both use the left side of the brain for speaking and grammar, in women it's the front part of the brain that handles these skills and in men it's the back and the front part of the brain. It seems that when one skill is concentrated in one area of the brain we are better at it, or at least we find it easier. When a skill is spread over two areas of the brain we find it more difficult.
J I suppose that would help to explain why men are better than women at mathematics and women are better than men at languages.
A Yep. But each person's different. Don't forget that not all men have a typical male brain, and not all women have a typical female brain.
N OK. I understand now. I'm not sure if I agree, but it's interesting.
J What about the answers then?
A OK. Question 1 …

- Allow students a few moments to work out what kind of brain they have. Your students may prefer to keep this information to themselves!

4 • Go through what the answers to the quiz mean on p.154 of the Student's Book explaining any new vocabulary.

▦ Have your say

This is an opportunity for students to discuss the topic.

1–2 Divide the class into groups of three or four.

• Check that students understand the three theories.
The sex of the brain theory
The type of job we do depends more on the sex of our brain than our gender. So men and women with male brains are more likely to be engineers and those with female brains are more likely to be nurses or teachers.
The education theory
Women are brought up to believe that certain jobs are suitable for men and certain jobs are suitable for women. They are not expected to be good at or interested in certain subjects like science and maths and are not encouraged to pursue careers like engineering.
The tradition theory
The reason why women don't do certain jobs is because traditionally these jobs have always been done by men. Men regard them as 'men's jobs' and women are discouraged from doing them.

• Elicit some opinions to round off the activity.

▦ Vocabulary

1–2 Students answer the question and compare ideas with a partner. If they have different ideas they should try to justify them. Point out there are no right or wrong answers.

▦ Pronunciation

3 • Ask students in pairs to decide where the stress is on the adjectives. Demonstrate different ways of marking stress on the board.
a'ggressive   <u>agg</u>ressive   aggre<u>s</u>sive
• Play **2.6** so that students can check their answers.
• Do a final check round the class.

2.6

<u>agg</u>ressive, a<u>ss</u>ertive, compe<u>t</u>itive, i<u>m</u>aginative, <u>prac</u>tical, <u>sen</u>sible, <u>sen</u>sitive, <u>talk</u>ative

Answers
See Tapescript **2.6** .

4 • Students do this speaking activity in pairs. They can use the adjectives from the list and any others they know.

▦ Speak

This is a final opportunity for discussion of the topic.

1–2 It is very important that students work on their own to answer these two questions.

3 • Students compare ideas with a partner and try to persuade them to their point of view.

4 • Students then work in groups of four and follow the same procedure.

5 • The presentation phase is a chance for them to share ideas, and need not be formal. Groups could either appoint a spokesperson to make the presentation, or could share the points between them.

— p. 20 —

Grammar extra

Adjective order

This non-verb grammar section looks at the order of adjectives before nouns. The short reading and speaking activities introduce the new theme – national costumes.

1–2 Ask students to read the short text and discuss the questions. Students from different countries can talk in pairs. If students are from the same country elicit ideas from the whole class.

• Encourage students to describe the costumes in as much detail as possible. Provide vocabulary where necessary but don't worry about correct order of adjectives at this stage.

▦ Exploring concepts

1 • Students work individually through 1. Check answers.

Answers
a <u>beautiful yellow silk</u> (sari)
b <u>smart knee-length cotton</u> (jacket); <u>tight-fitting white cotton</u> (trousers)
c <u>full red woollen</u> (skirt); <u>yellow, black, white or green</u> (stripes); <u>red woollen</u> (top); <u>short-sleeved white linen</u> (blouse); <u>white or red leather</u> (boots)
d <u>elegant Japanese silk</u> (kimono)

2 a Students work individually to list the adjectives under the headings. Check answers.

Answers
Where from	(Japanese)
Material	(silk), cotton, woollen, linen, leather
Colour	(yellow), white, red, black, green
Size / Age / Shape	(knee-length), tight-fitting, full, short-sleeved
Opinion	(beautiful), smart, elegant

b–c Students could work in pairs to answer the questions and then check their ideas in the **Language commentary** on p.126. Alternatively, you could elicit ideas from the class and write them on the board, and refer them to the **Language commentary** for later reference.

• Check answers.

Answers
b Opinion adjectives come before other adjectives.
c The correct order of adjectives before a noun is: Opinion, size, age, shape, colour, where from, material (noun). Point out that we do not usually use more than three adjectives before a noun.

Exploitation

1 • You can either do this as written practice, with weaker classes, or orally. Students work in pairs to describe the objects.
   • Check answers.

Possible answers
It's a large brown leather briefcase. It's a small black Japanese camera. It's a beautiful Chinese silk scarf. It's a small round wooden table.

Role play

2a–b Divide the class into pairs. Go through the example dialogue with the class. Then ask everyone to write down three things which have been stolen and three adjectives to describe each thing.
   • Tell students to take turns to be Student B. Remind them that it is Student B who asks the questions and builds up the adjective + noun pattern.
   • Monitor, but don't interrupt. Then elicit feedback from each pair of what was stolen. Correct any mistakes in adjective order at this point.

3 • This is primarily a fluency exercise which may allow students to use some adjective + noun combinations. Unless you want to turn it into another controlled practice exercise do not insist students use these language forms. Ask a couple of students to say what their partner told them.

— p. 21 —

Exploring words

Food and cooking

Students can do exercises 1–3 on their own or in pairs.

1 • Ask students what they know about Thanksgiving Day in the USA.

Background information
Thanksgiving Day is celebrated in the United States on the fourth Thursday of November. On that day families get together for a large celebration dinner. Strangers who have no families are also invited to join in the celebrations. Thanksgiving Day celebrates the Pilgrim Fathers' first harvest in New England in 1621. They celebrated this with native American Indians in a feast lasting three days. The Pilgrim Fathers were some of the first settlers in the United States. They were a group of 102 men, women and children who had sailed from Plymouth in England to make a new life for themselves in America.

   • Ask students to label the foods. Check answers and explain briefly what each food is.

Answers
a 6 **b** 2 **c** 3 **d** 5 **e** 1 **f** 4

2 a Students match ways of cooking food with the pictures. Students could use dictionaries to check the meanings of any words they don't know.
   • Check answers.

Answers
a 4 **b** 3 **c** 2 **d** 8 **e** 5 **f** 9 **g** 7 **h** 1 **i** 6
bake cook bread, cakes, biscuits and potatoes by dry heat in an oven
barbecue cook outside over a metal frame
boil cook sth in boiling water
fry cook in a frying pan in oil or fat
stir-fry cook by frying for a short time in very hot oil stirring all the time
grill cook directly over or under direct heat
roast cook meat or vegetables in an oven usually in a little oil or fat
steam cook in steam
stew cook meat or fruit slowly in liquid in a closed pan or dish

   b You could do this with the whole class. Elicit ideas and elicit or explain how the foods are cooked. You could put these on the board in a word web.

Answers
Potatoes baked, fried, mashed, boiled, roast, puréed
Eggs boiled, hard-boiled, soft-boiled, scrambled, poached

   c Students tell their partners how they usually cook the foods listed.
   • Have brief whole-class feedback.

3 • Read through the recipe ingredients with the class and explain any new vocabulary in the recipe.
   • Check answers.

Answers
1	peel … cut	6	Drain
2	Chop	7	mash
4	Add	8	Mix
5	Boil	9	decorate

4 • This is a fluency activity which gives students the opportunity to use some of the vocabulary which has been practised in the lesson.
   • Pair students from different countries or regions together where possible. If students are from the same country they can describe a different traditional dish to each other. Alternatively, they could describe the same dish but compare differences in ingredients and method of cooking. (If you have students who have no idea how their national dishes are cooked they can probably still describe them. If you want them to practise the cooking vocabulary, you could ask them to describe how to make something they can cook – it can be something simple like an omelette.) Monitor, helping with vocabulary where required.

5 • This can be set for homework. You could put the finished recipes on the wall or make up a class cookery book.

Writing

Describing a public event

In this section students write a description of a national or regional festival in their country for a tourist brochure.

Listen

1. • Ask students to look at the photographs on the page. Ask them if they recognize any of the festivals, and to describe what they can see in the pictures.
   • Play **2.7** once only. Tell students to match the descriptions they hear with two of the photos.
   • Check answers. You could elicit which words helped the students decide.

Answers
1 The large picture.
2 The picture top right.

2.7

1 People come to the village from all over the world to watch this annual event, and although most of the competitors are Finns, there are also entrants from Norway, Germany and Switzerland. The race itself is run over 235 metres. The runner – a man – runs over the obstacle course with a woman, who must be at least 17, on his back. They have to run over sand, grass, asphalt, up hills, over fences, and through water. If the man drops the woman they are given a 15-second penalty.

2 The Round-up, which attracts more than 30,000 visitors to the town each year, is held on the second weekend of March. The festivities begin on the Thursday with a parade through the town. This is followed by a dance. While this is going on, the hunters, working in groups of 25, go out in search of snakes. Each group is accompanied by an official, who carries anti-venom antidote just in case anyone is bitten. For obvious safety reasons, tourists are not allowed to join in.

2. • Before you play **2.8** explain to students that they will need to fill in the missing information in the table as they listen. Check the vocabulary in the table first.
   • Play the recording. Once should be enough as students don't have to understand everything. Then check answers.

Answers
Sweetwater, **Texas**
1958
To get rid of **snakes**
Second weekend in **March**
A parade, **snake** hunting, prize-giving, snake-handling exhibitions, **cooking** competition
Chilli, **beer**

2.8

The Annual Sweetwater Rattlesnake Round-up takes place, as its name suggests, in the town of Sweetwater in the state of Texas, USA. The event started in 1958 when a group of cattle ranchers and farmers paid people from out of town to round up the snakes and take them away from the area. The venomous snakes, which are found in particularly large numbers in this part of Texas, were proving a danger to humans and animals alike.

The Sweetwater Rattlesnake Round-up, which attracts more than 30,000 visitors to the town each year, is held on the second weekend of March. The festivities begin on the Thursday with a parade through the town. This is followed by a dance. While this is going on, the hunters, working in groups of 25, go out in search of snakes. Each group is accompanied by an official, who carries anti-venom antidote just in case anyone is bitten. For obvious safety reasons, tourists are not allowed to join in.

On the Friday, when the hunting groups return, and after a prize has been awarded to the group which has caught the most snakes, there are snake-handling exhibitions at which you can find out what to do if you come across a snake. Basically, don't play with it and don't run away from it either. Remember, it's more afraid of you than you are of it!

The big event on the Saturday is a cooking competition for the best chilli. A prize is given to the best chilli in several different categories, and you can try the end results for yourself. For the more adventurous there is rattlesnake chilli and for the less adventurous there is hamburger chilli, which you can wash down with a glass or two of beer if you like. The festivities don't end until the last bowl of chilli has been eaten.

Brainstorm and notes

• Divide the class into groups of three or four. If your students are from different countries, put students from the same country together. Any students who can't be partnered up in this way could form another group and describe a festival that they all know something about, e.g. Bonfire night, Christmas.
• Students should talk together to pool their ideas and make detailed notes in answer to the questions in 2.

Write

1. • Students work individually to write the first draft of their account.
   • Before they start, work through the **Reminder** box with them and check that they understand each point. You could give them, or elicit from them, a possible paragraph plan.
     1 Name of festival, when and where it takes place.
     2 Origins of festival and when it dates from.
     3 The main events; what people eat and drink.
   • Remind students that although this is a first draft other students will read what they have written.
   • Monitor and help with vocabulary where necessary but don't correct what students have written.

2a–b Students should exchange accounts with someone from a different group. They should read each other's accounts and suggest one or two improvements.
   • As they read they can ask themselves these questions: *Does the account answer all the questions a tourist would want to know? Is it clear?*
   c Students discuss their suggestions for improvement. Be available to answer any queries.
   • Students write their final version. This can be done in class or at home.

▶ **Writing model 2 (photocopiable) TB p.130**

Language in action

Invitations

This section practises the language used for inviting people to do things, and accepting and turning down invitations.

Introduction

1 a Divide students into pairs. Students have to write down mini-dialogues for three of the situations.
  - First, give an example using one of the situations. Ask questions like these:
    1 Look at **a**. Who is inviting? (*The woman on the left.*)
    2 What is she inviting the other person to do? (*To go to a birthday party.*)
    3 Does the other person want to go to the party? (*Yes*).
    4 What do you think the woman on the left says? (*It's Neil's birthday next Saturday. We're having a surprise party for him. Would you like to come?*)
    5 What do you think the other woman replies? (*I'd love to come. What time does it start?*)
  - Write up the students' suggested dialogue on the board, making any corrections. If students provide any other appropriate forms you could write these up too. Don't give any new forms though.
  - Allow enough time for students to do the activity (six to eight minutes). Then elicit a few examples for each situation. Don't worry about correcting mistakes at the moment. Treat this as an opportunity for you to see how much the students know.

b Students make lists of the language they already know for inviting, accepting invitations and refusing invitations. They could do this in pairs or you could elicit ideas from the whole class and write them directly onto the board.

2 a Tell students that they are going to hear five conversations about the people in the illustrations. The first time they should simply match the conversations with the illustrations in their books.
  - Play **2.9** and check answers.

Answers

1 a 2 d 3 e 4 c 5 b

2.9

1
B Hi, Sally. How are you doing?
S I'm fine. You?
B Oh, great! Actually, I'm glad I've bumped into you. You know it's Neil's birthday next Saturday?
S Oh, right.
B Well, it's his thirtieth, so we've decided to throw a surprise party for him. You will come, won't you?
S Yeah, great. What time?
B Nine-ish? Oh, and bring a bottle.

2
O Phil?
P Mm?

O Janice and I are going to stay at a friend's house for the weekend while they're away.
P That sounds nice.
O Yeah, well, actually it's in a really nice place, right by the sea. Would you and Martha like to come along?
P Oh, we'd love to, but we're busy this weekend. Thanks for asking, though.

3
S What's that you're reading?
M It's an invitation. Someone I was at university with is having an exhibition of her paintings. There's a party afterwards. It says 'Bring a partner'. Do you want to come?
S When is it?
M Saturday.
S This Saturday?
M Yes. From 8.00 p.m. on.
S Mm, Saturday night's a bit difficult.
M It doesn't matter. I'll ask Pete if he wants to come.

4
O Karen?
K Yeah?
O Sam and I are going to the cinema tonight. Do you fancy coming?
K Thanks, I'd like that.

5
L Hello, Sandra. It's Linda here. How are you?
S I'm fine thanks, Linda. And you?
L Not too bad. Look, the reason I'm ringing is that we're having a small dinner party a week on Friday and we'd like to invite you and David.
S Just a minute, Linda. I'll have to check my diary. Is that the 29th?
L Yeah.
S Oh, oh I'm really sorry, but we've arranged to go to the theatre that night.
L Ah, well, never mind … Some other time …

b Before you play the recording again check that students understand what they have to do. Student A should write down any of the language used to invite someone to do something. Point out that it is not necessary to write down the whole sentence. *Would you like to …?* is enough. Student B should write down any expressions used to accept and refuse invitations.

c Students tell each other their ideas and add the expressions to their lists. If you prefer, you could elicit ideas from the class and write these on the board for students to copy down.

Answers

Inviting	Accepting invitations	Refusing invitations
You will come, won't you?	Yeah, great.	I'm really sorry but …
We'd like to invite you …	Thanks, I'd like that.	We'd love to but …
Do you fancy (…) -ing?		(X) is a bit difficult …
Would you like to …?		
Do you want to …?		

This section looks at main sentence stress and sounding enthusiastic.

1 **a** Read through the information with the students, then demonstrate. Write this question on the board.
Did you have a nice holiday?
Ask students which words they think will be stressed and underline them.
Did you <u>have</u> a <u>nice</u> <u>holiday</u>?

• Ask them which word they think is the most important in the sentence (*holiday*). Underline it twice.

Note Syllable stress is left until the next unit. But you could deal with it here if you like. Ask students which syllable in *holiday* is stressed (**ho**liday) and underline the stressed syllable rather than the whole word twice.

• Now write up these two sentences, which are possible replies to the question, and follow the same procedure.
We <u>had</u> a <u>lovely</u> <u>holiday</u>.
The <u>hotel</u> was <u>really</u> <u>nice</u> / but …

b Allow students a few minutes to do the exercise in pairs then play **2.10** so that students can check their ideas.

2.10

1 A What are you doing on Saturday?
B I'm having a <u>party</u> on Saturday.
2 A When are you having a party?
B I'm having a party on <u>Saturday</u>.
3 A How are things between you and Peter?
B We're getting <u>married</u> next month.
4 A When are you getting married?
B We're getting married next <u>month</u>.
5 A I saw a red car parked outside your house last night.
B My <u>brother's</u> staying with us at the moment.
6 A Who's your brother staying with?
B My brother's staying with <u>us</u> at the moment.

Answers
See Tapescript **2.10** .

c Ask students to do the activity in pairs. You could elicit their ideas first before you play the tape or play the tape directly.

d Play **2.11** . Tell students to correct any answers which are 'different'. Their answers are not necessarily wrong.

2.11

1 /I'm having a <u>party</u> on Saturday./ You <u>will</u> come, /<u>won't</u> you?/
2 /We're going to the <u>theatre</u>./ Do you fancy <u>coming</u>?/
3 /We're getting <u>married</u> next month./ We'd like to invite you to the <u>wedding</u>./
4 /My <u>brother's</u> staying with us at the moment./ Would you like to <u>meet</u> him?/
5 /I've got two tickets for the <u>theatre</u>./ Do you want to <u>come</u>?/

Answers
See Tapescript **2.11** .

2 **a** This exercise gives students practice in sounding enthusiastic when accepting invitations. Play **2.12** and check students' answers.

2.12

1 **a** Yeah, great. (Enthusiastic) **b** Yeah, great. (Unenthusiastic)
2 **a** Thanks, I'd like that. (Unenthusiastic) **b** Thanks, I'd like that. (Enthusiastic)
3 **a** Yeah, all right. (Enthusiastic) **b** Yeah, all right. (Unenthusiastic)

Answers
See Tapescript **2.12** .

b Play **2.13** and drill the enthusiastic responses chorally and / or individually.

2.13

1 Yeah, great.
2 Thanks, I'd like that.
3 Yeah, all right.

■ **Practice** ■■■■■■■■■■■■■■■■■■■■■■■■ p. 23 ■■

• Divide the class into groups of four: A, B, C, D. Give each student a piece of paper with their letter on it. They can clip this onto their clothes.

• Each student's diary includes arrangements, things they want to invite others to do, and spaces. They each invite the others, accept and refuse, until they have filled their diaries. If you think it necessary, demonstrate the first part of the activity by being Student A.

• Get the class into the middle of the room and tell them to mingle. They should not ask more than one question at a time to each person and should not speak to anyone who has the same letter as them.

• Monitor the activity, but don't interrupt. You could note down one or two mistakes that you hear, write them on the board and get students to correct them at the end of the activity.

• Finish off by asking a few students to tell you some of their plans for next week.

■ **Language check** ■

To round off the unit, encourage students to read through the final **Language check** which summarizes the points covered in the unit. Students could tick points they feel confident about and highlight points they want to return to and revise.

3 Working practices

Theme

The overall theme of this unit is work.

Preview Current employment trends
Listening Teleworking – working from home
Skills Unusual jobs, including an ice sculptor
Grammar extra Zoo keeper
Writing Letters and faxes

Grammar

- Review of the Present continuous to describe trends
- Present perfect continuous with adverbs
- Word order: time and place words and phrases / adverbs of manner

Vocabulary

- Jobs and work

Writing

- Letters and faxes

Functional language

- Agreeing and disagreeing

Pronunciation

- Stress and linking

Workbook

- Grammar and functional language as above
- Topic vocabulary: work; figures; idioms to do with time
- Quotations about money

Preview

This provides a general introduction to the theme of the unit, work, by focusing on recent employment trends. The short reading texts also include examples of the Present continuous used to describe trends.

■ Your thoughts ■■■■■■■■■■■■■■■■■ p. 24 ■

1 a You could start by getting the class briefly to discuss the first of the five statements. How many agree, how many disagree?

- Students now work through the rest of the statements individually, recording their agreement or disagreement on the 1–5 scale suggested.

- Spend a few minutes on each statement finding out opinions. Students have an opportunity to practise the language of agreement and disagreement in the *Language in action* section of the unit, so there is no need to insist on specific language forms here.

b–c Ask students to write statements expressing their own attitude to work, then discuss them in pairs or small groups.

- Monitor their discussions and write any interesting statements you hear on the board just for interest or for possible later discussion.

■ Read ■

This task introduces students to the topic of the texts which follow, as well as vocabulary related to this theme.

1 • Check that students understand the words and phrases, then let them note down any current changes taking place in their country.

2 • Students read the four articles and match them with the headings.

- They could check if any of the trends they noted down are mentioned.

- Check answers.

Answers

Presenteeism* 3
Child labour 1
Women in management 4
Multi-job holders 2

* *Presenteeism* a new word referring to the phenomenon of people staying at work longer than they need to. It is related to *absenteeism* – people being away from work when they should be there.

- If you would like to exploit the texts further, you could ask these questions: *What jobs do you think the other child workers are doing?* (Text 1) *Why do more people than before need two jobs?* (Text 2) *What do you think the mental, physical and social effects of presenteeism could be?* (Text 3) *Why are American companies employing women managers?* (Text 4)

■ Vocabulary ■■■■■■■■■■■■■■■■■■■■■■■■■■ p. 25 ■

- Students work through these words individually or in pairs.
- Check answers.

Answers

a	current	e	effective
b	illegally	f	teamwork
c	(the) majority	g	glass ceiling
d	competitive		

- You could spend some time on other related words, e.g. illegally: *illegal / legal / legally*; competitive: *compete / competitor / competition / uncompetitive.*

■ Have your say ■■■■■■■■■■■■■■■■■■■■■■■■■■■■

1 • You may want to give them time to refer back to the text and note what the major trends referred to in each text are before they start the discussion.

2 • Students discuss possible future employment trends.
- Have brief whole-class feedback.

Possible answers

1 More children are expected to contribute towards family income. People can't afford to live on one income. Managers want to be seen to be the hardest workers. Women are good at management skills, but people are not willing to see them in the 'best' jobs. Generally, pressures to earn money are increasing.

2 Greater dependence on computers. More people working from home. People may have several jobs in their lifetime. Earlier retirement age. More unemployment.

—Grammar review — Present continuous for trends

1 • Work through this first question with the class to remind them of the basic difference between the two present tenses.
- Check answers.

Answers

a An action which is generally true.
b An action happening now.

Note If it helps to clarify the difference, use the words *permanent* and *temporary* to describe the two uses.

2–3 Students could now work individually or in pairs through 2 and 3. Remind them to refer to the **Language commentary** on p.127.
- Check answers.

Answers

2 a 2 (The speaker is spending some time redecorating. They may have started last week and expect to finish next week.)
  b 3 (Each year a growing number of people are retiring earlier.)
  c 1 (The speaker is probably feeding the cat twice a day for period of time the neighbour is on holiday.)

3 a 2 b 3 c 1

■ Check ■■■■■■■■■■■■■■■■■■■■■■■■■■■■■■■■■■

4 • Set a time limit of three to four minutes for students to complete these sentences.
- Check answers.

Answers

a	are working	(trend)	d	are paying	(trend)
b	start	(generally true)	e	works	(generally true)
c	are finding	(trend)	f	am walking	(repeated action)

5a–b This is a more open-ended practice exercise. Students think of their own endings for the four sentences, using the Present continuous.
- Elicit one possible ending for each sentence, then let students work on their own to think of answers.
- As they compare answers with a partner, monitor and correct any verb mistakes you hear.

c Finally, in pairs or groups, students discuss changes or trends currently affecting their lives.
- Start by giving an example of your own, then elicit one or two of their ideas, e.g. *It's taking me longer and longer to get to work. The traffic's getting worse and worse.*
- Again, monitor conversations but do not interrupt. Deal with corrections at a later stage.

— p. 26 —

Listening

This section is based on the topic of *teleworking* – the growing practice of working from home and communicating with your office by phone, fax or computer. The interview contains examples of the Present perfect continuous.

■ In your experience ■■■■■■■■■■■■■■■■■■■■■■■■■■■

1 • Find out how many people in the class know someone who works from home.
- Elicit some of the reasons why people do this.

2 • Let students work in pairs or small groups for a few minutes to discuss the pros and cons of this kind of work.
- Elicit their ideas.

■ Listen ■

1 a Introduce the word *teleworker* and elicit its meaning. You could ask what the prefix *tele-* means. What other words do students know that start like this? (*telephone / telescope / telegram / television / telepathy / telephoto lens*, etc.)

b Before students do the questionnaire, you could pre-teach these words: *independently; undisturbed; equipment.*

• Students do the questionnaire to find out if they could be teleworkers. They could either work through the questionnaire individually and then compare answers in pairs, or discuss each question in pairs as they go through the questionnaire.

c Conduct a quick survey: How many of the class could be effective teleworkers?

2 • **3.1** Students now listen to the interview with the teleworker and make a note of how his life has changed. You could ask them to listen for at least five points of change, then compare answers in pairs before listening for the second time.

• Don't pre-teach any words from the interview. Encourage students at this stage to listen for a general idea of what it is about. There will be a chance to focus on vocabulary later.

• Play the recording once or twice as necessary.

• Check answers.

Answers
– He no longer travels into the polluted city to work in a hot office.
– He has sold his car.
– He sees more of his family.
– He's less tired. / He gets more sleep.
– He sees friends more often. / He has become a more sociable person.
– He finds it easier to concentrate on his work. / He has fewer breaks.
– He no longer has meals at the restaurant. / He misses the gossip.

3.1

I You've been working from home for nearly a year now. What's it like?
T Brilliant! Absolutely brilliant!
I No regrets at all?
T None! I certainly wouldn't go back to spending three hours a day in my car just to work in an overheated office in the middle of a polluted city. In fact, I actually sold my car last month and since then

I've been putting the money I save on travelling into a separate bank account.
I OK, so what else do you like about teleworking apart from not having to travel every day?
T So many things. I mean, on the personal front, I see more of my family. I didn't use to get home until seven in the evening, by which time I was so tired I just staggered in, had a meal, watched TV for a couple of hours and went to bed.
I And now?
T Well, for a start, I'm much less tired. Since I started working from home, I've been getting more sleep. And I've been seeing my friends more often.
I What about work?
T You'll have to ask my boss about that, but I'd say I was better at my job than I used to be. I can certainly concentrate more easily, and I probably have fewer breaks than my colleagues at head office.
I How do you explain that?
T I'm not really sure, but I've heard several people say this. One thing, I suppose, is that there aren't as many distractions at home, so I usually finish a job before I have a break. I'm sure the company has been getting more work out of me. So far this week, for example, I've written three reports, and sent over a hundred e-mails and faxes, I've made fifty or sixty phone calls and I've been preparing for a business trip to the Far East next week. I haven't stopped!
I What about contact with other people? Doesn't it get lonely being at home all the time?
T That's something that used to worry me, but I can honestly say that I don't feel cut off at all. I mean most days I speak to my colleagues in the office. And of course, I'm in regular contact with our branches in other countries. Today, for example, I've been talking on the phone to colleagues in Australia and Japan – that was a three-way conversation that lasted nearly an hour.
I But what about face-to-face contact with other people?
T No problem. Two or three of my friends who live locally also work from home – so from time to time we have lunch together. And I certainly don't miss the boss breathing down my neck – I work office hours, you know, so he can contact me whenever he needs to. No, strangely enough, I think I'm a more sociable person than I was, I mean, I've got to know several of my neighbours really well.
I So is there nothing you miss about your old life?
T Not really, no. I mean the food in the restaurant was very good, there was always coffee around – and, of course there was office gossip – but that's all really.
I So, finally, what would you say to someone who's thinking about teleworking?
T I'd say 'Go for it'.

■ Vocabulary ■

• Students should work individually through this exercise, then compare answers in pairs.

• Check answers.

Answers
a 4 **b** 3 **c** 2 **d** 1 **e** 6 **f** 5

■ Understanding ideas ■

1 • Students should read through these comprehension questions and note down any of the answers they remember. They could work in pairs to do this.

• Play **3.1** again. Students check or complete their answers.

• Check answers.

Answers

a By car.
b He's less tired / concentrates more / has fewer breaks.
c When he's finished a particular job.
d Nearly an hour.
e Two or three friends who live near (and also work from home).
f Restaurant food / coffee / gossip.
g Do it. 'Go for it.'

2 • Students need to use their imagination to answer these questions. It should not be necessary to play the recording again. They could work through the questions individually or in pairs.
  • Elicit their ideas.

Possible answers

a Because he didn't need it for work. / Because he realized he did not need a car. / Because he decided cars were expensive causes of pollution.
b He can think more clearly because he's relaxed, not stressed after a dreadful journey. / He doesn't worry about his boss 'breathing down his neck'.
c Distractions at the office: People wanting a chat / gossip / breaks at specific times / telephone calls / general bustle of office life – people moving around and talking.
d He makes an effort to see people for social reasons. / He is not as tired as he was, so he feels more like socializing.

■ Have your say

  • Students could discuss this final question in pairs, groups or as a class.
  • You could conduct a final survey: How many students would like to work from home? Has anything they have heard changed their minds?

— Grammar – Present perfect continuous — p. 27 —

■ Exploring concepts

1–3 Students work through these questions individually or in pairs. If you are confident that they can deal with the questions and use the **Language commentary** on p.127 effectively, let them work through all the questions, referring to the **Language commentary**, before you check answers with the whole class. Alternatively, check answers after each part.
  • Check answers.

Answers

1 Sentence **a** refers to a completed action. (Present perfect simple) Sentence **b** refers to an incomplete action. (Present perfect continuous)

2 The present of *have* + *been* + *-ing* form of the verb.

3 Sentence **a** refers to a single, continuing action. Sentence **b** refers to a repeated action.

■ Exploitation ■

1 • Read through the example, then let students work individually through the exercise.
  • Check answers.

Answers

He started swimming twenty-five minutes ago. He's been swimming for twenty-five minutes.

She started exercising five minutes ago. She's been exercising for five minutes.

He started walking / jogging / running four and a half minutes ago. He's been walking / jogging / running for four and a half minutes.

She started cycling nine minutes ago. She's been cycling for nine minutes.

He started rowing seven and a half minutes ago. He's been rowing for seven and a half minutes.

2a–b Elicit the answer to 1 and check that students understand why *has just called* is correct. (The inclusion of *just* means that this is a completed action.)
  • Students work individually through 2–10, noting down their answers.
  • Students compare answers, and then work out together why the other answer is wrong.
  c Students listen to **3.2** and check their answers.
  • Finally, check answers and explanations.

3.2

L Jo has just called to say that her car's broken down on the motorway in the middle of nowhere.
K Has she phoned a garage for help yet?
L I don't know. I've been telling her to have her car fixed for ages, but she's taken no notice.
K It's not a very good car – it's been causing problems for ages.
L I know. She's been trying to sell it since her accident, but now she's given up because no one's interested in buying a twenty-five-year-old pink car.
K That's not surprising – it's in a dreadful condition. I know she's cleaned it several times, but she's only taken it to a garage once in the last five years.

Answers

1 ✓ *has just called*
  ✗ *has been calling* would mean she phoned several times.

2 ✓ *has broken down*
  ✗ *has been breaking down* would mean this happened repeatedly.

3 ✓ *Has she phoned*
  ✗ *Has she been phoning* would mean has she been making lots of phone calls.

4 ✓ *I've been telling her*
  ✗ *I've told her* would refer to a single completed action. (*for ages* suggests a continuous or a repeated action.)

5 ✓ *has taken*
  ✗ *has been taking* – it is unusual to talk about a repeated negative action.

6 ✓ *it's been causing*
  ✗ *it's caused* suggests a completed action, whereas this is a continuous state of affairs which has gone on for months.

7 ✓ *She's been trying*
✗ *She's tried* would suggest that she tried on only one occasion since the accident.

8 ✓ *she's given up*
✗ *she's been giving up* would suggest that she has given up repeatedly. (By its nature the verb *give up* refers to a single action.)

9 ✓ *she's cleaned*
✗ *she's been cleaning* suggests a continuous action. We are told that she cleaned it on several occasions. The phrase *several times* is not used with the Present perfect continuous.

10 ✓ *she's only taken*
✗ *she's only been taking* would suggest a repeated action, but we are told that she only took it once.

3 a Work through a couple more examples together with the class to make sure they understand the task. As the examples show, the information allows students to make Past simple, Present perfect simple and Present perfect continuous sentences.
  • Set a time limit for students to work in pairs to write more sentences from the chart.
  • Check answers.

Answers

Job	She's worked for IBM and Sony. / She worked for IBM for three years.
	She's been working for Sony for three years.
Home	She's lived in a flat in London. She bought a house two years ago.
	She's been living in the house for two years.
Relationships	She split up with Kris six years ago.
	She's been going out with Mario for four years.
Holidays	She's had / spent holidays in Poland and Spain.
	She didn't go anywhere / She didn't have a holiday four years ago.
	She's been going to Spain for the last three years.
Sports	She's played tennis and golf.
	Four years ago she was injured, but a year later she started playing tennis again.
	She took up golf two years ago and has been playing since then.

b Students now make their own chart like the one in their books.
  • When they have finished, they work in pairs, asking and answering questions. Demonstrate a few questions with the whole class before they begin, e.g. *How many sports have you played? How long have you been playing tennis?*
  • Monitor their conversations, listening for the correct use of the two Present perfect tenses. Only interrupt if students are repeating particular errors of use or form.

▶ **Photocopiable activity 5 p.155**

Skills

The theme now moves on to unusual jobs.

▌Speak ▌

1 • Check that students understand the four categories of work listed, then elicit other jobs for each category. Don't spend more than a few minutes on this, as the *Vocabulary* section on p.29 is devoted entirely to jobs and related vocabulary.

Possible answers

• **manual**	gardener electrician miner driver
• **office**	receptionist telephonist clerk manager
• **professional**	lawyer teacher dentist architect
• **artistic**	photographer illustrator composer fashion designer

2–3 Set a time limit of three or four minutes to discuss these questions.
  • Elicit a few ideas.

Possible answers

2 Work	**Disadvantages**
Manual	hard / tiring / boring / repetitive / badly paid dangerous?
Office	dull routine / repetitive / in unpleasant building?
Professional	long hours / demanding / stressful
Artistic	insecure / difficult to be successful / lonely

3 Reasons for changing: wanting a change / as a result of redundancy or early retirement / need for more money

▌Listen ▌

1 • Play **3.3** once, pausing briefly after each speaker to allow students to compare their ideas in pairs.
  • Play the recording once more. This time you could ask students to note down the clues that helped them to guess the job. If they don't know the exact name for the job, they can describe what the person does. Give students a few moments to discuss ideas and compare notes.
  • They could compare answers in pairs, giving reasons for their ideas.
  • Check answers.

3.3

Speaker 1 I spend all my time waiting for the phone to ring, which it does almost non-stop. You'd be amazed by the kind of questions people ask. It's quite difficult to stop yourself laughing sometimes. Someone rang me yesterday and said his mouse wasn't working. He moved it around but nothing happened. It turned out he had forgotten to connect it. Most of the problems are easy to put right. Most people ring because they're too lazy to read the manual. The hardest thing is being polite from nine in the morning till six in the evening.

Speaker 2 It's hard physical work, but I enjoy it 'cos it's out in the open and at that time of the year it's usually quite warm. The buses pick us up at seven in the morning and take us out of town to the fields. We start picking as soon as we get there – you've got to pick the fruit before it's too ripe. We put it into wooden boxes which are collected by tractor and taken to the sorting area where they're weighed and packed ready for the supermarkets.

Speaker 3   There are loads of people doing it now. It's so easy – all you need is a bucket of water and a cloth. The most important thing you've got to do is find yourself a really good place where cars have got to stop for at least half a minute. Traffic lights are best – especially in the rush hour when everyone's stopped or going very slowly. The money's not bad as long as you put the hours in.

Answers

	Job	Evidence
Speaker 1	Computer phone help-line worker / adviser	waiting for phone / questions people ask / mouse not working / read the manual
Speaker 2	Fruit-picker	hard physical work / out in the open / to the fields / start picking / fruit's too ripe / wooden boxes / collected by tractor / weighed and packed / ready for supermarkets
Speaker 3	Car windscreen washer	bucket of water and cloth / place where cars have got to stop / traffic lights

2 •   Students discuss this question in pairs or groups for a few minutes.
  •   They could finish by carrying out a brief class survey. How many students would like to try the three jobs?

Read

1 •   Ask students to read through the questions, then look at the photograph. Check answers, except for **d**, which they will find out in the next task.

Answers

a   Rubber gloves / to protect his hands. Other warm clothes.
b   Ice.
c   Chain-saw – usually used for cutting down trees or cutting up wood.
d   Students may come up with various descriptions of the man's job. Don't tell them the answer to this question. They are going to read the first paragraph of the article to find out.

2 a   Students read the first paragraph to check their guess. They may not know the word *sculpt*, but encourage them to guess what it might mean from the context and from the picture.
  •   Check answers.

Answer

He's an ice sculptor.

  b   As students read the rest of the text, they make a note of the man's attitude to his job. Encourage them to look for the words which show whether he likes or dislikes the job, and whether he is serious about it or treats it as a hobby.
  •   Check answers.

Answer

•   Enthusiastic: *watching them melt is beautiful. / It's brilliant. / I've been fascinated by ice since my late twenties ... / I loved the place ...*
•   Professional: he has a studio and specialist equipment / knowledgeable / he went to the Arctic to do a sculpture.

Vocabulary
p. 29

•   Allow students a few minutes to find the seven words in the article.
•   Check answers.

Answers

a exhibition   **b** (to) melt   **c** fascinated   **d** (to) die out
e scary   **f** fragile   **g** (to) charge

Understanding ideas

1 •   Before they read the text again, ask students to make a note of any answers they remember. They can then read the text again. Deal with vocabulary queries at this stage, but encourage students to guess the words they don't know rather than ask for an explanation of each word.
  •   Check answers.

Answers

a   His ice sculptures last only a short time – six or seven hours.
b   Since his late twenties. / For about 20–23 years.
c   He taught himself by practising in the car park of an ice factory.
d   In the first sculpture the woman was sitting down (*seated*); in the second she was *standing*.

2 •   Students will need to use their own ideas to answer these questions. Allow groups a few minutes to discuss their ideas, then pool ideas as a whole class.
  •   Check ideas.

Possible answers

a   While training to be a cookery teacher he may have come across ice-sculptures used as table decorations in hotels.
b   The piece of ice he is working on could suddenly slip, fall and hurt Duncan Hamilton. It could break any time he is working on it, so it is rather unpredictable. He could be finishing the final details when it cracks.
c   His work is very well-known. / He is very good at what he does. / Ice sculpture is coming back into fashion. / Hamilton is rich and successful.
d   It could have been physically challenging – working six days in freezing conditions. It could have been technically difficult to sculpt a human being out of ice.

Have your say

1–2   Before dividing students into groups to discuss the questions, have a quick brainstorm for art and material vocabulary. Give students one minute to come up with as many different types of art and material as they can, then elicit ideas and write vocabulary up on the board. Supply other ideas if necessary (see the list of possible answers below).
  •   Allow students a few minutes to discuss the questions.
  •   Monitor, giving help where necessary.
  •   Elicit students' ideas, noting any more useful vocabulary on the board.

Possible answers

1–2 Kinds of art	Materials
painting	paint (oil-paints / water-colours)
sculpture	metal (bronze / iron / silver / gold, etc.) / wood
drawing	pencil / charcoal / pastels
modelling	clay / plasticine
weaving / embroidery	cloth / silk / cotton / wool

Speak

1a–b Students should work in groups of at least four.
- Each student thinks of and makes notes on their best and their worst job.
- When they have made their notes, give them time to prepare a short presentation. You might like to give them, or elicit, a few guidelines on how to structure the presentation: *I have chosen … because … / What makes this my ideal job is … / The worst job I can imagine is …*

2 • Students take turns to describe their two jobs. Make sure they stick to the time limit suggested (one to two minutes about each job).
- Monitor, but do not interrupt the presentations.

3 • Each group chooses the best and the worst of the jobs that have been described.
- Have brief whole-class feedback.

▶ **Photocopiable activity 6 p.159**

— p. 30 —

Grammar extra

Word order: time and place words and phrases / adverbs of manner

Exploring concepts

1 a Look at the example and elicit a couple of suggestions for other time words. Students then read the article to find the eight time and place words and phrases in the text.
- Check answers.
b Elicit a couple more suggestions of place words before students circle the examples in the article.

Answers
a Time words and phrases
for over eight years [1], At the moment [2], in the past [3], during the day [4], at night [4], from 8.30 a.m. to 4.00 p.m. [5], for long [6], after dark [6]
b Place words and phrases
at Longleat [1], at the world-famous safari park [2], in an 80-acre enclosure [4], in a house [4], in the park [5], there [6]

2 • Check that students understand the terminology used in the descriptions of the three sentence patterns. If they do not, work through this task with the whole class.
- Check answers.

Answers
a Subject + Verb → Place → Time
Andrew Hayton has worked at Longleat for over eight years.
The elephants are in an 80-acre enclosure during the day (and in a house at night).
Andrew works in the park from 8.30 a.m. to 4.00 p.m.
… it can get dangerous there after dark.
b Subject + Verb → Time
He has also looked after rhinos in the past.
… he doesn't stay for long …
c Time → Subject + Verb → Place
At the moment he is an elephant keeper at the world-famous safari park.

3 This task focuses on adverbs of manner but also includes frequency adverbs to provide a contrasting word order.

a Students start by identifying the different kinds of adverbs in the text.
- Check their answers.

Answers
1 How? (adverbs of manner)
slowly carefully neatly patiently smartly politely well gratefully
2 How often? (frequency adverbs)
always usually

b You could elicit answers to these questions from the whole class.

Answers
1 After the verb or the object.
2 Before the verb.

- Remind students to refer to the **Language commentary** on p.127.

Exploitation

1a–b Write the first sentence on the board, and elicit suggestions for correction. Point out that there may be more than one possible 'correct' answer. Students continue working individually, then compare answers in pairs.
- Check answers.

Answers
1 I often get to work early on Friday mornings. / On Friday mornings, I often get to work early.
2 I sometimes go out to a bar with my boss after work. / After work, I sometimes go out to a bar with my boss.
3 I went to the cinema with a couple of friends last night. / Last night, I went to the cinema with a couple of friends.
4 I'm flying to Greece at the weekend. / At the weekend I'm flying to Greece.
5 My sister is meeting me there next Tuesday. / Next Tuesday, my sister is meeting me there.
6 We're staying in a five-star hotel until Saturday. / Until Saturday, we're staying in a five-star hotel.

2 a Do the first sentence as an example. Students continue working individually.
- Check answers.

Answers

1 Every morning Sylvia got up early, so she was *never* late for work.
2 She got up late this morning, so she walked to work *quickly*.
3 She tried to get into the office *secretly*, so that no one would see her.
4 Unfortunately the door closed *noisily* behind her and everyone turned round.
5 She smiled *sweetly* and pretended everything was normal.
6 Her boss came up to her *angrily* and said, 'Come into my office!'

b Give students a few moments to think of a possible continuation, elicit a suggestion for the first sentence to make sure that students understand the task, then let students continue working in pairs.
• Have brief feedback on possible endings.

Possible answers

7 Sylvia went *timidly* / walked *slowly* into the office.
8 'Now, Sylvia,' said her boss *slowly*. 'Why were you late this morning?'
9 'I had to see my doctor,' said Sylvia *nervously*.
10 'I hope it's nothing serious,' said her boss *kindly*.
11 'I'm going to have a baby,' Sylvia lied *convincingly*.
12 'Wonderful news,' said the boss. 'Let's go and tell everyone *immediately*.'

Additional activity

For homework, students could write a short story, creating atmosphere and interest by using adverbs of manner. Suggest a choice of these kinds of story:
– A ghost story
– A crime story
– A joke
– A true-life episode in their life
Suggest a word limit of 100–120 words. Brainstorm ideas in class first.

— p. 31 —

Exploring words

Jobs and work

1 a Set a time limit of five minutes for students to match the words with the people in the picture.
• Check answers.

Answers

1 e   2 g   3 h   4 j   5 i   6 a   7 b   8 c
9 f   10 d

b Read through the explanation with the students, then elicit other examples of job words ending in *-er* and *-or*. (Try to avoid the jobs in the list which follows.)

Note While there are no hard and fast rules about which job words end in *-er* and which end in *-or*, many of the words that contain the letters **ct** end in *-or*, e.g. *director* / *doctor* / *actor*.

• Students could either work through this exercise individually and then compare answers in pairs, or you could work through the first couple of questions with the whole class first.
• Check answers, getting students to mark the stress on the words then repeat them to practise correct pronunciation.

Answers

1	'caretaker	5	trans'lator
2	pho'tographer	6	hotel ins'pector
3	'hairdresser	7	refuse co'llector
4	'sailor	8	'gardener

c Students could work individually or in pairs on this activity. If you think it will take too long, limit the number of jobs students define, or set the exercise for homework. The aim of this activity is for students to build up sets of verbs associated with jobs, so try to elicit a range of verbs for each job.
• Elicit suggestions.

Possible answers

1 A *vet* treats sick animals / works with farmers.
2 An *electrician* installs electrical equipment / checks the safety of electrical equipment.
3 A *farmer* grows crops / raises animals.
4 A *mechanic* repairs cars / maintains machinery.
5 An *optician* tests people's eyes / sells people glasses.
6 A *decorator* paints houses / hangs wallpaper.
7 A *fire-fighter* rescues people from burning buildings / puts out fires.
8 A *road-sweeper* keeps the streets clean / collects rubbish.
9 A *surveyor* measures areas of land / examines buildings.
10 A *surgeon* performs operations / cures sick people.

2 a In *Skills*, we looked at the field of art. This exercise extends this to other types of creative artist. You could set a time limit for this activity to see how many words individuals could come up with in two minutes, then elicit suggestions.

Possible answers

music	composer	performer	musician	singer	
literature	poet	novelist	dramatist	playwright	
film	film star	director	screenwriter	actor	producer

b Students compare lists with a partner and tell each other about their favourite artists.
• Finish the activity by eliciting a few ideas or conducting a brief class survey, e.g. *Who's your favourite composer? Has anyone else chosen this composer?*, etc.

3 a This is a collocation exercise.
• Point out that some verbs from **A** go with several nouns from **B**. Remind students how important it is to learn words with the words they go with, not on their own.
• Students could work individually or in pairs.
• Check answers.

b As with other mini-discussion exercises, suggest a time
limit – for example, a maximum of two minutes for each
question. Alternatively, suggest that each pair or group
discusses two or three questions.

• Monitor conversations, listening for the appropriate use of
work-related vocabulary. Do not interrupt or correct at
this stage. Spend a few minutes after the discussions
clarifying any problems.

c Students make up two or three questions, then ask their
partner. You could also do this as a whole-class
mingle activity.

• Again, monitor but do not interrupt or correct.

4 • This is a final group or class discussion about the value of
work. Spend as much or as little time on it as you think fit.

• You could start by eliciting a few of the jobs implied by
the question, e.g. *sports personalities / pop musicians / film
stars / business executives*, etc.

— p. 32 —

Writing

Letters and faxes

▮ Read ▮

1–3 Give students time to read through the questions, then ask
them to read the three advertisements quickly to find the
answers. Encourage them only to look for the relevant
information. Check the answer to the first question, then
let students discuss questions **2** and **3** in pairs or groups.

Answers
a Salesperson (another word for a sales assistant) in the toy
  department of a department store.
b An entertainer on a cruise ship – this could involve singing,
  dancing, etc.
c Receptionist for a film production company.

▮ Different methods of writing ▮

1 • Students work in pairs to make a list of differences
between a fax and a letter, then check their ideas by giving
them the two models to look at (photocopiable from
p.130). Don't let students spend too long on this activity.
If they have any problems thinking about the style of
writing, ask them to think of when people use faxes and

letters; are they any different? The models show that there
is no difference in style; both faxes and letters can be
formal or informal.

• Check answers.

Answers
The only real difference between faxes and letters is format and
layout – the way the details are set out before the message itself.

2 • Students discuss their ideas in pairs. E-mails are discussed
in Unit 8, so avoid them in this discussion.

• Elicit ideas.

Possible answers
You might send a fax:
– when you have an urgent message or a tight deadline
– when you want a quick reply
– when presentation or appearance are not important
– when the message is short.
You might send a letter:
– when there is no urgency
– when you definitely do not want a quick reply
– when the appearance of what you send is important, e.g. a
  personal message / a love letter
– when you are sending an enclosure or a very long message.

▮ Write ▮

In this activity, students write a fax and a letter. It is
suggested that the two pieces of writing are done together,
but you might prefer to deal with them on two
separate occasions.

1 • Check that students understand what the task involves:
All students are going to write two replies – one to advert
a and the other to either **b** or **c**. The reply to **a** will be a
normal letter, the other will be a fax.

• Work through the plan with the class, eliciting useful
phrases and listing them on the board.

• Students write their basic letters, without worrying about
the formalities of fax or letter layout.

• Monitor this writing process, helping where necessary.

2 • Students now write first drafts of the letter and fax,
adapting their 'basic letter' to suit the job and the format.

3a–c Divide the class into groups of three. They exchange their
two pieces of writing with two different partners.

• Students follow the normal procedure of reading each
other's writing, and suggesting improvements to content
and layout.

• Students return the letters to each other and discuss the
improvement ideas.

• Be available at this stage to resolve any questions that
may arise.

• Students write the final versions of their letter and fax.
This is probably best done for homework.

▶ **Writing model 3 (photocopiable) TB p.130**

Language in action

Agreeing and disagreeing

The newspaper story about the effect the closure of a large company will have on a town provides the context for a role play in which students will agree and disagree with each other.

▌ Introduction ▌

1 • Students read the story to find the answers to questions a–c. This is a scanning task, so set a time limit of two to three minutes.
  • Check answers.

Answers
a 3,000 people.
b Sales fell by nearly 40% in the previous year.
c Employees who have worked for PZM all their working lives.

2 • Play **3.4** . As they listen for the first time, ask students to identify what the three speakers agree about.
  • Check answers. Don't spend time going through all the subjects on which speakers disagree at this stage.

Answers
They all agree that the closure will have a terrible effect on the town.

3.4

A Have you heard about PZM? I was absolutely amazed …
M Oh, so was I.
C I wasn't – they've been losing money for nearly a year now.
M Everyone knew they were losing money, but I didn't think they'd close down completely.
A Neither did I.
C Oh, I did.
M I thought they might make a hundred or so people redundant but this is going to have a terrible effect on the town.
C That's true. I agree.
A Yeah – you're right there.
C Will it affect your family?
A Yeah, my dad's worked there all his life.
M I don't know what my dad'll do. He's too old to get another job.
A I think my dad's quite pleased really, though he wouldn't actually admit it. He's never really liked working there.
M My dad won't know what to do with himself. His work is his whole life.
C I wonder what'll happen to the buildings.
M Maybe another company'll move into the town and buy it.
C I think that's a bit optimistic, Matt.
A I agree. It'll probably just stay empty until the council decide to knock it down and build houses on the site.
M I think it's so sad.
C Mm, so do I.
A I disagree – it's progress – nothing lasts for ever. If you ask me, PZM weren't very good employers – I mean lots of people work there but they pay really low wages and the working conditions are dreadful.
C Oh, I don't agree. I worked there for a while a few years back and I've got very good memories.

3a–b Allocate A and B roles before they listen again and make sure they know what they are listening out for. They note down the expressions of agreement and disagreement used by the speakers.
  • Play **3.4** again, pausing from time to time to allow students to note down the expressions.
  • Students share information, writing lists of expressions of agreement and disagreement. They could now add other expressions they already know to the two lists.
  • Check answers. (Don't add too many expressions to these lists – it is better for students to focus on and practise a smaller number of expressions.)

Answers

Agreeing	**Disagreeing**
So was I.	I wasn't.
Neither did I.	I did.
That's true.	I disagree.
I agree. (x2)	I don't agree.
Yeah – you're right there.	
So do I.	
Other expressions	**Other expressions**
True.	I'm not sure about that.
That's just what I was thinking.	I can't agree with you.
Absolutely!	That's nonsense!
You're right.	Rubbish!

Notes
1 You may need to revise the formation and use of expressions with *So* and *Neither*.
  For agreeing: *So / Neither* + auxiliary / modal verb + subject, e.g.
    I saw John. – So did I.
    I can't swim. – Neither can I.
  For disagreeing: Subject + auxiliary / modal verb, e.g.
    I saw John. – I didn't.
    I can swim. – I can't.
2 Listen for and correct the common error *I am agree.*

▌ Pronunciation ▌ p. 150 ▌

This section looks at stressed syllables, main stressed syllables and linking between words.

1 • In Units 1 and 2 we referred to stressed 'words' and main stressed 'words'. From now on students will be asked to identify the syllables which are stressed in the words rather than just the words themselves. These usually follow the normal rules for word stress.
  • Check students understand what a syllable is, and that they can identify which syllable is stressed.
  • Write the three sentences on the board and ask students which syllables they think will be stressed.
  • Play **3.5** for students to check their answers.

3.5

1 I a<u>gree</u>.
2 <u>That's</u> <u>true</u>.
3 You're <u>right</u> <u>there</u>.

Answers
See Tapescript **3.5** .

2 a Allow students a few moments to identify the main stress in B's replies. Elicit a few ideas but don't confirm whether their ideas are right or wrong.

b Play **3.6** for students to check.

• Check answers. Although both words are stressed in each reply, the most important word is *I* and this has the main stress.

3.6

1 A I think the government's doing a good job.
  B I don't.
2 A I was worried when I heard the news.
  B I wasn't.
3 A I didn't agree with what he said.
  B I did.
4 A I'm not surprised.
  B I am.

Answers
See Tapescript **3.6**.

• Play **3.6** again and drill the replies.

3 a Ask students to look at the examples of how some words are linked in their books. Play **3.7**.

3.7

1 So do I.   3 Neither did I.
2 So was I.   4 Neither am I.

b Play the tape again. Pause between each example and drill.

c Ask students to work out the rules of pronunciation. They can do this in pairs. Check answers. Point out the linking /w/ between *do* and *I*.

Answers
1 **b** (Sentence 3 – linking between *did* and *I*)
2 **d** (Sentence 1 – no linking between *so* and *do*)
3 **c** (Sentence 3)
4 **a** (Sentence 4)

d Students could either do this in pairs or you could elicit their ideas and write them directly onto the board.

• Play **3.8** and make any corrections to the version on the board.

3.8

1 I don't agree.   3 So have I.
2 Neither do I.   4 So will I.

Answers
See Tapescript **3.8**.

e Play the tape again, pausing after each response to drill.

Practice   p. 33

Divide the class into groups of up to seven students, and no fewer than four.

1 • Each group invents more details about the PZM closure. This will give students something more concrete to discuss in the role play. You could first elicit a few ideas from the whole class.

• Monitor, suggesting ideas if necessary.

2 a Each group appoints a chairperson to run the meeting. You might prefer to appoint the chairperson rather than allow each group to decide, as a strong student is needed for this role. This student turns to p.154 and reads the role card.

b Other students turn to p.156 and choose one of the other six roles.

c–d Allow a few minutes for students to prepare their opening statements. You could demonstrate this by giving an example yourself: *I have lived here all my life and I am very disappointed by the news. It's not going to be easy for other people to get jobs … etc.*

• Students take turns to make their statements. At this stage, others members of the group could agree or disagree briefly.

• One member of each group should make a written note of any points on which the majority agrees. If time is short, set a time limit for this part of the role play, but warn students in advance of this.

• The chairperson guides the group through the rest of the agenda.

• Monitor this stage carefully, but only interrupt to help the proceedings along. Listen for the appropriate use of agreeing and disagreeing language, but do not correct errors at this stage in order not to interrupt the flow. Make a note for later feedback.

e–f Each group decides on any action they could take and together writes a brief action plan.

• You could ask for quick feedback on their action plan from the different groups.

• To round off the activity, students write a report of their meeting. This writing activity could be done by students individually for homework.

Language check

Follow the usual procedure.

4 Journeys

Theme

The overall theme for this unit is journeys.
Preview Different kinds of journey
Reading The explorer Michael Palin
Skills Great journeys and human achievements
Grammar extra A balloon trip
Writing A journey where something went wrong

Grammar

- Review of the Past simple and Past continuous
- Past perfect
- Time clauses and sequencers

Vocabulary

- Air travel

Writing

- Describing a journey where something went wrong

Functional language

- Requests: making and responding positively and negatively to requests

Pronunciation

- Linking between words like *could you*, *would you* and *can't you*; polite intonation in requests

Workbook

- Grammar and functional language as above
- Topic vocabulary: planes and flying; roads and railways; phrasal verbs to do with travel
- Extract from a novel, *Four Letters of Love*

Preview

This section provides a general introduction to the theme of the unit by looking at different journeys – by plane, car, camel and train – as well as what makes a journey interesting, uncomfortable, boring, etc. The recordings and reading texts also contextualize the language used for describing events in the past: Past simple and Past continuous.

▮ Your thoughts ▮▮▮▮▮▮▮▮▮▮▮▮▮▮▮ p. 34 ▮

1 • You could introduce the theme briefly by asking students to look at the photographs and tell you what they can see in the pictures and where they think the places are. This is an opportunity to pre-teach some of the vocabulary which comes up in the reading texts and recordings if necessary: *shepherd*, *turban*, *flock of sheep*, *camel*, *queue of cars*. The name of the rock is Uluru, formerly known as Ayers Rock, in Northern Australia.

   • Check that students understand what the two statements mean by asking: *Which one means the person likes the journey, and which one means the person likes being in different places?* You could point out that *travel* is an uncountable noun.

   • If students don't agree with either statement they can write their own or you can supply some alternatives, e.g. *I love travel and I love travelling. / I hate everything about travelling. It doesn't interest me at all, I always look forward to going away but I'm always disappointed.*

2 • Let students mingle to find a partner who agrees with them. They are more likely to share the same ideas on the questions asked.

   • Set a time limit of five minutes for discussion of the questions. Ask them to make notes.

   • Have whole-class feedback.

   Possible answers
   – **Interesting or enjoyable**: beautiful scenery, the method of travel (helicopter, cruise ship), the people you meet.
   – **Boring**: uninteresting scenery, uninteresting people, waiting (e.g. at the airport, for the train to arrive, in a traffic jam), making the same journey every day.
   – **Uncomfortable**: the method of transport (e.g. camel), the weather, lack of space and not being able to move around (aeroplane).

▮ Read ▮

1 • Tell students to read the texts fairly quickly for general understanding. They could underline any parts of the text which helped them to choose their answers.
  • Students compare answers with a partner.
  • Check answers.

Answers

  a Text 3 (All the text from *occupants turn and stare* to the end).
  b Text 1 (*four days without a wash, walking like gorillas*).
  c Text 2 (The fact that the writer took lots of photographs).

2 • Ask students to read the text again, more carefully this time, but without using a dictionary. Explain that they need to get used to guessing the meaning of words they don't know from their context. Some of the vocabulary which may be problematic is checked in *Vocabulary*.
  • Give students a few minutes to discuss their ideas in pairs then check answers.

Possible answers

  a The writer seems to be sorry that she went on this trip. She says that on Day Two they asked themselves 'Why are we doing this?' She also describes difficult or unpleasant things.
  b Perhaps the shepherd didn't give the writer an address. If he did, he lives in a very remote place where it might be difficult to get mail.
  c The writer is probably either a child or a teenager. It probably felt as though they were driving fast (a) because the other cars weren't moving, and (b) because he felt that they shouldn't be moving.

▮ Vocabulary ▮   p. 35 ▮

  • Students can work on their own then compare ideas with a partner.
  • Check answers.

Answers

  a 1   **b** 1   **c** 2   **d** 1

  • For extra practice, you could ask students to discuss these questions about the words.
    1 Which is more difficult to *steer* – a car or a horse. Why?
    2 If you are in a vehicle which is *stationary* for a long time, what do you do? How do you feel?
    3 Why do people say things for the *umpteenth* time?
    4 How do you feel if people *stare* at you?

▮ Listen ▮

1–2 Ask students to read the questions. Check that they understand *memorable*.
  • Play ▮4.1▮. Ask students to compare answers in pairs. Play again if necessary.
  • Check answers.

▮4.1▮

Speaker 1   This time last year my family and I were travelling around Australia. One of the places we visited was the desert. We took a car from Alice Springs to Uluru. It was boiling hot outside and I can remember that the air-conditioning in the car wasn't working. I remember the first time I saw the rock in the distance it was glowing bright orange. It was absolutely spectacular!

Speaker 2   It was a really small plane. It was one of those planes where you go up about three steps and you're in the cabin. And erm I think there were about twenty of us and anyway the smoking section was at the back of the plane and when the stewardess came down to check all the passengers were on board everybody was erm sitting in the at the back in the smoking section. Erm, so she said 'Would some of you move to the front please? Would you like to move to the front?' and we said well nobody wanted to go because we thought well we all wanted to smoke. And since nobody put their hands up then she said, 'Well, I'm afraid I'll have to ask some of you to move to the front. You can smoke there if you like but we need to you know distribute evenly the weight of the plane.' And after she said that one er, one guy said 'She'll be asking us to put our hands out of the windows and wave our arms up and down next!' Everybody burst out laughing.

Speaker 3   I can remember the scene at the station very clearly. I was 22 I think, I'd never been away from home for any length of time and I was just about to go to Montreal to work there for a couple of years. My parents came to the station to see me off. I hadn't wanted them to, because I don't like long goodbyes. I remember my dad put his arm round me and told me to take care of myself. My mom was so upset she couldn't speak. She was hugging me and she was crying at the same time. When the train pulled into the station I was crying too. I felt really awful, really homesick. I got on the train and I cried all the way to Montreal.

Answers

Speaker 1	1	She was travelling by car.
	2	The rock (Uluru) looked spectacular.
Speaker 2	1	She was travelling by plane.
	2	It was an amusing experience.
Speaker 3	1	She was going to travel by train.
	2	She was going away, leaving home and her parents and was upset.

▮ Have your say ▮

  • Give students a few minutes to think of some ideas. Tell them that it could be a car, bus, coach, train, boat or plane journey. Check that everyone has a journey to describe. If students can't think of anything, they can describe the last journey they went on or even a journey that they do every day. Encourage students to ask each other questions. This should not be a monologue.

─ Grammar review ─ Past simple and Past continuous

1–2 If you are confident that your students will be able to answer the questions, let them work through questions 1 and 2 in pairs. Tell them to check their ideas in the **Language commentary** on p.128. Then check the answers with the class. Alternatively, you could go through each question step by step with the whole class.

Answers

1 **a** 1 As I <u>was climbing back</u> into the car … the driver <u>was</u> probably <u>wondering</u> if we would ever reach our destination.

2 When the stewardess (came) down to check all the passengers (were) on board, everybody <u>was sitting</u> at the back in the smoking section.

3 She <u>was hugging</u> me and she <u>was crying</u> at the same time.

4 When the train (pulled) into the station, I <u>was crying</u> too.

5 This time last year my family and I <u>were travelling</u> around Australia.

b A 5
B 2, 4
C 1, 3

2 **a** Carlos phoned Antonio after I arrived. We suppose that Carlos was waiting for me to arrive before phoning Antonio.

b Carlos was in the middle of phoning Antonio when I arrived.

- You could draw time lines on the board to make the difference in meaning clear.

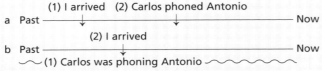

a Past —— (1) I arrived   (2) Carlos phoned Antonio —— Now

b Past —— (2) I arrived —— Now
      ~~ (1) Carlos was phoning Antonio ~~

- You could ask students to draw their own time lines to illustrate the difference in meaning between these pairs of sentences:

a When they arrived, we were eating dinner.
b When they arrived, we ate dinner.
a We drove to Miami when we heard the bad news.
b We were driving to Miami when we heard the bad news.

Check

3 • Students can do the exercise on their own, then check with a partner.
• Check answers.

Answers

a were you doing … was telephoning
b was living
c were arguing … broke in … ran away
d stood up … said … left
e woke up … went … was raining … was blowing … went
f finished … washed up

4 • Students could complete the sentences in pairs. Remind them to use the Past simple or Past continuous. Monitor, indicating mistakes and answering any questions students have.
• If time is short you could elicit ideas from the whole class.

Suggested answers

a was still sleeping / was getting up / had breakfast
b was walking up to the house / was breaking into my car
c answered it / ignored it / was having a shower
d slipped and fell / was wondering what excuse to give for being late
e were going to bed / was getting up
f cooked dinner, did my homework and washed the dog

▶ **Photocopiable activity 7 p.160**

Reading

This section looks at the theme of explorers and one person in particular – the English actor, writer and explorer Michael Palin.

- You could start off the lesson by asking students to look at the photo of Michael Palin and read the text underneath. Find out whether any students know who Michael Palin is and whether they have seen him in films or on television.

■ In your view

1–2 Ask students to read the questions. Check that they understand *explore* and *explorer*.
- Divide the class into pairs and ask them to discuss **1**. Elicit an idea from the class as an example. (See possible answers below.)
- Allow a few minutes for discussion then elicit ideas.

Possible answers

1 • Some people want to be explorers because
 – they want to find out about other cultures and ways of life, e.g. 'lost tribes' in the Amazon.
 – they like adventure and excitement.
 – they like to be the first to go to a place.
 – they like to discover new things.
• The kind of people who make good explorers are usually curious, adventurous, determined (single-minded), people who don't mind 'roughing it' (living in uncomfortable conditions).
 You could teach some of these adjectives if students don't provide them.

- Get students to ask each other the questions in 2. After a couple of minutes ask several students to report back on what their partner said.

■ Read

1 • Ask students to read the information about Michael Palin under the photo if they haven't already done so, and to read questions **a–d**.
- Tell them to try to predict or guess the answers to the questions and write these down. Elicit a few ideas but don't tell students whether their answers are right or wrong. This is the purpose of the while-reading activity which follows.

2 **a** Ask students to read the article and check their ideas.
b When students have read the article and answered **2a** they should decide on the best summary. Students who finish before the others could compare ideas with their neighbour or you could ask them to do the *Close up* questions.
- Check answers.

Answers

1 **a** His favourite subject was geography.
    b His hobby was stamp-collecting.
    c He first went abroad when he was 19.
    d Jobs and relationships were more important to him than travel.

2 The best summary is the second one. The article explains the importance of exploration to Palin when he was a child (how it influenced his hobbies and interests); how it took a back seat until his personal and professional life were more stable; how it became more important again.

■ Close up

- If you want to do this activity fairly quickly, elicit ideas from the whole class. Alternatively, students could work in pairs and use dictionaries to find the answers.

Answers

- Babies *crawl* because they can't walk. *Crawl* also has a metaphorical meaning as in *traffic crawls* = to go slowly.
- *Sort out* means 'to put in order'. Other things which people *sort out* are their lives, problems.
- Students will probably know the meaning of *take off* for a plane. They can use this knowledge to work out the related meaning of *take off* in the text (become a successful actor). Another meaning which students at this level will probably know is remove (of clothes).

■ Understanding ideas p. 37 ■

1–3 Deal with any other vocabulary questions before students work through these questions. Check the meaning of: *urge, irresistible, desire, influenced, preacher, missionary, taste.*

- Ask students to answer the questions in pairs. Remind them that they will have to use their imagination as well as the information in the text.
- Allow students enough time to do the activity then elicit ideas from the class.

Possible answers

1 It would make the missionary more interesting to the writer. The writer could enjoy imagining how he had lost it (a lion had attacked him?) or the missionary might even explain how he had lost it in gory detail.

2 It could mean that he sees travel as adventure, and had never travelled in this way before.
It could also mean that he had only travelled before in his imagination or had second-hand experience of travel through books and TV.

3 – a child: His hobbies and interests related to exploring: geography, church; stamp-collecting.
    – a student: Girls.
    – in his 20s: Getting his career off the ground and forming a stable relationship with someone.
    – in his 30s and 40s: His career and travel. He was lucky to be able to combine the two.

■ Have your say

1–2 Students can discuss the questions in pairs. Ask them to give reasons for their answers. Elicit opinions from the class to round off this skills section.

Possible answers

1 Michael Palin is probably not most people's idea of a typical explorer. He was more interested in his career and his personal life when he was in his twenties – the age at which young people usually travel and explore the world. Typically explorers would put that before anything else.

2 – It is better to get an idea of lots of countries. It gives you a general picture of what the world and the people who live in it are like.
    – If you don't spend long in a place you get a very superficial and sometimes wrong idea of what a place is like. If you spend time in a place you can begin to understand the people who live there.

— Grammar – Past perfect

■ Exploring concepts

- If your students are more confident by now about working on these grammar sections on their own they could answer the questions in pairs, then check their ideas in the **Language commentary** on p.128. Follow this up with a whole-class check. If your students are still not confident or you think that they will find these questions difficult, you can work through the exercises with the whole class. Then read the **Language commentary** through together.

Answers

1 The Past perfect is formed with *had* or *had not* (*hadn't*) + the past participle. Point out that the contraction of the affirmative form is *'d*, which is the same contraction as for the conditional form *would*.

2 **a** 1 being eight (situation); deciding on my future (event).
        2 being excited (situation); not going abroad (non-event).
    b The Past perfect – either to emphasize that one event happened before another or to give an explanation for a past situation or event.

3 The adverbs *already*, *just* and *never* come between *had* and the past participle. *Before,* which combines with *never,* comes at the end of the sentence.

4 There is no difference in meaning in the sentences in **b**.
The difference in meaning between the other pairs of sentences is:
    a *When I was eight, I decided on my future.* = At the age of eight (during the year when I was eight years old) I decided on my future.
        When I was eight, I had (already) decided on my future. = I decided on my future some time before I was eight, for example when I was five, six or seven.
    c *When the police arrived, the party finished.* = The party finished the moment the police arrived or just after.
        When the police arrived, the party had finished. = The party finished before the police arrived.

Exploitation

1 • Divide the class into pairs for this controlled practice activity. Demonstrate the activity by asking the students to ask you the questions and answering yourself. Encourage students to use the contracted forms 'd and hadn't.
   • Tell students to answer the second question with something they actually did later in the day.
   • Monitor the activity, correcting any mistakes you hear.

2 • Divide the class into groups of four (or three if you don't have enough students). Ask students to read the instructions and check that they understand all the vocabulary in questions a–g.
   • Read the example with the class, and elicit a couple of other reasons why Maria was late. Tell students to give reasons which are events and to use the Past perfect.
   • Monitor, but don't correct or interrupt. You could note down some mistakes that you hear as you go round the class, write these on the board and ask students to correct them at the end.

3 a Divide the groups of four into pairs for this activity.
   • Monitor. You could either correct as you go round the class or when each pair finishes, you could look at their answers, tell them how many mistakes there are and give them a few minutes to try to correct them.
   • Check answers.

   Answers

2 was	9 had broken in
3 got out	10 put down
4 paid	11 had bought
5 walked	12 returned
6 looked	13 found
7 had closed	14 had died
8 sensed	15 had forgotten

   b This is a final opportunity for you to see how well students are using the Past perfect and Past simple. Monitor, helping with vocabulary when required and correcting mistakes. Round off the lesson by hearing as many endings as there is time for.

— p. 38 —

Skills

The theme of this section is great journeys and human achievements.

Speak and listen

1–2 You could introduce the theme by asking students what important events are shown in the photographs. Be careful not to ask who did them or when they happened. Alternatively, you could do this after the listening.
   • Ask students to read the quiz questions. Explain any new vocabulary. Tell students to answer the questions on their own, then compare ideas with a partner. Point out that they should make a guess if they have no idea.

• Before you play the tape, warn students that the information on the tape is not in the same order as the quiz. Tell them to correct any wrong answers as they listen. Play **4.2**, twice if necessary.
• Check answers.

4.2

Good afternoon. In today's programme we are going to look back at some of the great achievements of the twentieth century. Let's start by mentioning important breakthroughs in flight and space travel. The most important of these was the first powered aircraft flight in 1903. The flight, though it lasted just twelve seconds, marked an important technological advance, and made Orville and Wilbur Wright household names overnight. Just thirty years later, in 1933, the first solo round-the-world flight was accomplished by another American, Wiley Post, with the first non-stop round-the-world flight being achieved in 1949.

Such advances in aviation technology paved the way for the space revolution and on 12th April 1961 Yuri Gagarin made history by being the first person to orbit the earth, doing so in a time of one hour and 48 minutes. Another important first in space travel was the first moon landing on 20th July 1969, with the American astronaut Neil Armstrong becoming the first person to walk on the moon.

But not all of the great achievements of the 20th century were technological. Some marked important triumphs of man over nature. For instance, the expeditions to the North Pole in 1909 and the South Pole in 1911. However, the race to the South Pole, which was won by the Norwegian Roald Amundsen, had unfortunate consequences for the British expedition team led by Captain Robert Scott, who died on the return journey from the Pole.

Another achievement we shouldn't forget was the first ascent of Everest. On 29th May 1953 the New Zealander Edmund Hillary, and the Sherpa, Tenzing Norgay, became the first two people to stand at the top of the highest mountain on earth.

In the field of sport there were major achievements too …

Answers

1 Tenzing Norgay and Edmund Hillary in 1953.
2 Roald Amundsen in 1911.
3 Neil Armstrong in 1969.
4 Yuri Gagarin in 1961.
5 Wiley Post in 1933.

Note The photographs on the page show Orville Wright flying over Tempelhof, Berlin; Tenzing Norgay on the summit of Everest; Scott and his team at Amundsen's tent at the South Pole and Buzz Aldrin on the moon in 1969. The main photograph is of the Breitling Orbiter.

Read

• Ask students to read the instructions. Check that they understand the words achievements, achieve.
• For the first reading, ask students to read through quickly to find the 'new' achievements. Tell them not to worry about vocabulary at this stage; they will have a chance to read the text in more detail later.
• Allow students about five minutes to read the text and tick the achievements which were not mentioned in Speak and listen. Check answers and explain any related vocabulary which students don't know, e.g. circumnavigation, ascent, sound barrier.

44 Unit 4

Answers

Paragraph 1 – First non-stop round-the-world balloon journey.
Paragraph 2 – First circumnavigation of the world by Magellan.
Paragraph 3 – First time the sound barrier on land was broken.
Paragraph 4 – Sir Chris Bonnington's attempt to climb Everest.
              – Reinhold Messner's solo ascent of Everest
                without oxygen.
Paragraph 5 – Breaking the sound barrier on water.
              – Reaching 1,600 km an hour on land.
              – Reaching 800 km an hour on land in a wheel-
                driven vehicle.

■ Vocabulary   p. 39 ■

- Students can either do this exercise in pairs or on their own, then check answers with a partner. Remind students to look at the words in context. This will help them to choose the correct meaning.
- Check answers.

Answers

a 5   b 4   c 3   d 1   e 2

■ Understanding ideas

1–3 Students read the text again, then work in pairs to answer the questions. If there are a lot of vocabulary queries, set a limit of, say, eight words.

- Allow students enough time to answer the questions in pairs. Remind them that not all the answers are in the text and that they will have to use their own ideas as well.
- Check ideas.

Possible answers

1 It was a record that still hadn't been broken at that time – everybody wanted to be the first to break it.

2 – Going to the moon has increased our knowledge of the universe.
   – The first great aircraft journeys have revolutionized travel. People can now travel longer distances in a shorter time.

3 The 1981 ascent was a more difficult thing to achieve: it is harder for one man to climb alone than to climb with a team; also it is much more difficult to climb Everest without oxygen than with it. People possibly saw the 1975 ascent as a repetition of the 1953 climb, although it was a more difficult route.

■ Have your say

1–2 You could divide the class into new pairs or small groups to discuss these questions.

- Allow students about five minutes maximum to do this activity. Then get feedback.

Possible answers

1 If students come up with different ideas you could use the ideas below as a mini-quiz. Ask students when it happened, etc.
   – First animal in space (dog, 1957)
   – First woman in space (Valentina Tereshkova, Russian, 1963)
   – First manned balloon flight (The Montgolfier Brothers, French, 1783)
   – First explorer to land in the Americas (Christopher Columbus, Italian, 1492)
- 'Firsts' still to be achieved: first flight beyond our universe, first person to walk on the ocean floor, first solo non-stop round-the-world balloon flight.

2 – Many 'firsts' were achieved before or at the beginning of the 20th century when women had fewer opportunities to climb mountains, explore, etc.
   – Many 'firsts' have involved machines, where women traditionally had few opportunities to work: space travel, flight, breaking of land-speed records, etc.
   – Men are physically stronger than women.
   – Some might say that women are more sensible than men!
- The divisions between what women and men can do are less rigid than they used to be; both women and men now have similar opportunities.

■ Speak

1 • Depending on the time available students can discuss one, two or all of the situations. Allow six to eight minutes for the final feedback.

- Divide the class into groups of three or four. Check they understand the situations, and depending on the time available, ask them to choose two or more situations to discuss. They should all take notes.
- Monitor, supplying vocabulary where necessary.

2 • Give groups time to decide who will present what (they could each take a situation, or divide the situations between them) and to prepare a short presentation of their ideas.

- Groups present their ideas. Take a vote on which group has the best ideas.

──────── p. 40 ────────

Grammar extra

Time clauses and sequencers

1 • This question introduces the theme. If no one has been on a balloon trip you could briefly elicit whether they would like to go on one, and what they think it would be like.

2 • Ask students to look at the drawings.
- Students can work in pairs to decide what they think is the correct order and number the drawings 1–8. You could begin by checking number 1 (c).

3 • Play **4.3** , twice if necessary, for students to check their answers.

Note The technical word for the inflatable part of a balloon is *envelope*; we have not used this in the recording.

4.3

Everybody who was going on the balloon trip met in the car park. Then we were taken to a field. The balloon was actually on the back of a lorry and we all had to help to get it ready. First of all, we took the balloon off the lorry. Then four of the women had to get into the wicker basket – one in each corner – to balance it. The men then helped to inflate the balloon with a wind-machine. As soon as it was inflated, everyone climbed in. It started to rise when the pilot turned on the gas burners. It lifted off the ground very gently but went up extremely quickly – much faster than I'd expected – about 100 metres a minute – and then when the pilot decided we were high enough he turned down the burners a bit so we stayed at more or less the same height. While the pilot was flying the balloon, he was talking to the lorry driver, who was following below. He also gave us some information – told us how fast we were flying, pointed out some landmarks and so on, and people chatted and took photographs. I was waiting for the champagne, but there was no sign of any – much to my disappointment. One thing that surprised me was the fact that there wasn't any wind at all, and it was also extremely hot, I suppose because we were standing right under the burners. Anyway, when the hour was up the pilot started looking for somewhere to land. I was a bit worried about the landing but it was OK. It was quite straightforward really. Once the pilot spotted an appropriate site, he turned off the burners and the balloon started to descend. I was scared we were going to fall like a stone but it was quite gradual. Just before we landed he told us to crouch down and hold tight on to the ropes. We had to have our backs facing the direction the balloon was travelling in so that if it fell over we'd fall backwards rather than forwards. Anyway, it was a very gentle landing. After we landed, we got out and helped to deflate the balloon. Then we had to roll it up and after that, we put it on the back of the lorry again. And finally, we celebrated our safe return with a glass of champagne, and we were given a certificate to prove that we'd been on a balloon flight. It was great. I really enjoyed it.

Answers

1 c **2** h **3** g **4** e **5** f **6** b **7** d **8** a

▮ Exploring concepts ▮

1 • Ask students to read sentences **a–i**. Explain any new vocabulary.
   • Read through the instructions with the class. Make sure they can distinguish a sequence word or expression (one(s) which tell you the order in which something happens) – *First of all* (sentence **a**) from a time clause – *As soon as the envelope was inflated* (sentence **c**).
   • Allow students a few minutes to do the exercise then check.

Answers

1 a (First of all), we took the balloon off the lorry.
  b (Then) four of the women had to get into the wicker basket to balance it.
  c As soon as the balloon was inflated, everyone climbed in.
  d The balloon started to rise when the pilot turned on the gas burners.
  e While the pilot was flying the balloon, he was talking to the lorry driver, who was following below.
  f Just before we landed, he told us to crouch down and hold tight onto the ropes.
  g After we landed, we got out and helped to deflate the balloon.
  h (After that), we put it on the back of the lorry again.
  i (Finally), we celebrated our safe return with a glass of champagne.

2–3 Students can either do these exercises in pairs, then check their ideas with the **Language commentary** on p.128. Or you can work through them with the whole class.

Answers

2 a Time clauses can come at the beginning or end of a sentence. When they come at the beginning, they are followed by a comma.
  b *As soon as* tells us that the next action happens <u>immediately</u> after the one described.
  c *While* tells us that two actions happen at the same time.

3 a Sequence words usually come at the beginning of a sentence. *Then* doesn't need a comma after it.
  b *first of all*: First, Firstly, To start with
    then / after that: Next, Later, Afterwards
    finally: In the end

▮ Exploitation ▮

1 • Divide the class into pairs. Explain the task.
   • Allow students enough time to put the sentences in the correct order. Then check answers.

Answers

1 e **2** h **3** b **4** g **5** d **6** i **7** a
8 c or f **9** f or c

2 • Elicit names of activities which are adventurous, exciting or interesting and write them on the board. You could give an example from this list and use prompts to elicit the others: *parachuting, gliding, scuba-diving, caving, skiing, snowboarding, water-skiing, bungee-jumping, rock-climbing* or even a fairground ride like *The Big Dipper (Rollercoaster)*.
   • Make sure that everyone in the class has something to talk about. (It doesn't have to be anything very exciting.) Then allow students a couple of minutes each to describe their experience to their partners. Encourage them to ask each other questions.

3 • Students can work together to write the short story in class or this can be set for homework. Provide any vocabulary you think your students won't know.

Possible story

While Alan and Pete were waiting for the train they chatted about the football match they were going to see. When the train arrived they got on but it was very busy so they had to stand. Then before the train had left the station it stopped suddenly. An inspector came into the carriage. He wanted to know who had pulled the emergency brake. An American tourist said it had been him. He had thought the brake was a handle and had pulled it by mistake. The train started again. Alan and Pete were late for the match and some of the other passengers were looking angrily at their watches. As soon as the train got to their station, they got off and ran towards the exit. When they got out of the underground they heard the cheers. Someone had scored a goal. They had arrived too late to see it.

— p. 41 —

Exploring words

Air travel

You could introduce the topic by finding out which students have flown, who flies the most, who has been on the longest flight, etc.

1 a Divide the class into pairs. Where possible, pair any students who have never flown with students who have. Students can either do this exercise on their own then compare ideas with a partner, or do the exercise together.

• Ask students to read the text. Allow students a few minutes to do the exercise. Any students who finish before the others could check any phrasal verbs they are not sure about in their dictionaries.

• Check answers.

Answers

get away	7	see off	3
stop over	4	take off	5
pick up	1	nod off	2
drop off	8	touch down	6

b Ask students to discuss the questions with their partner.

• You could ask students to tell you what their partner has said.

2 a Check students understand *airport terminal building*, then ask them to make three separate lists under the headings given. This is a good opportunity for dictionary work. If students have monolingual dictionaries they can look up any words they don't know.

• Elicit an example for each category and write these on the board.

• Allow students enough time to do the activity. (Students who finish before the others could add some words of their own to the list.) Then check answers.

Answers

In or on a plane
wing, aisle, cabin, cockpit, hand-luggage, hold, seatbelt

Inside an airport terminal building
arrivals hall, baggage reclaim, check-in desk, conveyor belt, customs, departure lounge, gate, (hand-luggage), passport control

Outside an airport terminal building
air-traffic controller, runway, control tower

• Check that students understand all the words.

b Students do the exercise in pairs. Check answers.

Answers

1 False. He sits in the cockpit. The passengers sit in the cabin.
2 False (True). Hand-luggage usually goes in the cabin but it can go in the hold.
3 True.
4 True.
5 False. The runway is strictly for taking off and landing.
6 False. The wing is outside the plane. Passengers can walk up and down the aisle.

c Allow students a few minutes to write some questions of their own to ask another pair. If time is short each pair could think of one question which they could ask the whole class.

d Students work in pairs. Tell them to try to answer the questions first and only use a dictionary to check their ideas. Students could do the questions in small print after the vocabulary questions have been checked or at the same time.

• Check answers and ideas.

Answers

1 jet lag
  jet lagged
2 airline
  Depends on the country. For example, Qantas (Australia).
3 taxi
  Before take-off when the plane is getting into position and after landing.
4 scheduled
  charter (flight)
5 connection
  Bad weather, missing passengers, etc.
6 flight-attendant
  air-hostess; steward / stewardess

3a–c Ask students to read the instructions. Give an example by describing a flight you have been on and asking students to guess what three 'mistakes' you told them.

• Allow students a few minutes to prepare what to say. Students who have not flown could describe a bus or a train journey.

• Make sure that both students have the opportunity to speak. Give each student a time limit of two minutes for their topic.

• To round off the activity you could find out who guessed the most 'lies'.

▶ Photocopiable activity 8 p.161

Writing

Describing an incident

The theme of this section is journeys where things went wrong.

Read and write

1 • Ask students to read the five descriptions and tell you which they liked best and why. Deal with any vocabulary students don't know.

2a–b Divide the class into pairs. Ask them to read the instructions in their books.

• Tell each pair to choose the three descriptions they like best, then discuss what they think happened next in each one. Finally, they should write the next two lines for each of the descriptions they chose. (It is important that they don't bring the description to an end.) Monitor, helping with vocabulary where necessary.

c–d Students exchange descriptions, and guess which extracts are being continued. They return them to check.

e Pairs now discuss possible endings to one of the three extracts and complete the description. Set a time limit as this is not the most important writing phase in the lesson. Monitor, helping where required. You could read out the best descriptions to the class.

Brainstorm and notes

1 • Divide students into groups of three or four for this speaking activity. Ask them to read though the instructions.

• Allow them three or four minutes to think of what they are going to say then let them discuss in groups. Students who are going to describe something that went wrong might find the questions a useful starting point. Monitor the discussions, but don't interrupt. Tell students they can ask you for vocabulary later.

2 • Students now work on their own to use any of the ideas they heard to write notes for their description. Set a time limit of about five minutes.

3 • As students finish, or after five minutes, set the writing task. Remind students to make their descriptions interesting.

4a–c Get students to exchange descriptions with one of the students who was in their original group. Tell them to follow the usual procedure as described in their books.

• Set the final writing task for homework.

▶ **Writing model 4 (photocopiable) TB p.131**

Language in action

Requests

Introduction

1 • Divide the class into pairs. Read the introduction and ask pairs to write down three or four things they think the woman will ask the other passengers to do. Provide vocabulary where necessary but not the request language.

• You could elicit ideas and write these on the board in note form, e.g. *Put her luggage on the rack.*

2 • Play **4.4** to check ideas.

4.4

W Excuse me. Is this seat free?
M Yes.
W Would you mind helping me with my suitcase?
M Not at all. Where would you like it?
W Could you put it up there?
M No problem.
W Thank you very much. The train's very busy today, isn't it?
M Yes, it is.
W Don't you think it's a bit stuffy in here? (To woman) Excuse me. I wonder if you could open the window a bit? Thank you. That's much better.
(To teenage boy) Excuse me! EXCUSE ME. CAN YOU TURN THAT DOWN A BIT PLEASE? Thank you.
I Tickets please? I'm sorry madam but this ticket's out of date. It's for yesterday.
W Oh. I am sorry. Can you change the date on it?
I I'm afraid not. Thank you, 'kyou, 'kyou …
W Well, can't you just turn a blind eye? I am getting off at the next station.
I I'm sorry but that's not possible, madam.
W Oh, all right. How much is it?
…
W Excuse me. I'm sorry to bother you again but could you possibly get my case down for me?
M Certainly.
W That's very kind of you. Thank you.

3 a Ask students in pairs to write down any request expressions they know under the three headings given. They should each make a copy of these. You could monitor to see how familiar students are with this language, but don't correct or help at this point.

b Before you play the tape again divide the pairs into A and B. Make sure they understand what they have to do. Remind them that it is not necessary to write down the whole sentence. Play **4.4** again.

• Ask students to tell their partners what they heard. Then ask for ideas and write them on the board.

Answers

Making requests
Would you mind (help)-ing …?
Could you (put) …?
(Excuse me.) I wonder if you could …?
(Excuse me.) Can you (turn) …?
Can't you …?
Could you possibly …?

Responding to requests positively
Not at all.
No problem.
Certainly.

Responding to requests negatively
I'm afraid not.
I'm sorry but that's not possible.

Pronunciation p. 151

This section looks at linking between words like *could you*, *would you* and *can't you* and polite intonation in requests.

1 • Play **4.5** .

4.5

a Would you mind helping me with this chair please?
b Could you put that over there please?
c Can't you forget I told you?

Answers

a /wədju/ b /kədju/ c /kaːntʃu/

2 a Read the instructions through with the class. Play **4.6** . Check answers after each pair of requests.

4.6

1 a Could you carry this upstairs?
  b Could you carry this upstairs?
2 a I wonder if you could carry this upstairs?
  b I wonder if you could carry this upstairs?
3 a Can you carry this upstairs?
  b Can you carry this upstairs?

Answers

1 b 2 a 3 b

b Tell students that they are going to hear six requests. Play the first request of **4.7** , which is the example in their books. Indicate the intonation pattern and ask students to repeat. Remind them of the pronunciation of *could you*.

• Play the remaining requests. Pause after each one and drill. Insist on polite intonation.

4.7

1 Could you carry this upstairs?
2 I wonder if you could carry this upstairs?
3 Can you carry this upstairs?
4 Would you mind helping me with this chair?
5 Could you put that over there?
6 Can't you forget I told you?

Practice p. 43

Role play

Here is a suggested procedure.

• Divide the class into A and B groups. You could give students B a piece of paper to pin to their clothes (to distinguish them from students A).
• Ask students to read their instructions for Situation 1 on the appropriate page in their books. Check that there are no problems with vocabulary. Make sure students decide which country they are going to and write it down. Give an example of what Student A asks and Student B replies and vice versa.
• Students mingle to find someone who can help them. If you want to make the activity last longer you could tell students that they must refuse one request. Stop the activity when you see that several students have finished.
• Repeat the procedure for Situation 2.

Language check

Follow the usual procedure.

5 Away from it all

Theme

The overall theme of this unit is getting away.
Preview People in different places
Reading Small islands
Skills A year out
Grammar extra Living out of town
Writing Places

Grammar

- Review of *will* and *going to* for predictions, expectations, arrangements and intentions
- Other uses of *will* and *going to*: predictions, offers, promises, etc.
- Articles

Vocabulary

- Describing places

Writing

- Describing a place

Functional language

- Opinions: asking for, giving and avoiding giving opinions

Pronunciation

- Unpronounced sounds and linking /r/, /w/ and /j/

Workbook

- Grammar and functional language as above
- Topic vocabulary: places; prepositions; *in, on, off*; towns
- Extract from a travel book about Antarctica

Preview

This section is a general introduction to the theme of the unit – getting away. It looks at a variety of reasons why people go away to other places and at the advantages and disadvantages of living or staying in different types of places. The recordings and reading texts also contextualize the language used for talking about the future: *will*, *going to* and Present continuous.

▮ Your thoughts ▮ p. 44 ▮

1 • Divide the class into pairs for this activity. Students work in pairs to discuss which alternative they prefer and why.

2 • Still in pairs, students decide an advantage and disadvantage for each of the three alternatives. Have brief whole-class feedback.

▮ Read ▮

- Ask students to read the extracts and match them with the situations. Check answers.

Answers
1 b1 **2** c2 **3** b2 **4** a1 **5** c1 **6** a2

▮ Listen ▮ p. 45 ▮

1 • Tell students that they are going to hear three people talking about three of the situations in the reading. For this first listening, students should just listen to get the general idea.
- Play **5.1** once, then check answers.

5.1

Speaker 1 This year I'm doing the same as I did last year 'cos I enjoyed it so much. I'm going to Tenerife with three friends. We're going back to Playa de las Americas, where we were last year. We're even staying in the same apartment 'cos it's really handy for everywhere; it's near the beach and it's not far from the town centre. There's loads to do there. We go clubbing every night. There are some really great clubs. And there are hundreds of bars too. The nightlife is brilliant. You never get bored. You meet loads of people.

Speaker 2 It's quite hard being so far away from home, actually. The people I work with have been extremely nice, very hospitable, inviting me to their homes for meals and so on. But it's not the same as having your own family around you. I miss my kids a lot. Another thing is the language. Although most people in the company can speak some English, it's a different thing once you're outside the office. I'm afraid my Italian isn't very good yet. I can understand more than I can speak, but I feel a bit left out in conversations. I'm sure I'll feel more at home soon – once my Italian improves.

Speaker 3 We've always wanted to live in another country and my husband's always wanted to run his own business so we're going to combine the two. We're going to run a bar in Fiskardo on Cephalonia. We first went there for a holiday five years ago and we fell in love with the place. It's so quiet, so peaceful! My husband's already over there – there are one or two problems to sort out – and I'm going to fly out next month. I think our lives will change for the better once we've made the move. We'll get more job satisfaction 'cos it's our own business. And life will be much less stressful.

Answers
Speaker 1 – someone on holiday in a lively resort.
Speaker 2 – someone working in a foreign country.
Speaker 3 – someone working in a tourist resort.

2 • Play **5.1** again. This time students note down the advantages and disadvantages the speakers mention. (Not all the speakers mention disadvantages.) It is a good idea to stop the tape after each speaker. Students could compare ideas in pairs then check.

Answers

	Advantages	Disadvantages
Speaker 1	The apartment is handy for everywhere – the beach, the town centre. There's plenty to do. Good nightlife. Easy to meet people.	
Speaker 2	The people he works with are very nice – hospitable.	He is away from his family. His Italian isn't very good and most people don't speak English.
Speaker 3	It's quiet and peaceful. They'll get job satisfaction from their own business. Life will be less stressful.	

■ Vocabulary

1 • You could elicit answers from the whole class or students could discuss the words with a partner, followed by a check.

Answers
a convenient
b lots and lots (Point out that *loads* is an informal word.)
c excluded (not included)
d manage

2 • Allow a short time for students to practise the vocabulary by discussing these points in pairs. Do quick feedback if there is time.

Suggested answers
a A house or flat could be handy for the shops, the children's school, the office, the university, the underground, etc.
b Personal answer.
c When everyone is invited to something, e.g. a party, except them. When everyone knows who or what someone is talking about except them.
d Personal answer.

■ Have your say

1 • Students continue working in pairs for this short speaking activity. If you want to extend **1**, ask students to think of possible advantages and disadvantages for each option.

2 • Students who have never been away from home can be asked to think about who or what they would miss most. Allow a few minutes for discussion then get some feedback.

—Grammar review — The future – predictions, expectations, arrangements, intentions

1–2 Students should be able to work through these review exercises in pairs, referring to the **Language commentary** on p.129 to check their ideas.

• Before they start, check that they understand the words *predictions, expectations, arrangements, intentions.* You could give or elicit an example of each.
Predictions What we say will happen (from evidence): *Experts can predict who will win an election before the election takes place.*
Expectations What we believe will happen: *If we study hard for an exam and we are good at the subject we expect to pass.*
Arrangements Plans for the future which have been organized: *I can't see you tomorrow night. I've arranged to go to the cinema with David.*
Intentions Definite plans to do something in the future: *I intend to retire before I am 60.*
• Check answers.

Answers

1 a We're going back   d We're going to run
   b We're even staying   e things will be quieter
   c I'll feel

2 a 3 (predictions and expectations)
   b 1 (intentions)
   c 2 (arrangements)

■ Check

3 • Students can do the exercise on their own then check with a partner.
• You could check each pair's answers as they finish and indicate where they have made mistakes. Allow everyone a few minutes to correct wrong answers. Then do a final check. It may help to elicit the function of the future form – prediction, arrangement, etc.

4a–b Students do the controlled practice activity in pairs. You could demonstrate the activity by giving a couple of examples yourself.

- When students have finished, you could elicit some examples from different students and the class can guess whether they are true or not.

5 • Divide the class into groups of three or four. Demonstrate the activity by eliciting an idea for a couple of categories and writing them on the board, e.g.
Science and technology *I think there will be day-trips to the moon.*
Space *I don't think people will live on other planets.*

- Ask students to keep a note of points they all agree with.
- Monitor, but don't interrupt. You can correct at the feedback stage if necessary. Finally, elicit some statements from each group that everyone agrees with.

▶ **Photocopiable activity 9 p.162**

— p. 46 —

Reading

The theme of this section is living on a small island.

■ In your experience ■

1 • Give students a few minutes to look at the photographs and answer the questions in pairs. Get feedback from the class.

2 • Either get students to discuss the questions in pairs, then hear their ideas, or elicit ideas from the whole class.

■ Read ■

1 • This is an information exchange so you need to divide the class as far as possible into two equal-sized groups. The activity works best if there are three or four students in each group, (it can be done with pairs too), so subdivide the original groups if necessary. If you prefer not to do the activity as an information exchange, simply work with one of the texts. The other text could be set for homework.

- Explain to the class that each group is going to read a different text, answer the questions on that text, and finally exchange information on the text they have read with a student from the other group. Emphasize that it is important that they work on the comprehension questions as a group and that everybody notes down the answers.

2 • Check that each group knows which text they are going to read, and ask them to read the questions in 2 on the appropriate page. Check vocabulary. You may also like to pre-teach the following words:
Group A: *inaccessible, seafood, to be cut off, to get away (from something), success.*
Group B: *a new era, invest, 'green' tourism, mains (gas, electricity), rubbish dump.* (Eigg is pronounced /eg/.)
Alternatively, let students use their dictionaries.

- Tell students to write brief answers to the questions in 2 as they read. Each group should then check that everyone agrees on the answers. You could check these quickly with each group before they go on to the *Close up* questions.

Answers
2
Group A
a Tory Island is in the North Atlantic 8 miles off the coast of County Donegal in Ireland.
b 180 people live on the island.
c The islanders speak Irish as a first language.
d The ferry service operates four or five times a day in summer. It doesn't say how often it operates in winter.
e The climate is stormy, wet and windy.
f The main problems the islanders have are unemployment and being cut off from the mainland in winter.
g A hotel will soon open on the island. It should provide work for ten people.
Group B
a 63 people live on the island.
b The island is 12 miles off the north-west coast of Scotland.
c The islanders speak Gaelic.
d The main problems are there is no mains gas or electricity or rubbish dump.
e The islanders have recently bought the island, which was previously owned by millionaires, who did nothing for the island and the people who lived there. More people are coming to live on the island – new families are coming and old families are returning. New businesses are being set up.
f The ferry service operates every day in summer and three times a week in winter.

- Students should spend a few minutes answering the *Close up* questions as a group. Check each group's answers before they do 3. Any group which is lagging behind the others can be asked to go straight on to 3 without doing *Close up*.

■ Close up

Possible answers
Group A
- The following things can make a place *inaccessible*:
  its situation (in a mountain region); bad weather (storms;
  snow); no roads; no airstrip or airport; no railway; no harbour
  or beaches where boats can land.
- The name of the person is a *specialist*. The name of the thing
  is a *speciality*.
- *Seafood* is fish and shellfish. Examples of fish are: salmon,
  cod, trout. Examples of shellfish are: oysters, lobster,
  crabs, mussels.

Group B
- A gift / donation / phone call / letter can be *anonymous*.
- 'Green' tourism is tourism for people who are interested in
  the environment, for example, walkers, bird-watchers.
- The opposite of *encourage* is *discourage*.

3 · Tell students that the questions in 3 require them to use
their imaginations as well as the information in the text.
When each group has finished 3 check their answers.

Possible answers
Group A

3 a Patrick Doohan probably left the island because he couldn't
get a job. He probably returned because he realized the
island's economic possibilities and because he wanted to.
b The three shops are probably small so only give work to the
owners. Someone probably runs the community centre or
looks after it. The same person might run the bar. The other
activities mentioned (fishing, growing vegetables, keeping
sheep and painting) are not really jobs although they bring
in enough money to help people get by.
When the hotel opens there will probably be jobs for a
cook(s) / chef(s); barperson(s); chambermaid(s); receptionist(s);
waiter(s) / waitress(es).
c People who like peace and quiet would want to visit Tory
Island – possibly famous people, writers or painters. People
who like places where there is a lot going on wouldn't want
to come, nor would people who like to sunbathe and enjoy
the sun.

Group B

3 a Perhaps she used to live on the island, or she had connections
with Scotland, or she is a nature lover.
b The previous owners possibly bought the island because they
could afford to (to be able to say 'I own my own island',
which sounds very grand). They probably never lived on the
island because of its location, the weather or the lack of
infrastructure. They probably didn't invest in the island
because they never lived there and because they realized it
wouldn't be profitable.
c Old families may be returning because there will be more
opportunities now, and new families may be arriving because
they see it as an exciting adventure and challenge which they
want to be part of.

4 · Allow students to decide on four or five key facts. It is
probably better not to check ideas to this as to some extent
it is a matter of personal choice.

■ Information exchange

1 · Divide the class into A / B pairs. If there are any extra
students you could put a weaker student together with a
stronger student from the same group.
· Allow students enough time to exchange information. Tell
them they can refer to their notes but not the text.

2 · Using the information they now have on both texts
students have to decide which island they think has a
better future and why. Elicit ideas from the class to round
off the activity.

—Grammar — *will* and *going to*: ———— p. 47 —
other uses

■ Exploring concepts

1–2 Students can work in pairs to answer 1 and 2. They can
then check their ideas in the **Language commentary** on
p.129. Do a final check with the whole class.

Answers

1 · We use **will** to talk about future facts.
· We use **going to** to make predictions which are based on
what we already know or can see.

2 a 1 **b** 1 **c** 1 / 2 **d** 2 **e** 3 **f** 1 **g** 2 **h** 3

■ Exploitation

1 · Students can do this as a written exercise. Check that
they know which form they will be using (*will*). Hear
some answers.

2 · Students can do this exercise orally in pairs. You may want
to pre-teach some of the following vocabulary first: *Big
Dipper (Rollercoaster), scream, run into someone, coconut,
fortune-teller, fortune.*
· Monitor, supplying vocabulary and correcting where
necessary. You could feedback ideas onto the board.

Possible answers

- The Big Dipper is going to go down really fast.
- Some people are going to buy ice-cream.
- Somebody is going to drop an ice-cream.
- Some people are going to buy tickets for the Big Dipper.
- It's going to rain.
- The man in the green jumper is going to steal the other
  man's wallet.
- The child's going to run into a man.
- The man at the shooting range is going to win a soft toy. He's
  going to give it to his girlfriend. She's going to be pleased.
- The man in the red jacket is going to hit the coconut.
- The man in jeans is going to see the fortune teller.

3 · Students in pairs can take turns to make as many offers as
they can. Demonstrate with the example sentence. (See
suggested answers below.)
· Monitor, correcting where necessary. Then elicit ideas.

Suggested answers

Example

I'll do the washing up; I'll make the beds; I'll take the dog for a walk.

a I'll open the window; I'll turn on the air-conditioning; I'll get you a cold drink.

b Sit down, I'll get you a drink of water (an aspirin); I'll call the doctor.

c I'll lend you the money; I'll pay.

d I'll close the window; I'll turn up the central heating; I'll get you a hot drink; I'll make you a cup of coffee.

e I'll have a look at it; I'll give you a push; I'll phone the garage.

4 • Students work in pairs to do this mini role play.

5a–b This activity is a free practice activity which gives students the opportunity to practise the different future forms they have studied in this unit. Unless you want to make it just another controlled practice activity we suggest that you don't tell students what language to use or correct as you monitor. It will give you the opportunity to assess how well students are using the future forms. If students do not use the forms correctly you could remind them of appropriate forms at the end of the activity.

▶ **Photocopiable activity 10 p.163**

— p. 48 —

Skills

The theme of this section is taking time out. In Britain, the United States, Canada, New Zealand and Australia it is quite common for young people to take a year out either between finishing secondary school (High School) and going to college or university, or between finishing university and starting their first job, in order to travel. Other people may take time out during their working lives to continue their studies.

Speak

1–2 If your students are young and unlikely to have taken time out it is probably better to do this as a quick whole-class activity. If they are 18 or older they could discuss the questions in pairs.

• Have brief whole-class feedback.

Possible answers

1 Personal answer

2 • Between school and university – this is a good time to take time out. Most people of this age have no real ties. The experience may make them more mature. Young people can 'rough it' quite happily.

• Between university and your first job – this is also a good time. Most people are not married yet so have no real ties. It is better to get travel out of your system before you get on the career ladder, when it may be difficult to get off.

• After one year in a job – this is probably not a good time; you need to establish yourself in the job and your employer would probably think you were not a serious employee. However, if you didn't like the job and were thinking of changing anyway, it would be an ideal time.

• After eight to ten years in a job – this is probably a good time; you will have established yourself in your job; you may be a bit stale – a change will do you good. However, you may well have other ties – a partner and children; and commitments – a mortgage to pay, a family to support, etc. so it could be difficult.

Read

1 • Ask students to decide whether they think statements a–d are True or False. You could ask for a quick show of hands to see what people think, but do not confirm or deny at this stage.

2 • Ask students to read the article to check their ideas. Tell students not to worry about any words they don't know but just to get the general meaning of the text.

• Check answers.

Answers

a False Neither of them was worried about what they would do on their return.

b True Both of them worked as they travelled around.

c True They both say the experience has changed them.

d False They both plan to travel in the future.

Guessing meanings ▬ p. 49 ▬

• Students can answer the questions in pairs or on their own, then check their ideas with a partner. Check answers. They should use the prompt questions and the context to help them guess.

Answers

a The suffix *-less* means *without*. So *homeless* = without a home; *jobless* = without a job, and *penniless*, which literally means without a penny, = with no money. You could elicit any other adjectives students know with this suffix ending, e.g. *careless, smokeless, worthless, painless, endless, meaningless, hopeless, friendless, treeless*.

b *Swap* means to exchange something for something else. Point out that it is an informal word. You could either elicit or give ideas of things you could swap, e.g. addresses, telephone numbers, seats, ideas, a bar of chocolate for a packet of crisps.

c A *snap decision* is a decision which is taken quickly without careful thought.

d *Laid-back* is an informal word which means very relaxed in manner and character.

e The meaning of *bug* here is a keen interest.

• Before students go on to *Understanding ideas* you could check whether there is any other vocabulary in the text which students want to know the meaning of and deal with that now.

■ Understanding ideas

1–4 Students should read the text again if necessary, and then work individually, then compare with a partner, or in pairs.

- Check ideas.

Possible answers

1 Fiona and Andy were probably not worried about what they were going to do on their return because it was a long way in the future (they were thinking about the trip); the job situation might have been all right at that time; they might have been the sort of people who don't worry about things.

2 Fiona is probably referring to the excitement of seeing her friends and family again after such a long time.

3 She means that everyone else was living life at a fast pace whereas she was living life slowly and in a relaxed manner. (You drive fast on a motorway. You can't drive very quickly on a minor road; also people often take minor roads so that they can take their time and enjoy the scenery.)

4 Andy will probably go abroad again if the company he works for gives him time off; Fiona may go abroad again – it is less sure, but we get the impression that she would like to.

■ Have your say

- If students are from different countries they could work in pairs to swap information and opinions. If students are from the same country, you could do this as a whole-class activity.

Possible answers

Possible benefits: It would keep employees happy (a happy employee works better than one who isn't and wishes they were in the Himalayas, for example); a break in a stressful job could benefit the health of the employee and indirectly the company – they would work better, take less time off for illnesses, etc.

■ Listen

1 • Ask students to read statements **a–h**. Tell them that they need to correct the statements as they listen the first time.

- Play **5.2**. You could allow students a few moments to compare ideas with the person next to them, then check answers.

5.2

I decided to take a year off after finishing High School before I went to university and considering I was going to be studying French at university I thought the best way to improve my the way I spoke French was to go to France. Erm, I went for five months in all and I went with a programme which meant I was going to be staying with another with a French family for that time. At the beginning of my stay of course I felt homesick because France to Australia is a very long way. Erm, I wasn't with my family of course, and I missed my family and my friends. Erm, I was I couldn't I wasn't able to telephone them very often because of course it's very expensive and being surrounded by French all the time and me not being that wonderful at speaking French I had a few difficulties but once I got over that and started making friends and fitting in it was it just improved significantly.

I'm really glad I went because it gave me a lot more independence because I had to stand on my own two feet on my own without my family in a foreign country where I didn't necessarily speak the language very well. Er the distance from Australia meant that I had to be fully independent because I couldn't ring my parents all the time and say 'What do I do now? I don't understand' because Australia is a long long way from France and of course the telephone bills would have been enormous. Erm of course my French improved. Erm before I went I couldn't speak very well at all and when I left I can I can hold a conversation now in French er so of course that's good. It's definitely improved my confidence er as well. Er, now I go into life with the attitude that if I managed to do something in a country where I didn't speak the language as my mother tongue then I can do it here. It's, It's not that hard. And I definitely think I'm a more mature person now. I can handle what life throws at me.

Answers

a Lisa is going to study French ~~and German~~ at university.
b She went to France for five ~~weeks~~. **months**
c She stayed with ~~other Australian girls~~. **a French family**
d She missed her ~~school~~ in Australia. **family and friends**
e She **isn't** sorry she went to France.
f She **didn't** spend a lot of money on phone calls.
g She can ~~write~~ French better now. **speak**
h Lisa thinks going to France was a ~~negative~~ experience. **positive; good**

2 • Tell students to take notes in answer to the questions as they listen for a second time. Play **5.2** again. Allow students a few moments to compare ideas, then check answers.

Answers

a She felt homesick; she wasn't able to phone her family and friends much; she couldn't speak French very well.
b It has given her more independence; she is more confident; she is more mature.

3 • You could elicit ideas from the whole class.

Answers

a *to stand on one's own two feet* means to manage to live life without help from anyone else.
b *what life throws at me* means any difficult problems that happen in the future.
c *in all* means in total.

■ Speak

1 • Divide the class into pairs and make sure they understand the task. Tell them to set a realistic budget! Set a time limit for the activity.

2 • With a large class, pairs should share their ideas in groups.

Grammar extra

Articles

The theme for this section is living out of town – in the suburbs or in the country.

■ Read

1 • Tell students that they are going to read two short texts about the advantages and disadvantages of living in the suburbs and living in the country. You could elicit some ideas from the class before they read and write these on the board.

• Ask students to read the texts and find the advantages and disadvantages of living in each place. They can compare ideas with a partner before you check answers.

Answers
Living in the suburbs
Advantages
– The children can walk to school and it is handy for the underground.
– Jake can go to work by underground. It only takes him 20 minutes.
– Because they are near the underground they can get into the city centre easily and enjoy all that Warsaw has to offer.
Disadvantages
Anna has to drive to work.
Living in the country
Advantages
– They can have a garden.
– It's quiet and it's close to nature.
Disadvantages
– It is very cold in winter.

• If you haven't already done so you could elicit more advantages and disadvantages from students.

Possible answers
Living in the suburbs
Advantages   Flats are cheaper; you can sometimes live in a house instead of a flat.
Disadvantages You can spend a lot of time travelling to work; travelling can be expensive.
Living in the country
Advantages   It is healthier; you have more space and privacy.
Disadvantages It can be noisy (sheep and other animals) and smelly; you are further from amenities like shops, cinemas and hospitals.

2 • Short pairwork discussion. If your students already live in one of these places then they could consider the option of living in the city centre.

■ Exploring concepts

• Students can work on their own or in pairs. There are a lot of articles in the text and students only need to find one example of each one; set a time limit. Follow this up with a class check. Remind them about the **Language commentary** on p.130.

Answers
Indefinite article (a / an)
1 Line 2 a block of flats
2 Line 31 a small house
3 Line 10 an American
  Line 12 a university lecturer
Definite article (the)
1 Line 32 The house
2 Line 10 The city centre
3 Line 13 The biggest disadvantage
4 Line 19 the River Vistula
  Line 29 the Bieszczady mountains
5 Line 12 the USA
6 Line 23 the cinema
No article (Ø)
1 Line 43 Temperatures
2 Line 41 nature
3 Line 4 Warsaw
4 Line 6 school
  Line 18 work (= place of work)
5 Line 16 by underground

Note There are many more articles in the text. The task, however, is only to find one example of each.

■ Exploitation

1 • Students can work on their own, then check with a partner. As you monitor you could indicate which sentences contain mistakes. Finally, check answers.

Answers
a a teacher; an architect
b The capital of France, Paris; the River Seine
c school; to university
d Mount Everest is the highest mountain in the world; in the Himalayas
e hospital; an operation; The doctor; the operation
f the sun; the beach; a picnic
g dogs; cats
h food; the (a) fridge

2 • Divide the class into small groups of three or four students. Delegate one student in each group to keep the time. Ask students to read the instructions and demonstrate the activity with one of the groups. It is probably better not to remind students that this exercise is to give them practice in the use of articles or to correct mistakes as you monitor. Simply use it as a gauge of how well they use articles when they speak. If you like you could note down some mistakes that you hear and draw attention to them at the end of the activity, or at the beginning of the next lesson.

Exploring words

Places

1 • Ask students to match the geographical features with the letters on the map. They could use dictionaries to check the meaning of any words they don't know.
• Check answers.

Answers

coast f   desert j   estuary g   gulf e   island c
mountain range k   ocean b (or d)   peninsula a   plain h
plateau l   sea d (or b)   lake i

2a–b Students can do **a** and **b** on their own, then compare with a partner, or do the exercises in pairs. Check ideas.

Answers

2 a The preposition *on* is used before a river (1), a gulf (5). The preposition *in* is used before a country (2), an area of a country (3, 4), a sea (6), a mountain range (7), an ocean (8).
b If a place is situated *on* the coast it is on the land; if it is situated *off* the coast it is in the sea.

c Divide the class into groups of three or four students. Demonstrate the activity with the whole class first. As you monitor, correct any incorrect use of prepositions.

3 • Students can either continue to work in groups or you could divide the groups into pairs again and leave them in the same pairs for the remainder of the activities in this section.
• Some of this vocabulary will be unfamiliar to students so it is a good opportunity for dictionary work. You could suggest that students first of all look up any words they don't know and pass on their meanings to their partners or the rest of the group before they do the activity.

Possible answers

a *port* because it is a town or a village where ships load and unload their cargo.
b *pool* because a stream is a small river.
c *path* because it often has no proper surface; also there are no buildings on either side of it.
d *sand* because it is the 'material ' you find on the beach or the shore.
e *cliff* because the other two are pieces of rock.

4 a Again students can use their dictionaries to check the meaning of words they don't know, or you could elicit ideas from the whole class if time is short. Check answers.

Answers

crowded < > deserted   narrow < > wide
deep < > shallow   straight < > winding
high < > low

b Set a time limit for pairs to work though the list, then have whole-class feedback, adding other words as necessary.

Answers

a road – deserted, narrow, straight, wide, winding
a river – deep, fast-flowing, shallow, narrow, wide, winding
a beach – crowded, deserted, golden, narrow, palm-fringed, pebbly, sandy, wide
a mountain – high, low, snow-capped
the sea – deep, turquoise

5 • This fluency activity gives students the opportunity to use some of the vocabulary from the lesson.

a–c Ask students to read the instructions and then go through a–c with them. Suggest that they draw in pencil so that any changes of mind or differences of opinion can be rectified more easily, and set a time limit.

d Match up pairs of students. Pairs should take turns to tell the other pair as much as they can about their island pointing out features, etc. on their map as they do so. When each group has finished they should agree on the main differences between the two islands. You could limit this to a maximum of five differences.
• Monitor the activity, but don't interrupt. Then elicit feedback on the differences from selected pairs.

Writing

Describing places

■ Read ■

1 • Ask students to read the description of Granada. (Granada is situated in the south of Spain.) If your students are from different countries, you could pair different nationalities together to exchange information. If your students are from the same place they could discuss the similarities and differences together. Alternatively, you could simply elicit ideas from the whole class. Get feedback.

2 • Ask students to read the text again, this time underlining the adjectives. An example is given in their books.
• Check answers and explain any new vocabulary. Finally, elicit ideas on how the adjectives improve the description.

Answers

snow-capped, beautiful, sandy, old, the most interesting, narrow, winding, cobbled, small, modern, the latest, brightly-coloured, freshly-caught, sweet-smelling, dark-coloured, open, red, pink, white.

The adjectives bring the description to life. They help us to imagine Granada: the sights and smells, etc.

■ Vocabulary ■

• Students will probably be familiar with some but not all of this vocabulary. You could either ask students to look up the words they don't know in their dictionaries or you could explain them yourself. Students could either do the activity in pairs or you could do it with the whole class. Write up ideas on the board. As this is not the main focus of the lesson spend no more than five minutes on this activity.

Possible answers
- In a town or city: fountains, grass, parks, statues, trees.
- At the seaside: rocks, rock-pools, seaweed, shells.
- In the country: fields, grass, pine trees, rapids, rocks, trees, wild flowers.
- In the mountains: pine trees, rocks, wild flowers.

■ Brainstorm and notes

- Students are going to write a description of one of the four places mentioned. Ask them which one they would like to write about, then form groups or pairs.
- Tell students they need to decide exactly which place they are going to describe. Remind them about the vocabulary they studied on p.51. They will find these words as well as those on this page useful for their description. Monitor, helping with vocabulary where necessary.

■ Write

1 • Before students begin writing you might like to go through the model text and guidelines with the class. The text is particularly useful for students who have chosen to describe somewhere in the country. Alternatively, you could look at it at the end of the lesson before students write their final drafts as a reminder of the sort of features they should include in their descriptions.
  • Students now write the first draft of their description. They could either do this in pairs or on their own. Set a time limit for this, depending on the time you have available.

2a–b Ask students to exchange descriptions with someone from another group and suggest improvements.
  c Students now return the descriptions and tell the other student(s) their suggestions.
  d Set the writing task for homework.

▶ Writing model 5 (photocopiable) TB p.131

— p. 53 —

Language in action

Opinions

■ Introduction

1 a Ask students to look at the pictures for a short time, then play **5.3** for them to match the conversations with the photographs.

5.3

1
A Do you think it's a good idea for parents to send young children to nursery school?
B How young?
A Two or three years old.
B It's difficult to say.

2
A What's your opinion of children living at home with their parents until they get married?
B I don't think they should. I think it's a good idea to live on your own for a bit – it helps to make you independent, think for yourself, learn to manage your money, learn to cook, even.

3
A Do you have an opinion on young people having to do military service?
B It's not something I've really thought about.
A But don't you think it's unfair that boys have to do military service but girls don't?
B I'm not sure. Maybe. Anyway, girls do have to do military service in some countries.

4
A What do you think about this idea of taking a year out between school and university?
B I'd say it's a brilliant idea. I think the best time to travel is when you're young and have no ties.

Answers
1 b **2** d **3** a **4** c

b Before you play the tape again, divide the class into groups of three and indicate who is A, B, C. Make sure everyone understands what they have to do.
  • Play **5.3** again, stopping after each dialogue to give students time to write the language down. You could play each dialogue twice if necessary.
c Students exchange information. Then write the headings on the board and elicit the expressions from the class.

Answers

Asking for opinions	Giving opinions	Avoiding giving opinions
Do you think ...?	I don't think ...	It's difficult to say.
What's your opinion of ...?	I think ...	It's not something I've really thought about.
Do you have an opinion on ...?	I'd say ...	I'm not sure.
Don't you think ...?		Maybe.
What do you think about ...?		

2 • Students in pairs or groups give their personal views on the topics. Monitor, but don't correct. Use this as an opportunity to assess how well students can use the opinion language. You could listen out for typical mistakes, note these down and draw attention to them during feedback.

Pronunciation   p. 151

This section looks at unpronounced letters and linking /r/, /w/ and /j/.

1 a Ask students to read the words in their books. Tell them to cross out any letters which they don't hear as they listen to the tape.
   • Play **5.4** once straight through. Ask students to compare answers. Play again. Pause and check answers after each one.

5.4

1 wha~~t~~ do	5 I don'~~t~~ think
2 ha~~d~~ to	6 no~~t~~ something
3 can'~~t~~ go	7 difficul~~t~~ to
4 no~~t~~ true	

Answers
See Tapescript **5.4**.

b You could elicit the rule completion from the whole class. Point out that this is a general rule for normal speech; people who are speaking carefully and slowly may pronounce these sounds. The *t* and *d* are often replaced by soft glottal stops when we speak quickly.

Answer
a consonant

2 a This exercise introduces the linking sounds /w/ and /j/. The linking /r/ was introduced in Unit 3. Go through the instructions with the class. Point out that the letters *w*, *y* and *r* are not pronounced when they are at the end of a word which is standing on its own, but they are sometimes pronounced when they are followed by other words. If your students know phonetics you could demonstrate this by writing the words in phonetic script: *say* /seɪ/, *know* /nəʊ/, *your* /jɔː/.
   • Play **5.5**. Then check answers.

5.5

1 a What would you sa**y**?
  b I'd sa**y** it's a good idea.✓
  c I'd sa**y** they were stupid.
2 a I don't kno**w**.
  b I don't kno**w** what I think.
  c I don't kno**w** if it's a good idea.✓
3 a Is that you**r** opinion? ✓
  b Is that you**r** view?
  c Is that what most people you**r** age think? ✓

Answers
See Tapescript **5.5**.

b Ask students to complete the rule by choosing the correct alternative.

Answer
a vowel sound

3 a Students can either do the exercise in pairs or you can do it with the whole class. If students are working independently of you it is a good idea to do the first sentence with everyone as an example.
   • Write the sentence on the board or on an overhead transparency. Ask students to tell you which sounds are not pronounced when we speak quickly, and where there is linking between words. Indicate these on the board. Repeat this procedure for all the sentences.

5.6

1 What do you think about͜ this ͜idea?
2 It's difficul~~t~~ to say.
3 I'm no~~t~~ sure.
4 It's not something I've really thought about.
5 I'd say ͜it's a stupid ͜idea.
6 Do you have ͜an opinion ͜on military service?

Answers
See Tapescript **5.6**.

b Play **5.6**. If students were working on their own, tell them to make any changes as they listen. Then go through the answers with the whole class following the procedure above.

c Ask students to repeat each sentence after the tape. Insist on correct linking.

Practice   p. 53

1 a Divide the class into pairs. Tell them to decide on a topic for their survey and decide on a question to ask. Check that everyone's question is correctly phrased.

b Everyone designs a questionnaire. Each person will need their own copy.

c Before you get students into the middle of the room and start the activity, you could write some conversation starters on the board, e.g. *Excuse me? Have you got a minute? I'm doing a survey on (zoos). Would you mind answering a question? It won't take long.* Remind them to say thank you at the end.
   • Set a time limit, then split pairs up. Each of them should ask as many people as possible their question.
   • Monitor the activity from the front of the room. Again, you could note down one or two mistakes if you like and refer to them at the end of the activity.

2 • Students return to their seats and exchange information. They should first of all check that they haven't both interviewed the same person. It doesn't matter if they have, but they need to make the necessary adjustments to their report, i.e. *We interviewed nine (not ten) people.* Monitor, helping out where necessary.
   • Hear the results of all the surveys if possible. If your class is too big for this to be feasible hear a selection on different topics.

Language check

Follow the usual procedure.

6 Relationships

Theme

The overall theme for this unit is relationships.
Preview Love and marriage
Reading Arranged marriages versus love matches
Skills Cars
Grammar extra Friends
Writing Keeping in touch with friends

Grammar

- Permission, obligation, prohibition
- Permission and obligation: the past
- Indefinite pronouns: *someone*, etc.

Vocabulary

- Love and marriage

Writing

- Personal letters

Functional language

- Permission: asking for, giving, refusing permission

Pronunciation

- Sounding willing

Workbook

- Grammar and functional language as above
- Topic vocabulary: relationships; cars and driving
- Extract from a children's book: *The Iron Man*

Preview

This section looks at the theme of love and marriage. The reading text and the recordings also contextualize the language used for talking about permission, obligation and prohibition: *must, mustn't, can, can't, have to, don't have to.*

■ Your thoughts ▬▬▬▬▬▬▬▬▬▬▬ p. 54 ■

1 • Divide the class into pairs and ask them to read the three quotations (by John Lennon and Paul McCartney, Jane Austen and Michel de Montaigne in that order). Clarify any vocabulary and allow pairs a few minutes to exchange opinions. Tell them to try to back these up with examples or arguments. Elicit some opinions from the class.

2 • Ask if students know any other sayings, and elicit opinions about them.

■ Listen ▬▬▬▬▬▬▬▬▬▬▬▬▬▬▬▬▬▬▬▬▬

The song *Where have all the cowboys gone?* is by the American singer Paula Cole. It is quite fast but only fairly easy words have been gapped. It helps to set the context for the lesson.

1 • Students can stay in the same pairs for this activity. Together they should decide where they think the missing words go in the text. Tell them to ignore any vocabulary they don't know for the moment.

2 • Play **6.1** from beginning to end. Students should check their answers as they listen. Check answers and explain any vocabulary students want to know.

6.1

Oh, you get me ready in your '56 Chevy
Why don't we go sit **down** in the shade?
Take shelter on my front porch,
Dandelion, sun-scorched
Like a **glass** of cold lemonade?
I will do the laundry
If you pay all the **bills**

Where is my John Wayne?
Where is my prairie son?
Where is my happy ending?
Where have all the cowboys gone?

Why don't you stay the evening?
Kick back and watch the **TV**
And I'll fix a little something to eat
Oh, I know your back hurts
From working on the tractor
How do you take your coffee, my sweet?
I will raise the children
If you pay all the **bills**

(Repeat chorus)
I am wearing my new **dress** tonight
But you, but you don't even notice me …

We finally sold the Chevy
When we had another **baby**
And you took the job in Tennessee
You made **friends** at the farm
And you join them at the bar
Most every single day of the **week**
I will wash the **dishes**
While you go have a beer

(Repeat chorus)

Where is my Marlboro man?
Where is his shiny gun?
Where is my lonely ranger?
Where have all the cowboys gone?

Answers

down, glass, bills, TV, bills, dress, baby, friends, week, dishes.

You may find these definitions useful:
front porch: American houses (but not flats) have a front porch. The porch extends from the front of the house, has a wooden roof and wooden floor but no walls. There are usually chairs for people to sit on there.
kick back: sit back in a relaxed way
fix: make
Marlboro man: The cowboy who featured in the ads for Marlboro cigarettes.
lonely ranger: This is a reference to a TV western called 'The Lone Ranger', which was popular in the 1950s and early 1960s.

■ Understanding ideas ■ p. 55 ■

- Elicit ideas from the whole class. If students don't provide an answer straightaway you could give them the following alternatives to consider: *Is she a modern woman? A romantic? A traditionalist?*

Possible answers

She is a traditionalist. (She wants the man to go out to work while she looks after the children and does the housework.)
She is also a romantic. (She dreams of a good-looking cowboy (like the one in the Marlboro ads) who will look after her, pay attention to her, and love and protect her.)
She isn't happy because her husband doesn't compliment her (he doesn't even notice that she's wearing a new dress) and because her husband goes out drinking with his friends every night leaving her at home with the children.

■ Listen ■

1 · Ask students to answer the three questions quickly and compare answers. While discussing **c**, you could pre-teach *church wedding, registry office wedding*.

2 · Play **6.2** stopping after each speaker to allow students time to note down the information. It should only be necessary to play the tape once. Students can compare ideas with a neighbour before you check answers. Or you can check answers after each speaker.

6.2

Speaker 1   In the United States you can get married without your parents' permission when you're 16 or 18. It depends on the state. Every state has its own laws. I guess that the average age that people get married is about 25. That's the first marriage of course. As you probably know, we have a very high divorce rate in the States and an awful lot of people get married more than once. The actual wedding can be well anywhere – church, City Hall, in your own home. I had a friend who got married in a bowling alley – 'cos that's where she met her husband.

Speaker 2   Britain apparently has the highest divorce rate in Europe but marriage is still very popular here. You can get married when you're 18 without your parents' permission, but I'd say most people wait until they're in their mid-twenties. You can actually get married in lots of places nowadays – at a football ground if you want – or even sky-diving – if you can find a vicar who's a sky-diver of course! But most people still get married in church or in a registry office.

Speaker 3   In Japan women can get married when they are 16, but they have to have their parents' permission. I don't know about men. When you are 18 you are free to choose who you marry. I suppose the average age that people get married is around 24 for women and 30 for men, but I'm not really sure. You don't have to get married in a church. You can get married in a registry office if you prefer.

Note Speaker 3 is from New Zealand.

Answers

		United States	Britain	Japan
a	Average age	25	mid-twenties	Women: around 24 Men: around 30
b	Marriage age without permission	16 or 18 (Depends on the state)	18	18
	Marriage age with permission	XXX	XXX	Women: 16 Men ?
c	Place	anywhere, e.g. church, City Hall, in your own home, at a bowling alley	Lots of places: church, registry office, football ground, while you are sky-diving	Church; registry office

■ Read ■

- Before students read the text you could ask them if they know anything about the Amish community. Some of them may have seen the 1985 film *Witness* starring Harrison Ford.

Background information
The Amish are a strict sect, most of whom live in rural Pennsylvania (USA). They wear the same type of clothes as worn in the mid-19th century and do not make use of modern technology. (For example, they do not use machines to farm, do not have electricity, etc.)

- Ask students to read the text. Tell them to tick anything which surprises them as they read.
- Hear some views and explain any vocabulary students want to know.

Grammar review – Permission, obligation, prohibition

1–2 You may prefer to do most of these activities as whole-class activities if time is short. Alternatively, students can work as usual on their own or in pairs. Then, depending on the time available, you could either check answers with the class directly or refer them to the **Language commentary** on p.130 first.

Answers

1 • We use *can* to talk about permission and *can't* to talk about absence of permission.
  • We use *must* and *have to* to talk about obligation and *don't have to* to talk about absence of obligation.
  • We use *mustn't* to talk about prohibition.

2 There is no real difference in meaning between the pairs of sentences in **a** and **c**. At this level it is acceptable to say that *must* and *have to* are more or less synonymous. *Can't* and *mustn't* are more or less synonymous in the example given but not always. For example:
*Amish brides **must** wear blue* is more or less the same as *Amish brides **have to** wear blue.*
*Amish couples **can't** tell anyone they are going to get married* is more or less the same as *Amish couples **mustn't** tell anyone they are going to get married.*
In sentence **b** *mustn't* = not allowed, prohibited, and *don't have to* = there is no obligation; it is not necessary.

■ Check

3 • Ask students to do this exercise on their own. You could monitor, indicating mistakes. Then allow students a few moments to try to correct their mistakes before checking answers with the whole class.

Answers

a can
b mustn't
c don't have to
d can't
e must / have to

4 • Set up pairs or small groups for this activity, which is best done orally. You might like to elicit some more ideas from the class first using the 'parks' situation. If students don't come up with more ideas give some prompts, e.g. *What about walking your dog in parks? (You can walk your dog but you must keep it on a lead / you mustn't let it off its lead.)*
  • Tell students to take turns and say one sentence each until they run out of ideas for each situation. Monitor the activity, getting students to correct any mistakes they make.
  • Elicit a couple of examples for each situation.

5 • Divide the class into small groups, and ask for some ideas before giving them a few minutes to exchange ideas. Ask for a few examples at the end.

▶ **Photocopiable activity 11 p.165**

Reading

The theme of this section is the advantages and disadvantages of arranged marriages as opposed to love matches. Don't tell students what the theme is as the pre-reading activity involves them working it out for themselves. If you want to introduce the theme, you could simply say that you are going to look at different aspects of marriage in this lesson.

■ In your experience

1 • Ask students to read the instructions. Check that there are no problems with vocabulary.
  • Ask students to decide how important each of these factors is to them when they choose (or chose) the person they want to spend the rest of their life with. Tell them they can add other factors to the list if they like.

2 • Students compare answers with their partner. If there are any very big differences, they should try to explain why a particular factor is or isn't important to them. You could write up people's scores on the board.

■ Read

1 • Ask students to look at the title of the article and elicit what they think the article will be about. Confirm whether their ideas are right or wrong and check that they understand *arranged marriage*, the difference between *marriage* and *wedding*, and *love match*.

Answers

– The title tells us that the article is going to be about the advantages (and possibly also disadvantages) of arranged marriages (where parents choose the husband or wife for their daughter or son) compared with love matches (where people marry the person they fall in love with).

2 • Ask students to read the article and check their predictions.

■ Close up

Answers

– *fail to understand* means not understand. Another meaning of *fail* is not pass (an exam).
– *fragile* means easily broken. Anything made of glass or pottery is fragile.
– *To be off your head* means to be crazy. Other expressions are *out of your mind, round the bend.*
– The verb is *choose.* (chose, chosen)
– *throw away* means waste in this context. Another meaning is to get rid of something you don't want any more. You can throw away rubbish, paper, old clothes, etc.

■ Understanding ideas ■ p. 57 ■

1–4 Ask students to work in pairs to answer the questions. Allow enough time for students to work out the answers (eight to ten minutes) then check.

Possible answers

1 Nimu seems to be independent – she announces her decision, doesn't ask anyone's permission. She also seems to be a modern woman. She doesn't share her mother's traditional view of marriage and is not prepared to put herself last in a marriage.

2 They can see that love-matches don't always work. They can see that their parents' marriages have been successful. They want a marriage that is going to last and not end in divorce.

3 Suraya may be referring to the chance to live your own life according to what you want, not according to what your husband wants or what the family expects of you. She is also possibly referring to the chance to have a career.

4 For arranged marriages:
   – Parents know what qualities are needed for a marriage to work. They therefore choose husbands who will be responsible and respect their wives.
   – Arranged marriages last.
   Against arranged marriages:
   – Daughters had no choice in who they married.
   – Wives always had to put their husbands first and couldn't complain. They had to pretend to be happy if they weren't.

■ Have your say

- Allow students a few minutes to discuss the question in pairs. Then, if your students are interested in the topic, open it up for a mini class debate. Otherwise hear a selection of views.

— Grammar — Permission and obligation (2) ——

■ Exploring concepts

1–3 You can do these exercises with the whole class. Alternatively, students can work in pairs and check their ideas in the **Language commentary** on p.131 before a final check.

Answers

1 Sentences **a** and **d** refer to obligation in the past.
Sentences **b** and **c** refer to permission in the past.
Check that students know which forms are used to talk about obligation in the past (*had to* and *didn't have to*) and permission in the past (*could* and *couldn't*).

2 There is no real difference in meaning between the pair of sentences in **b**. In **a** the first sentence means women weren't allowed to choose who they married; the second sentence means they weren't obliged to choose (someone else chose for them).

3 **a**

Present	Past	Future
must	had to	must or will have to
mustn't	—	mustn't
can	could	can or will be able to
can't	couldn't	can't or won't be able to
have to	had to	will have to
don't have to	didn't have to	won't have to

b **Did you have to** (get married to him)?
Didn't you have to (accept your parents' choice of partner)?
Could you (get married to anyone you liked)?
Couldn't you (get married to your cousin)?

■ Exploitation

1 • Ask students to do the exercise on their own, then compare ideas with a partner.
  • Check answers.

Answers

1	didn't have to	5	couldn't
2	had to	6	could
3	didn't have to	7	had to
4	didn't have to	8	could

2 • Divide the class into pairs or small groups and go through the instructions and the example with the class. If you have a mixture of nationalities in your class it will make the activity more interesting if you mix them up.
  • Students can now work in pairs to talk about the situation in the past in their own country or countries. Monitor the activity. Use your own judgement whether it is better to correct any mistakes in the target language now or later during feedback.
  • Hear a selection of responses from each group.

3 • Students can stay in the same pairs or groups for this activity. Read through the instructions and, if you like, demonstrate the activity by talking about yourself. Don't simply give sentences containing these structures – add other information too. The activity should be an exchange of experiences rather than simply a controlled practice exercise. Monitor without interrupting. Then hear some examples to round off the lesson.

— p. 58 —

Skills

The theme of this section is cars and our relationship with them.

■ Speak

1–4 Before students start the speaking activities, make sure that they understand the following words: *make* (e.g. Ford, Fiat), *model* (e.g. 306, Punto) and *fuel consumption* (how much fuel the car uses per kilometre). You might also like to pre-teach the words *petrol* (*leaded* and *unleaded*) and *diesel*. Elicit some examples of features which a car might have, for example: *air conditioning, sun roof, tinted windows, CD player, alloy wheels, electric windows, power steering, central locking system.*

- Divide the class into small groups of three or four students.
- Allow students a few minutes to think about their answers before they start speaking. When students have had enough time to exchange their ideas, stop the activity and hear a selection of answers.

■ Listen

- Before you play the tape, check that students understand the words *reliability* and *registration number*.

Background information
In Britain, car registration numbers are a combination of letters and numbers. Each area has a range of different possible letter combinations (e.g. MAD, DAD, CAD) and all cars have a letter which indicates the year of manufacture (A–Z).

- Tell students that they should listen for specific information only the first time they hear the tape. They should put a tick in the appropriate place in the table when a particular feature is mentioned.
- Play **6.3** straight through without stopping, then allow students a few moments to compare answers with a partner. Unless your students have found the exercise very difficult, it is better not to play the tape twice as they will be hearing it again before they answer the questions in *Understanding ideas*.
- Check answers with the whole class.

6.3

Speaker 1 My car is a wonderful blue Fiat Panda, which is about 12 years old and it's been all over Europe. It's lived in Italy, Hungary and travelled many miles. It's a dear friend. It never lets me down and it always starts.

Speaker 2 My favourite car was a black mini. It was my first car and it had a lovely wooden dashboard and I think that's why I liked it so much. It was very special. I was quite fond of of this car because the registration number was TFN so we called it Tiffany and it had a name and a little personality so yes I was quite fond of that car. It was special.

Speaker 3 Er, my favourite car was a red Vauxhall Astra which I had for several years until it stopped working. I liked it best because it was reliable, it was comfortable and it had a good stereo.

Speaker 4 Erm when I was a student, I inherited my grandfather's Volkswagen Beetle and it was an orange one and it was very old. In fact it was older than than I am and em he'd looked after it really really well though and so it was, it was a really nice car to drive – not for going on long journeys …

Speaker 5 My favourite car is actually the the car I've got at the moment. It's a Peugeot 306 – petrol not diesel – and I suppose I like it mainly for two reasons. It's a lot faster than the car I had before and it's very good going round corners and also it's bigger so it's it's quite comfortable. A friend of mine was quite surprised when she saw it for the first time. She said, 'I didn't think of you as em a red car driver. I thought of you more as a blue car driver,' which rather upset me at the time although I got over it later.

Answers

Features \ Speaker	1	2	3	4	5
colour	✓	✓	✓	✓	✓
make	✓	✓	✓	✓	✓
age	✓			✓	
reliability	✓		✓		
comfort			✓		✓
stereo			✓		
registration number		✓			

Understanding ideas

1–3 Play **6.3** again then ask the students to answer the questions in pairs. Remind them that they will need to use their imagination for some of the answers.

- Check answers.

Possible answers

1 Speaker 1 thinks of her car as a person.

2 A car can *let you down* by not starting, by breaking down. If you like you could elicit examples of how people can let you down, for example, by not doing something they promised to do or by doing something wrong.

3 The friend was surprised to see that Speaker 5 had bought a red car. She thought she would have bought a blue car. Speaker 5 interprets what her friend says as a negative comment on her personality. Speaker 5 obviously equates red with positive qualities (e.g. exciting, dynamic) and blue with qualities like calmness and reliability, which she regards as rather boring.

Have your say

- You could either allow students a few moments to think of some ideas, then discuss them with their partner, or you could do this as an open class discussion.

Possible answers
Some people are fond of their car because:
- it's their first car.
- they've had it a long time.
- it's associated with happy times: when they were in love, when they were a student.
- it's a classic car.
- it is a fantastic car (like a Porsche or a Ferrari).
It is probably more likely to happen with old cars but not necessarily.

Read

1 - Students can guess how these words from the article might be used on their own or in pairs, or you can elicit ideas from the whole class.

2 - Students will have more than one chance to read the article, so ask them to read it the first time simply to get a general idea and to check their ideas from 1.
- Find out how many of their ideas were the same or similar.

Guessing meanings p. 59

- Students can answer these questions in pairs. They should use the prompt questions and the context to help them. Check answers, then deal with any other vocabulary in the text which students want to know. You may want to limit this to six to eight words.

Answers
a *use up* means to finish a supply of something. The particle *up* with the verbs *drink* or *eat* means finish what you are eating or drinking.
b *common* means the same in many places. *Commonplace* means ordinary, not different or unusual.
c *inspiring* means it fills you with interest and enthusiasm. The related noun is *inspiration*.
d *blood-pressure* is the pressure of blood as it travels round the body. If a person has *high* blood-pressure it is an indication that their heart is beating too quickly.
e a *chore* is a dull, boring, routine task like doing the housework, weeding the garden, ironing.

Understanding ideas

1–4 Students can continue working in the same pairs as before. Allow students enough time to answer the questions. Then check their ideas.

Answers

1 c

2 The writer thinks mass-market cars are ordinary, boring and ugly with the exception of the Mini, the Fiat 500 and the VW Beetle.

3 The writer probably doesn't have a car because he refers to car owners as 'they' and not 'we'. He would probably like to have a classic car, which he would drive occasionally.

4 • an environmentalist – No. He doesn't mention the environment except to say that it is difficult to admit that you like cars nowadays because of their negative effect on the environment.
  • a snob – Yes. He looks down on people who own ordinary cars like Fords and Nissans.
  • a car enthusiast – No. He doesn't like most modern cars.
  • a classic car enthusiast – Yes. He admires the early models and he mentions a classic Rolls Royce in his fantasies.

Have your say

• If you have little time available you can do this as a quick class opinion check. Otherwise you can allow students a few minutes to express their ideas, then hear a variety of opinions.

Speak

1 • Read through the instructions with the class, then divide them into groups of three or four to compile a list of features. Set a time limit for this part of the activity.

2 • Groups can either appoint a spokesperson or share the presentation. You could make this stage fairly formal, with an opportunity for others to ask questions about the reasons. Then take a quick vote on which ideas were best.

— p. 60 —

Grammar extra

Indefinite pronouns

The theme of this section is friends.

• Ask students to read the text quickly and answer the question.

Answer

No, Nicholas and the writer aren't friends any more.

Exploring concepts

1–4 Students can answer the grammar questions on their own or in pairs. Check answers to **1** before students go on to **2**. They can then work through **2–4**, checking their ideas in the **Language commentary** on p.131 before you do a final check.

Answers

1 everybody, nothing, someone, everywhere, everything, anything

2 1 We use *some* in affirmative sentences.
  2 We use *any* in negative sentences and in questions when we don't know whether the answer will be *yes* or *no*. (**d**)
  3 We use *some* in questions which are offers (**b**) or requests (**a**), and when we expect the answer *yes*. (**c**)

3 a *Anything* is used with a negative verb form; *nothing* is used with an affirmative verb form.
  b *Everybody* is followed by the verb in the third person singular form.

4 a *Anyone* can be President …
  b *Anyone* can win the lottery …
  c *Everyone* I spoke to …

Exploitation

1 • Students can do this exercise on their own. Check answers before they do **2**.

Answers

a someone / somebody, anyone / anybody, no one / nobody
b anyone / anybody, everywhere, anywhere, somewhere
c Everyone / everybody, anything, everything, something, nothing

2 • Students can work in pairs or threes and continue the sentences in as many different ways as they can. Point out they should be careful with word order in **b**. Get them to say the continuations rather than write them. Set a time limit of four to five minutes.
  • Elicit several examples for each sentence.

Possible answers

a like that film / be so stupid / want to be a dentist.
b how old she is / who did it / how much it's worth.
c listens to your problems / cheers you up when you are sad / will pick you up from the airport at 3.00 a.m.
d him / chocolate / getting letters from friends.
e she goes too / I hear that song / they follow.
f sunbathing on the beach / sitting under a tree drinking cold lemonade / driving a car with the roof down.

3 • If students aren't already working in groups of three set these up or put pairs together to make groups of four.
  • Demonstrate the activity. Tell students that the person who answers should only say *yes* or *no*.

▶ Photocopiable activity 12 p.166

Exploring words

Love and marriage

1 • Divide the class into pairs for this activity, which provides a good opportunity for dictionary work. Allow enough time for students to do the exercise then check answers.

Answers

a *wedding* the ceremony when you get married.
  marriage the legal union between a man and a woman which makes them husband and wife.

b *girlfriend* the girl / woman a boy / man is going out with.
  fiancée the woman a man is engaged to.

c *date* planned meeting with someone of the opposite sex (usually a girlfriend or boyfriend or someone who might become your girlfriend / boyfriend).
  appointment formal arrangement to meet or visit someone on a particular date at a particular time (e.g. the dentist, the doctor, a lawyer).

d *bride* the woman who is getting married (used on or just before her wedding day).
  groom the man who is getting married (used on or just before his wedding day).

e *husband* the man a woman is married to.
  partner the person a man or woman is married to or living with. (In class: the person you are doing an activity with; in business: one of the owners of a business.)

f to *like someone* find someone pleasant.
  to *fancy someone* find someone sexually attractive.

g *father-in-law* the father of your husband or wife.
  god-father (in the Christian religion) man who promises at the baptism ceremony to look after the child in religious and moral matters.

h *maiden name* woman's surname before she gets married.
  married name woman's surname after she gets married (i.e. her husband's name).

i *relationship* close emotional or sexual friendship between two people.
  relation person who is related to you (e.g. uncle, cousin).

j *half-sister* sister with only one parent in common with the other.
  step-sister female child of one's step-mother or step-father by an earlier marriage.

k *widow* woman whose husband has died.
  widower man whose wife has died.

l *polygamy* custom of having more than one wife at the same time.
  monogamy custom of having one wife at a time.

2 a Ask students to match expressions 1–8 with the illustrations. Check answers and explain any new vocabulary before students go on to **b**.

Answers
1 c 2 g 3 d 4 h 5 b 6 e 7 f 8 a

b–c It is worth checking quickly that students know the Past simple forms of the verbs before they do the exercise.
• Play **6.4** for students to check their answers. Then deal with any new vocabulary.

6.4

Julian met Emily at a friend's party. He fell in love with her the moment he saw her. She was extremely pretty. He decided to go over and speak to her. 'Haven't I seen you somewhere before?' he asked – not the most original chat-up line – but Emily liked the way he smiled, and at the end of the evening agreed to go out with him. They went to the cinema on their first date, and got engaged six months later. They got married in a local church the following June.

They wanted to have a family while they were still young. Their first child was born a year later and two others followed in quick succession. Unfortunately, though, things didn't work out, and they split up just after their fifth wedding anniversary. They got divorced two years later. Julian admitted, 'We got married too young.'

Answers

1	met	5	got married
2	fell in love with	6	have a family
3	go out with	7	split up
4	got engaged	8	got divorced

3a–e Allow students a few minutes to discuss the questions in pairs then elicit ideas from the whole class.

4a–d This brief writing activity is a variation on the game 'Consequences'. You could demonstrate points 1 and 2 by eliciting ideas from the class and writing them on the board.
• Tell students that their story must fit with what the previous students have written.
• You can either monitor the activity, correcting mistakes as you do so, or treat this as a free writing activity and simply let students get on with it.
• When the stories are finished the students can read them out to the class and the class can vote on the best one.

— p. 62 —

Writing

Personal letters

The theme of this section is telling a friend personal news.

Read

• Tell students that they are going to read a personal letter from a young man (Jamie) who is writing to a male friend (Tony) for the first time in over two years. Ask them what sort of things they think Jamie will write about, (for example, his work or his studies). You could write these on the board.
• Ask students to read the letter, without trying to put it in the correct order, and see which of their ideas he did write about.

Answers
Jamie wrote about his new job, Eva (his ex-girlfriend) and Anita his new girlfriend.

- You could ask students to decide on the correct order of the letter extracts on their own then compare ideas with a partner. Check answers.

Answers

1 c 2 f 3 j 4 b 5 e 6 m 7 h 8 l
9 a 10 k 11 d 12 g 13 i

Brainstorm and notes

- Do this as a whole-class activity. Elicit the types of questions students can ask themselves for each topic and write these on the board as a reminder.
  Your studies: *Have you finished your studies? When did you finish them? Are you still studying? If so, what are you studying? What are your study plans for the future?*
  Work: *Have you got a job? Have you got a new job? Have there been any big changes at work? Are you happy in your job? Are you going to look for another job?*
  Family: *Is everybody in your family well? Has anything important happened? (Has anyone got married / had a baby, etc?)*
  Friends: *What news do you have about friends you have in common? Have you made any new friends?*
  Relationships: *Are you in a relationship with someone? Is it someone new? Have you any plans? (to get engaged, married?)*
  Purchases: *Have you made any big purchases? Have you bought a house / flat / car?*
  Future plans: *What plans have you got for the future?*
- Allow them time to write down what they are going to say in note form. Tell them they should not try to write about everything but should limit themselves to two or three important topics.

Write

1 - Allow students enough time to write a first draft of their letter. Either put a possible layout on the board for them to follow or read through the model letter with them. Remind them to follow the **Reminder** on their page.

2a–c Tell them to exchange letters with another person, read their new letter and make some suggestions for improvement. Students should then discuss these ideas together.
- Ask students to write the final version of their letter for homework.

▶ **Writing model 6 (photocopiable) TB p.131**

Language in action

Asking for permission

Introduction

1 - Students work in pairs to write how they would ask for permission in the situations. They will probably already know several expressions.
- Monitor to give yourself an idea of how much students already know, but don't correct. Students can make corrections themselves when they listen to the conversations.

2 a Play **6.5** without stopping. Ask students to tick the expressions which are the same on their lists or to make any corrections to their ideas.

6.5

1
J Sue? Hi, it's Jack.
S Hi, Jack. How are you?
J Fine. Erm, Sue?
S Yeah?
J Could I borrow your 'Best Rock Music Ever' CD? I'll let you have it back tomorrow.
S I suppose so. But make sure you remember.
J I will, don't worry. Can I come round to get it now?
2
A Is it OK if I join you?
B Of course. I think you know Alan, don't you?
A Hi.
C Hi.
3
A Do you think I could borrow your car tonight for a couple of hours?
B What for?
A I promised Jenny I'd give her some extra driving lessons.
B Jenny? No way! Anyway I'm using it myself tonight. Why don't you ask David?
A (Shouts) David?
D (From another room) Yeah?
A Any chance of borrowing your car tonight?
D My car?
A Yes. I said I'd pick Jenny up from college.
D Sure. Go ahead. I think the keys are on the table.
4
I Do you think I could possibly leave early tonight, Sara? It's my girlfriend's birthday.
S I'm afraid not, Ian. We need to get this finished today.
5
A Do you mind if I take this chair?
B No, not at all.
A Hi, Sue! Come and join us!
S Is it all right if I take this chair?
B No problem. I'm just leaving anyway.

b Allocate A / B roles and check that students know what to do.

c Allow students a few minutes to exchange ideas.
- Check answers.

Answers

Asking permission	Giving permission	Refusing permission
Could I borrow ...?	I suppose so.	No way!
Is it OK / all right if ...?	Of course.	I'm afraid not.
Do you think I could ...?	Sure. Go ahead!	
Do you think I could		
possibly ...?	No, not at all.	
Do you mind if ...?	No problem.	

- Draw students' attention to the affirmative response to *Do you mind if ...*, i.e. *No, not at all.*

d Elicit answers to this question from the whole class.

Answers

- The most formal expression used to ask for permission is: *Do you think I could possibly ...?*
- The most informal expression is: *Is it OK / all right if ...?*
- The expressions which show that the speaker is happy to give permission are all those listed under **Giving permission** above except *I suppose so*, which tells us the speaker doesn't really want to give permission.

▨ Pronunciation ▨▨▨▨▨▨▨▨▨ p. 152 ▨

This section looks at appropriate intonation for giving permission.

1 a Before you play tape **6.6** check that students understand the instructions.
   - Play once straight through. Check answers then elicit the difference between the speakers who sound happy to give their permission and those who don't.

6.6

1	All right.	✓	4 Yeah.	✓
2	All right.	✗	5 OK.	✓
3	Yeah.	✗	6 OK.	✗

Answers
See Tapescript **6.6** .

- The speakers who sound happy to give their permission start higher than those who don't.

b Play **6.7** . Pause between each response and drill.

6.7

1 All right.
2 Yeah.
3 OK.

2 a Students can either work in pairs or you could do the exercise with the whole class. Write up the sentences on the board, underline stressed syllables and double underline main stressed syllables (in bold).

b Play **6.8** and check answers.

6.8

1 Go ahead.
2 Of course. (*Of* could also be stressed)
3 Sure.
4 No problem.
5 I don't mind at all.

Answers
See Tapescript **6.8** .

c Before you play the tape again, ask students to look at the diagrammatic representation of the intonation pattern in their books. Read through this with them then play **6.8** again and drill. Insist on a 'happy' intonation pattern.

3 • Tell students that they are going to hear eight requests for permission. They should reply to the requests using the expressions in **1a** (once only) and **2a** in that order. You could nominate one or several students to respond.
   - Play **6.9** .

6.9

1 Can I borrow your pen for a minute?
2 Can I borrow your ruler?
3 Could I borrow your book till tomorrow, please?
4 Could I borrow this CD for a few days?
5 Is it all right if I pay you back on Friday?
6 Is it all right if I use your phone?
7 Do you think I could leave early today?
8 Do you think I could change my day off?

▨ Practice ▨▨▨▨▨▨▨▨▨▨▨▨▨ p. 63 ▨

▨ Role play ▨▨▨▨▨▨▨▨▨▨▨▨▨▨▨▨

- Divide students into A / B pairs. Tell Students A to read the information on the page and Students B to read the information on p.154. Deal with any vocabulary queries.
- Allow pairs a few minutes to think about the language they are going to use to ask permission in their situations. They also need to try to think of how they will persuade their partner to say *yes*.
- Ask students to role play both situations. Monitor unobtrusively.
- You could round off by giving feedback on any points you noted during monitoring.

▨ Language check ▨▨▨▨▨▨▨▨▨▨▨▨▨▨

Follow the usual procedure.

7 Seriously funny

Theme

The overall theme of this unit is humour.
Preview Different senses of humour / jokes
Reading Laughter
Skills Extract from a Bill Bryson book about Britain
Grammar extra Comic actors
Writing Humorous short stories

Grammar

- Review of modal verbs *can* and *could* to express ability and possibility
- *can, could, may, might* to express degrees of certainty and uncertainty
- Relative clauses (1): defining and non-defining clauses; *who, which, that*

Vocabulary

- Body language / Extreme adjectives

Writing

- Writing narratives (short stories)

Functional language

- Making suggestions

Pronunciation

- Silent letters; sounding enthusiastic

Workbook

- Grammar and functional language as above
- Body language; extreme adjectives; prepositions; idioms with parts of the body
- Short stories

Preview

Humour can be a tricky subject in the classroom. It's well-known that 'humour doesn't travel'. For this reason we have chosen material that should work whether students find it funny or not. Don't spend extra time explaining the cartoons, the jokes or the stories – it will probably slow things down and make your students feel inadequate – and they still may not laugh!

▉ Your thoughts ▉▉▉▉▉▉▉▉▉▉▉▉▉▉ p. 64 ▉

1a–c Students rank the cartoons in order, according to how funny they find them, then compare ideas with other students. They could do this in pairs or as a whole-class mingle.
- Elicit their ideas. Is there any consensus in the class about which cartoons are the funniest or the least funny? Don't ask students to try to give reasons for their choices.

2a–b Divide the class into pairs to think about and discuss what makes them laugh.
- You could start with a class discussion about films and TV programmes, then let students work through the rest of the list in pairs.

c–d Elicit students' answers to **c**. At this stage, accept any words students use to describe their sense of humour. (They will come across some of the commonly-used terminology in *Listen* 1).
- Do a quick class survey to find out to what extent students share the same sense of humour.

▉ Listen ▉▉▉▉▉▉▉▉▉▉▉▉▉▉▉▉▉▉▉▉

1 • Explain the first listening task, then play **7.1** .
- Check answer.

Answer
There are several possible questions:
- What kind of humour do you like?
- What's your favourite kind of humour?
- How would you describe your sense of humour?
- What do you find funny?
- What makes you laugh?

7.1

Speaker 1 Well I suppose I've got rather an individual sense of humour. All sorts of things can make me laugh – not always the things that are meant to be funny. For instance, I often laugh at things people say or do in real situations. I can't stand prepared jokes, you know the sort of corny jokes people tell in bars – jokes that you feel you ought to laugh at.

Speaker 2 Mmm, that's a really difficult question. I can tell you what I don't like – that's easy enough. I can't stand slapstick humour, you know like clowns, people slipping on banana skins, that kind of thing. There are a few comedians on TV I find funny – but it's difficult to say why they're funny – perhaps you could call it ironic humour.

Speaker 3 There are a few people I know, you know, friends of mine, who are just naturally funny. They can make me laugh at almost anything – but I'm not sure that's a particular kind of humour, is it? It's just an ability some people have got to make you laugh – a sort of natural wit. On the other hand, I'm not very keen on professional comedians – I just don't find them funny.

Speaker 4 Actually, I think humour's to do with age, I mean there's almost nothing on television that I find funny – it's all so middle-aged – especially sit-coms – they can be really dreadful, but my parents watch them and think they're absolutely hilarious. I sometimes go to the theatre – when there's a stand-up comedian on – some of the young ones are quite funny – pretty mad humour, but it makes me laugh.

Speaker 5 Mm, good question. I er, I don't like humour that's too obvious. I suppose what I really like is black humour – you know when you can see the funny side of something that is normally quite serious or er, even sad. Some people might call it sick humour, I suppose.

Speaker 6 My favourite kind of humour is something to do with words – definitely – I think people who can make jokes with words are really clever – you know – words with double meanings. I'm afraid I don't really like a lot of modern humour – to me it's just not funny.

2 • One of the aims of this task is to introduce the vocabulary of humour, so check students' understanding of the table, referring back to different kinds of humour that students talked about in *Your thoughts* 2c.
  • Play **7.1** again. Students complete the table.
  • Check answers.

Answers

Finds funny	Speaker	Doesn't find funny	Speaker
• the natural humour of friends	3	• slapstick, banana-skin humour	2
• stand-up comedians	4	• comedy programmes on TV	4
• black humour	5	• modern humour	6
• people in real situations	1	• obvious humour	5
• word humour	6	• the kind of jokes people tell in bars	1
• ironic humour	2	• professional comedians	3

■ Read ■ ■ ■ ■ ■ ■ ■ ■ ■ ■ ■ ■ ■ ■ p. 65 ■

1 • Introduce this reading activity by teaching the expression *a corny joke* (a prepared joke which has been repeated so often that it is no longer funny). People often *groan* rather than *laugh* when they hear a corny joke. Do students have *corny jokes* in their language? Elicit one or two.
  a In preparation for reading the jokes, get students to work through the three vocabulary questions, either in pairs or as a whole class. Don't spend too long on these questions.
  • Check answers.

Answers

1 People *walk* short distances and *fly* a long distance.
2 It's the British way of saying: *I am Paul* or *Paul is speaking.*
3 Something we eat as a vegetable.
   been – the past participle of the verb *be*.

  b Students read the three jokes, choose the funniest or the least funny, then compare ideas with a partner.
  • Do a quick class survey to find out which jokes students find the most and the least funny. Don't be tempted to explain jokes if students don't find them funny.

■ Have your say ■

1–2 Divide the class into pairs or small groups to discuss the two questions.
  • Elicit their ideas, e.g. do they have the same sense of humour as their parents?
  • If students are interested and willing, ask for one or two volunteers to translate into English a well-known joke (in their country / language) for the rest of the class.

— Grammar review — *can / could* —

The main focus here is on *can* and *could* to talk about abilities and possibilities, but students are also reminded about the other uses of these verbs.

1a–b Introduce this first task by checking that students understand the difference between *ability* and *possibility*.
  • Students work through a1–6 and b individually or in pairs. Remind them about the **Language commentary** on p.132.
  • Check answers.

Answers

a 1 P   2 A   3 P   4 A   5 A   6 B
b
1 time in general   4 present / present
2 present / time in general   5 past
3 future   6 present

  c Remind students that *can* and *could* have other uses.
  • Elicit answers to this exercise from the class.

Answers

1 c   2 a   3 b

■ Check ■

2 a Read through the example with the class and elicit a few other examples before they work in pairs. Set a time limit for this activity.
  • Monitor, correcting any errors you hear.
  • Students could tell the class about some of their partner's abilities. You could develop this into a survey to find out the youngest ages at which students could *walk, talk, swim, ride a bike*, etc.

b Working individually or in pairs, students finish sentences 1–3 in two or three different ways. These express definite possibilities.

• Check answers, and correct if necessary.

Possible answers

1 Watching television can … give you a headache. / send you to sleep. / make you a boring person. / teach you things. / keep you informed about world events.
2 Smoking can … help you to relax. / kill you. / make you unpopular in public places. / give you cancer and heart disease. / be very expensive.
3 Eating too much can … make you fat. / make you feel sick. / make you sleepy.

c Students work in the same way on sentences 1–3 with *could*.

• Check answers.

Possible answers

All the possible answers are expressions of speculation.

1 My car's making a strange noise. It could be … running out of petrol. / about to blow up. / a serious problem. / a flat tyre.
2 Chris and Sophie are very late. They could … be stuck in a traffic jam. / still be at work. / be in some kind of trouble.
3 What's that strange shaped thing in the sky? It could … be a flying saucer. / be a large bird. / be an alien spaceship.

3 • This is a more open-ended activity which depends on students' imagination.

• Students think of suggestion ideas in pairs. Each suggestion should include *could*.

• Elicit a few ideas from the class for each cartoon.

—— p. 66 ——

Reading

■ In your experience ■

• You could introduce this section and work through questions 1 and 2 with students' books closed.

1 a Students start by listening to a recording of four people laughing in different ways. This introduces the next theme of the unit, laughter, in a direct way.

• Play **7.2** without preparation. Students should have their books closed.

• Ask them what the four people were doing. Were they all doing it in the same way?

• You could elicit or teach the words for the different types of laughter they hear.

Answers

1 This is a *snigger* – the person is laughing unkindly or secretly at something they shouldn't find funny.
2 This is a *giggle* – the person is laughing quietly and uncontrollably like a child, maybe because they are nervous or embarrassed.
3 This is a polite *laugh* – the person may be laughing because they feel they ought to.
4 This is a *belly-laugh* – the person is laughing in a loud uncontrolled way.
Laugh is a general word which includes *snigger* and *giggle*.

b Elicit situations in which students might *snigger*, *giggle* or *laugh*.

2 • This is a chance for the class to discuss their reactions to hearing people laughing. Did any students laugh? Did other students join in? In other words was the laughter *infectious*?

• Students can now open their books.

■ Read ■

1 • Students are now going to read extracts from four articles related to laughter.

• You could pre-teach these words: *fitness*, *therapy*, *receptive*, *tension*.

• Students read the texts and match them with appropriate headlines. Allow only three or four minutes for this skimming task.

• Check answers.

Answers

Laugh away your aches and pains	4
Beware! Laughter can be catching	2
Laugh your way to university	3
Keep fit by laughing	1

2a–b Students read the extracts again and underline five facts about laughter. The key word here is **facts** – this means they should not choose sentences which include the words *may* or *might*.

• They then choose the two most interesting pieces of information, and compare choices with a partner.

• Elicit their ideas. If students suggest information which is not presented as factual in the texts, question them, e.g.

Student *Laughter may relieve pain.* (Text 4)
Teacher *Is this a fact?*
Student *No, it's a possibility.*
Teacher *How do you know?*
Student *Because the writer uses **may**.*

Close up

Answers

- *Patient* is also an adjective which means tolerant, can wait for something without getting annoyed – the opposite of *impatient*. (Here *patient* is a noun – someone who is being treated and looked after because they are ill.)
- *being alive* = living / not dead
  feeling alive = feeling energetic
- These words usually describe diseases: *infectious* (adj.) can be caught easily / can spread easily. *Flu is a highly infectious disease.*
  epidemic (noun) the appearance of a disease in a large number of people at the same time. *The flu epidemic of 1918 killed millions of people world-wide.*
  to spread (verb) move from one person to another. *The disease spread quickly – by Friday half the children were away from school.*
- In Britain children go to *primary* school at the age of 5. After that, they go on to *secondary* school.

Understanding ideas   p. 67

1–3   Remind students that the answers to questions like this are not in the texts: they will need to use their imagination to come up with possible answers.
- Allow students time to think up their own answers and compare ideas with a partner.
- Elicit possible answers.

Possible answers

1 Women take themselves less seriously than men. They are more often in informal social situations where laughter is acceptable. Women are more easy-going.

2 Laughing at an unfortunate situation can make it seem less serious. Laughter can dissolve stress.

3 They could treat patients with certain painful conditions by making them laugh instead of prescribing traditional medicines. This kind of treatment would not have the side-effects associated with drugs – it might also be less expensive. They could employ comedians to make patients laugh.

Have your say

- Students discuss the questions in pairs or groups.
- Monitor, but do not interrupt.
- Have a brief whole-class feedback session.

Grammar – Modal verbs: *can, could, may, might*

Exploring concepts

1–3   Students work through this 'new' grammar section in the usual way. The difference between definite facts and possibilities may already have come up in *Read* 2a. If so, encourage students to work quickly through questions 1 and 2 and check their ideas in the **Language commentary** on p.132. You may in any case prefer to check answers to 1 and 2 with the class before they move on to 3.
- Monitor, helping where necessary.
- Check answers.

Answers

1 Sentences **a** and **c** express definite facts. They contain simple verbs.

2a–b 1 Sentences **d** and **e** express possibilities (modal verb *can*).
      2 Sentences **b** and **f** express uncertainties (modal verbs *may* / *might*).

3 Present or future time?
   a P   b F   c P   d P or F   e F   f F

Exploitation

1a–b Students practise talking about possibilities and certainties using *can, may, might* or the Present simple.
- Elicit endings for one of the five beginnings, then let students continue by writing their own answers. They could write answers which apply to themselves, e.g. *Drinking coffee keeps me awake*, but should also try to make sentences which refer to less certain facts in order to use the target modal verbs.
- Students compare ideas in pairs and try to write more sentences together. You could run this as a competition to see which pair can produce the most correct completions within a time limit.
- Check answers, correcting errors related to the use of modal verbs.

Possible answers

1 Drinking coffee … makes my hands shake. / can keep people awake. / may be one of the causes of migraine.
2 Doing regular exercise … keeps people fit and healthy. / can be very time-consuming. / may prevent heart disease.
3 Lack of sleep … makes me irritable. / can lead to illness. / might cause accidents on the roads.
4 Watching violent films … gives me nightmares. / can be frightening for children. / may encourage people to commit violent crimes themselves.
5 Listening to loud music … gives me a headache. / can make people deaf. / may result in brain damage.

2a–b This task provides practice in *may* and *might* to talk about uncertain future events.
- Explain the task, then give students a few minutes to note down their definite and possible plans for the next four or five months.
- They then compare plans with another student. Pairs should ask and answer questions as in the example.
- Monitor this oral phase, listening for the correct use of the modal verbs. Correct if necessary.
- So far, this has been a very controlled exercise, so you could round it off by giving students a few minutes to find out more interesting information about each other's plans.
- Some of this information could be shared with the whole class.

Role play

3 This is a freer practice task which allows students to use *may* and *might*.

- Check that students understand the situation and character differences between the two roles. Student A is a worrier and thinks of all the things that could go wrong on their holiday. Student B is more confident and tries to reassure A.
- Encourage students to concentrate on the meaning of what they are saying; there is no need for the repeated use of *may* or *might*.
- Monitor their conversations, but do not interrupt.
- If you noted errors during the role play, you could deal with them quickly now or go over them at the beginning of the next lesson.

— p. 68 —

Skills

The theme of this section is nationality jokes. The jokes students listen to and the reading text make gentle fun of British and American people. This is potentially a tricky subject which should be handled with care. You may want to work quickly through *Listen and speak*.

■ Listen and speak ■

1 a Establish the idea that nationalities telling jokes about each other is a universal phenomenon and that such jokes are usually based on stereotypical characteristics.
- Find out who people in students' countries make jokes about.
- If you feel that it can be done in good taste and without causing offence, ask students to tell a few of these jokes.
  b Ask students to work in pairs to speculate about the cartoon.
- Elicit their ideas, but do not tell them yet whether they are right or not. (They will understand the cartoon when they hear the recording.)
  c Read the instructions with the students and explain the task: they should guess the last line of the three jokes they hear. You could teach them the expression *punch-line* (the last few words of a joke or story which make it funny) at this stage.
- Play **7.3** , twice if necessary, then let students discuss possible endings in pairs.

7.3 and **7.4**

1
Q How many Americans does it take to change a light bulb?
A I don't know. How many Americans does it take to change a light bulb?
Q Three – one to change the bulb and two to tell the rest of the world (on a chat show).

2
Jock, from Glasgow, went into the newspaper office. His wife had just died and he wanted to put a notice in the paper.
'What would you like to say?' asked the clerk.
'Jane's dead,' replied Jock.
'You can have five more words for the same money,' said the clerk.
'OK,' said Jock. 'I'll have: (Jane's dead. Red Toyota car for sale.')

3
An Englishman, an Irishman, a Scotsman and an American who were complete strangers were shipwrecked on a desert island. The inhabitants of the island welcomed the four men and soon the American was building a small railway, the Scotsman had opened a shop, the Irishman was making whiskey, while the Englishman (was still waiting to be introduced).

d Play **7.4** , the recordings of the complete jokes, so that students can check their guesses.

Note Don't worry if students don't find the jokes funny – and don't be tempted to explain them!

2 • If students are from the same country, this might work best as a class discussion. If students are from different countries, suggest they work in mixed nationality groups. Don't spend too long on this discussion, especially if there was little response to question 1a. Again, make sure you deal with this phase sensitively.
- Monitor group discussions and if appropriate, have a brief whole-class feedback session.

■ Read ■

1 a Read through the introductory rubric with the class. (Bill Bryson's *Notes from a Small Island* was a best-seller in Britain for some time. British people seem to enjoy being made fun of by amusing foreigners.)
- Draw attention to the photographs of Yorkshire and elicit students' impressions of the place and the people who live there. Do not confirm or deny any of their ideas at this stage.

Background information
Yorkshire is large county in the north of England with a variety of landscapes:
- gentle, agricultural land
- wild hilly areas (The Pennine Hills)
- heavily industrialized areas
- large cities (some with large ethnic minority populations) – e.g. Leeds, Bradford
- some of the last remaining coal mines in Britain
- the historic city of York with its Roman origins and impressive cathedral (York Minster)
- popular seaside resorts
The people of Yorkshire are often said to have
- a direct way of talking (*They call a spade a spade.*)
- rather traditional ways (especially about men's and women's roles)
- fierce pride in coming from Yorkshire
- a suspicion of people from outside Yorkshire, especially anyone from the south of England.

b Students read the extract to find out if any of their ideas about Yorkshire and its people are confirmed. They should try to get a general idea of how Bill Bryson regards Yorkshire people.
- Check their ideas.

Answer

The extract is full of irony. The writer seems to feel affection for Yorkshire people even though everything he says seems critical of them. He sees them as very different from other groups of people he has lived with. They seem very friendly (they come into your house without knocking) and are honest (although he says they are honest because they are quite happy to tell you what they think is wrong with you).

2 • Ask students to work individually or in pairs to answer the vocabulary questions. Get them to check ideas with each other before checking in a dictionary or with you.
   • Check answers.

Answers

a *dart* – to move very quickly / rush / hurry
b *cowered* – bent / crouched down in fear, as if trying to hide
   breathless – out of breath / finding it difficult to breathe
c *clumping around* – walking noisily and heavily with slow steps
d *shortcomings* – faults / weaknesses / inadequacies / personal failings

3 • Students now read the text again and match the four characteristics with the examples of behaviour.
   • Check answers.

Answers

a 3   **b** 4   **c** 1   **d** 2

■ Speak and write ■ p. 69 ■

1–2 Divide the class into groups, then read through the instructions with them to make sure they understand the task. You could give an example from your own experience to start them off.
   • Allow them about five minutes to think and make notes, then ask them to tell the rest of their group about the people they have chosen. Remind them not to say who they are talking about, but simply to describe their characteristics and behaviour. If you think that members of the group will not share enough experience to guess what is being described, they could omit the guessing phase of this activity and simply do the descriptions.
   • Monitor this speaking phase, but do not interrupt.

3 • Set this final writing activity for homework. Suggest a word limit of 100–120 words.

— p. 70 —

Grammar extra

Relative clauses (1)

This lesson deals with the following aspects of relative clauses:

• The distinction between defining and non-defining relative clauses.
• Relative pronouns *who*, *which*, *that*.
   Relative clauses (2) in Unit 10 deals with *where*, *when*, *whose* and *why*.

■ Exploring concepts ■

1 a If you are confident that students understand the term *relative clause*, allow them to work through this section in the normal way, checking their ideas in the **Language commentary** on p.132.
   • However, you may prefer to start by going through the basics more carefully with the class. With their books closed, follow this procedure:
   • Write the two sample sentences on the board with the relative clauses underlined:
     Woody Allen, who was born in New York in 1935, started his career as a TV scriptwriter.
     The film which first made Woody Allen famous was What's New Pussycat?
   • Ask: *What are the underlined sections called?*
   • Ask: *What is the difference between the relative clauses in the two examples?*
     Do not mention the use of commas at this stage; emphasize the idea that without the relative clause the second sentence has no meaning. The clause gives necessary or essential information.
   • Once you have established the idea of essential and non-essential information, let students continue with **1b** independently.

b Allow time for students to answer **1–6**, then compare and discuss their answers in pairs.
   • Check answers.

Answers

1 N   **2** E   **3** N   **4** N   **5** E   **6** E

   • You could introduce the terms *defining* (i.e. they include essential information) and *non-defining* (i.e. they include non-essential information) to describe the two kinds of relative clause if you wish. These terms are used in the **Language commentary**.

c Now draw attention to the use of commas in sentences with non-defining relative clauses. Show how commas are similar to slight pauses used when we say sentences which include non-defining relative clauses aloud. You could point out that non-defining relative clauses are rarely used in informal conversation.

2 • Draw attention to *who*, *which* and *that* in sentences **1b1–6** and ask students to discuss the question.
   • Check answers.

Answers

• *who* refers to people. (1 / 4 / 6)
• *which* refers to things. (3)
• *that* refers to people or things. (2 / 5)

■ Exploitation ■

1 This exercise provides personalized practice in constructing sentences containing non-defining relative clauses.

a Introduce the new topic by asking students which films they have seen recently. Elicit some of their favourite films and actors.

- Now get them to write a sentence for the rest of the 'favourites' in the list.
- They could compare and discuss lists in pairs before going on to **b**.

b Demonstrate the next stage by pointing out the example in the book, or by using one of the films students mentioned previously. Build up one or two sentences which contain extra information on the board.
- Students now use their list of favourites to write sentences with non-defining relative clauses.

2 In this exercise students practise making sentences which contain defining relative clauses.

a Start with the definition in the book or your own definition of a good film, then elicit a few more definitions from the class.
- Students could think of unusual or funny definitions for 1–3.

b Students compare definitions with a partner and decide whose is the better in each case.
- Elicit a selection of answers, correcting grammar where necessary.

c With the same or a different partner, students now think of more definitions – this time of people. Remind students that the relative pronouns *who* or *that* can be used to refer to people in *defining* relative clauses, but only *who* can be used in *non-defining* relative clauses.
- Elicit a few sample definitions from the class, then allow students to continue.
- Check answers, correcting grammar.

3 a Demonstrate this game, using the example from the book and one or more examples of your own.

b Monitor the pairwork stage, but don't interrupt or you may spoil the game element. Students could use dictionaries to help them with their definitions, but should not copy definitions out.
- Draw attention to and correct any relative clause errors after the game has finished.

▶ **Photocopiable activity 13 p.167**

4 a Ask students to read through the extracts and deal with any vocabulary queries before they answer the questions. You could let them work in pairs to answer the questions or allow them time to think about them before discussing them as a whole class.
- You could get students to put their hands up to show what kind of person they are.

b Students work in pairs to think of more pairs of people who are opposites. Set a time limit for this activity; do not allow students to spend too long on it, but use it as a quick final check. Ask for a couple of sentences from pairs to round off the lesson.

p. 71

Exploring words

Body language; extreme adjectives

1 Before students look at their books, you could show them some pictures of people (e.g. photographs from magazines), get them to describe the expressions on their faces and then say what their mood is. This will introduce the topic and may elicit some of the vocabulary that is going to be introduced.

a Students match the verbs with the photographs.
- Check answers and clarify any confusion between verbs with similar meanings, e.g. *laugh / smile*.

Answers
cry b   frown g   giggle f   laugh a   smile e
wink c   yawn d

b If you started the lesson with your own photos, use one or two of them again to introduce this task. Read through the example, then ask the class to explain the expressions of a few of the people in your photographs.
- In pairs, students explain the photographs in their books. Their explanations will show whether they have understood the meaning of the body verbs.
- Elicit ideas, correcting any misunderstandings about meaning.

2 This task introduces *extreme* or *ungradable* adjectives and contrasts them with *normal* or *gradable* adjectives.

a Students could read the cartoon conversation to themselves, or you could ask students to read aloud the parts of the three women.
- Elicit students' answers to the questions.

Answers
The woman in the middle was most amused – she found it *absolutely hilarious.*
The woman on the right was least amused – she found it *quite amusing.*

- Write the three adjectives *amusing / funny / hilarious* on the board to establish the example set of three adjectives. Establish which is the 'strongest' adjective in this group.

b Students now work individually or in pairs to find the strongest (ungradable) adjective, and to decide on the difference in meaning between the two remaining adjectives.
- Encourage them to guess before checking in a dictionary.
- Check answers.

Answers

1 *furious*; *angry* is stronger than *annoyed*.
2 *astonishing*; *surprising* is stronger than *unexpected*.
3 *starving*; *hungry* is stronger than *peckish*.
4 *freezing*; *cold* is stronger than *cool* / *cool* is warmer than *cold*.
5 *terrified*; *afraid* and *frightened* are similar in meaning, but *afraid* cannot be used in front of a noun. (You can say: *the frightened child*, but not *the afraid child*.)
6 *unique*; *rare* is stronger than *unusual*.
7 *brilliant*; *intelligent* and *clever* have slightly different meanings: *intelligent* describes a high level of mental ability; *clever* describes an ability to learn and do things quickly.

c Read through the explanation with the class. Elicit other sentences (you could base these on the list in **b**) for each of the two examples. You could then quickly provide other examples of your own, e.g. *An hour ago I was very hungry. Now I'm absolutely starving*.

d Working in pairs or individually, students complete the conversations. Make sure they know that they have to use the extreme adjective related to the first one in each case.
• Monitor, checking for the correct extreme adjective.
• Finally, check answers.

Answers

1 ... it's absolutely / really freezing.
2 ... I was really / absolutely terrified.
3 ... I was absolutely / really furious.

e Divide the class into pairs. Set a time limit for them to make similar conversations. If necessary, model an example exchange first with one student.
   Teacher *I suppose you're very hungry, Daniel.*
   Student *Hungry? I'm absolutely starving!*
• If time is short, or students are slow at this kind of activity, set it as a dialogue-writing homework.

f This is a personalized speaking activity which allows students to use some of the adjectives from the sets above.
• Ask students to decide quickly which subjects to discuss, then start talking. This is primarily a fluency task, so monitor discreetly and do not interrupt conversations.
• If you wish you could call *Time!* each time you want students to change topics.
• If one topic seems to catch students' interest more than the others, you could round off this section with a whole-class discussion.

▶ **Photocopiable activity 14 p.168**

Writing

Short stories

• Before referring to the coursebook, get students to talk in pairs or groups about some of their favourite stories. They could think of any kind of stories: a children's fairy tale / an episode from a TV programme / a novel / a play / a personal story of something that happened to them or someone they know.
• After a few minutes elicit different types of story with a few examples. Then refer students to p.72.

▐ Read

1 • Students read the three texts and answer the questions. This is a gist-reading task, so set a time limit and tell students not to worry about understanding every word.
   • Check answers.

Answers

a Story 3 is a complete story (It is an example of a *mini saga* – in this case a story written in 55 words.)
b Story 2 is the beginning of a personal anecdote. We are not told the end of the story.
c Story 1 is part of a new version of an old story – the story is *Little Red Riding Hood*.

2a–b Divide the class into pairs to discuss the questions. Do not spend too long on this part of the lesson.
   • Check answers.

Suggested / possible answers

a This story is from a book of confessions. The actual end of the story is:
   The writer and Phil both took their end-of-year exams. The writer passed and Phil failed. Even though he revised for eight hours a day, he also failed the resit and had to leave the university. Eventually Phil found a job as a milkman.
b The old story has been modernized, by being made politically correct.

▐ Brainstorm and notes

1–2 Divide students into groups to do this activity.
   • Give them time to choose a story type and think of a few ideas – they can note these down if they want.
   • As they tell their stories, other members of the group can, of course, ask questions and might even suggest improvements or give their own versions of a similar story.
   • Monitor this speaking activity, encouraging students to tell their stories in an interesting way.

3 • The reason for students to make notes before they start writing is to encourage them to think carefully about the sequence of events and the structure of their story.
   • Monitor this stage, checking particularly that students have thought about the beginning, middle and end of their stories. You could ask them supplementary questions about their notes.

- The full version of the story based on the sample notes in their books is in the **Writing model**.

Write

1 · As usual, you may want to save class time by getting students to write their first drafts for homework. Alternatively, you may prefer to allow a limited amount of class time in which students should concentrate on the structure and interest of their stories, rather than on grammatical accuracy, spelling, etc.
  · Before they start writing, refer students to the model story if you have not already done so.

2–3 Students read each other's stories. To make this task more interesting, get them to read stories they have not already heard in their groups.
  · This should be a quiet reading phase. During activities like this, some teachers find that playing quiet music aids concentration.
  · Students discuss their reactions to each other's stories and suggest improvements.
  · Monitor the discussions and be available to give help and advice.

4 · Remind students that they should incorporate the improvements discussed with their partners in the final version of their story, and also think carefully about grammatical accuracy, spelling, punctuation, paragraphing, etc.

▶ **Writing model 7 (photocopiable) TB p.132**

— p. 73 —

Language in action

Making suggestions

Introduction

1 a Ask students to read through the questions, then to read the text.
  · Check answers.

Answers

1 The activity is flying / travelling by air.
  Which words or phrases tell us this? *travellers / passengers / touch down / stewards*
2 Serving meals / films / electronic games / gambling / cabin crew add humour to their announcements / juggling

b–c Divide students into pairs to think about and discuss more ways in which air travel could be made less boring. They need not include suggestion expressions at this stage. They could simply write brief notes.
  Examples:
  – *competitions*   – *fashion shows*   – *live music*

- Each pair now tells another pair their suggestions. In these conversations, remind students to use any suggestion expressions they know. Elicit an example, e.g. *What about …? / Why not …? / They could …* Tell them to avoid suggestion expressions which include the speaker – *Let's … / Why don't we …? / We could …* They should react positively or negatively to the other pair's suggestions.
- Monitor these discussions but do not interrupt or correct. Use this as a chance to check for yourself how much suggestion language students remember.

2 a Explain that students are now going to listen to a group of passengers having the same discussion they have just had.
  · Play **7.5** for the first time. Students should listen for any of their own ideas that are mentioned by the speakers.

7.5

R   So, you're all in favour of the basic idea, then?
All Yeah!
    Absolutely!
R   And have you thought of any other ideas you'd like us to consider in the future? We're planning now for next year.
TB I think everyone should get a free CD player and two CDs to listen to during the flight.
R   If we did that, we'd have to put up air fares, I'm afraid.
M   What about putting on a magic show – the kids would love that.
TB I wouldn't.
TG Nor would I.
M   Then why not have general knowledge quizzes – one of the cabin crew could read out the questions and the passengers could all write down the answers and hand them in before the end of the flight.
W   Mmm – that's not a bad idea.
TB You could give the winner a prize?
TG Yeah, like a free flight to New York.
R   I'm not so sure about that. I don't think the company is quite that generous.
W   How about fashion shows? The attendants could model the latest designer clothes.
Y   No, I'm not keen on that idea – they've got enough to do without having to change their clothes every five minutes. No, I've been thinking, what about Karaoke competitions?
R   Brilliant!

b–c The aim of this task is for the class to build up a list of expressions used for making and reacting to suggestions.
  · Play the recording again, pausing from time to time to allow students to note down the expressions they hear.
  · They tell each other their expressions and make lists under the headings given.
  · Finally, they should add any other suggestion expressions they have already used.

Answers

Making suggestions
I think (everyone) should …
What about (putting) …?   What about + -ing
Why not (have general   Why not + infinitive
  knowledge quizzes) …?
You could (give the winner a prize).   You could + infinitive
How about (in-flight fashion shows)?   How about + noun
What about (Karaoke competitions)?   What about + noun

Accepting suggestions
That's not a bad idea.
Brilliant!

Rejecting suggestions
I'm not so sure about that.
I'm not keen on that idea.

■ Pronunciation ■■■■■■■■■■■■■■■■■ p. 152 ■

This section looks at unpronounced sounds, linking and
sounding enthusiastic.

1 a As this is revision, students should be able to do the
   exercise on their own or in pairs. However, if you prefer,
   you can do it with the whole class.
  b Ask students to identify the stressed syllables and the main
   stressed syllables. Tell them there is one main stressed
   syllable in each sentence.
  c Play **7.6** so that students can check their ideas and
   make any changes.
  • Write up the sentences on the board or on an overhead
   transparency and check answers.

7.6

1 I'm not so keen on that idea.
2 That's a good idea.
3 That's not a bad idea.
4 I'm not so sure about that.

Answers
See Tapescript **7.6** .

  d Play **7.6** again. Pause after each sentence and drill
   chorally and / or individually.

2 a Play **7.7** , which gives students practice in distinguishing
   an enthusiastic response to a suggestion from an
   unenthusiastic response.
  • Check answers.

7.7

1	a Yeah!	(E)	b	Yeah!	(U)
2	a Great!	(U)	b	Great!	(E)
3	a Fantastic!	(U)	b	Fantastic!	(E)
4	a Brilliant!	(E)	b	Brilliant!	(U)
5	a Absolutely!	(U)	b	Absolutely!	(E)

Answers
See Tapescript **7.7** .

  b Play **7.8** and get students to repeat enthusiastically after
   the tape.

7.8

1 Yeah!
2 Great!
3 Fantastic!
4 Brilliant!
5 Absolutely!

3 • Tell students that they are going to hear some suggestions.
   They must respond with any of the expressions in **1a** and
   2a. You might want to check the following: *DJ (Disc
   jockey), entrance fee, fancy-dress party.*
  • Play **7.9** . Pause after each suggestion and nominate one
   or more students to reply. Insist on an appropriate
   intonation for the response.

7.9

1 How about having a party?
2 We could have it at my place.
3 What about having a proper DJ?
4 We could charge a small entrance fee to cover costs.
5 So you're all in favour of the idea?
6 We could have a fancy dress party.
7 How about inviting our teachers?
8 We could all cook something.

■ **Problem-solving** ■■■■■■■■■■■■■■ p. 73 ■

  • Divide the class into groups to think about and discuss
   ways of making other routine activities less boring.

1 • Groups must first decide which activity or situation to talk
   about. Brainstorm for any alternatives to the activities
   listed in the book.
  • Once the activity has been chosen, allow students a few
   minutes to think up their own ideas.

2 • Make sure students take it in turns each to suggest an
   idea. This way they will get involved in the activity and the
   discussion will become more like a natural
   everyday conversation.
  • Monitor discussions, listening for the use of suggestion
   language, but do not interrupt or correct as this will
   reduce the fluency practice element of the task.

3 a As the discussions start to subside, ask groups to make a
   list of the suggestions that the group agrees about.
  • These suggestions could be displayed on the wall or passed
   from group to group.
  • Alternatively, groups could chose a spokesperson to report
   their agreed suggestions to the rest of the class.
  b Everyone responds to everyone else's suggestions, by
   choosing the best ideas for each activity.
  • At this stage or at the end of **2**, give feedback on any errors
   you have noticed while monitoring.

■ **Language check** ■■■■■■■■■■■■■■■■■■■■

Follow the usual procedure.

8 Making contact

Theme

The overall theme of this unit is communication.

Preview Communications: by telephone, mobile phone, fax, e-mail, letter

Attitudes to mobile phones

Listening Shyness and how to fight it

Skills Being bilingual

Grammar extra Answerphones

Writing e-mails

Grammar

- Review of Reported speech (1): Statements
- Reported speech (2): Questions
- Expressing quantity: *many / a few*, etc.

Vocabulary

- Everyday expressions
- Adjectives
- Telephone language: phrasal verbs
- *say, speak, tell*

Writing

- Writing e-mails

Functional language

- On the telephone

Pronunciation

- Strong and weak forms

Workbook

- Grammar and functional language as above
- Topic vocabulary: telephones; feelings; *say, tell, speak*
- Quiz: are you a winner or a loser?

Preview

This introduces the first theme of the unit – modern methods of communication. The short reading texts compare e-mail with letters and phone calls, while the vox pop recordings are of people expressing their opinions about mobile phones.

Your thoughts — p. 74

1 • Before students open their books to start the new unit, introduce the topic in your own way. Here are two ideas:
- If you have a mobile phone, get someone to phone you as the lesson begins. Talk for a few seconds, then say you have a class waiting for a lesson.
- Conduct a quick class survey: *How many students have mobile phones? How many mobile phones are there in the class now? How many members of their families have mobile phones? How much did their phones cost?*
- Don't get into the pros and cons of mobile phones at this stage – there will be opportunities to discuss these later.
- Check that they understand the term *snail mail* and why this is an appropriate name.
- Students look at their books then, in pairs or small groups, think about and discuss the methods of communication listed.

2 • You could do this as a class discussion, or students could continue working in pairs or groups.

Read

1 • In pairs, students brainstorm the advantages of e-mail and make a brief list of points.

2 a Students read the text and check whether any of their advantages are mentioned.

b Give students time to read the text again if necessary and note answers.

• Check answers.

Answers

e-mail	phone calls
– respects more urgent demands	– intrusive / calls always interrupt something
– allows for differences in time zones because it waits (in a mail-box) to be read	

e-mail
- less formal – you can write very short messages
- writers can change their mind
- you can communicate equally easily with someone on another continent or in the next room

letters
- more formal

- You could elicit any other comparisons between e-mail and the other two forms of communication, e.g. *quicker / more immediate / cheaper / easier to use / more convenient / you know it has arrived.*

■ Listen ■ p. 75 ■

This returns to the subject of mobile phones. If you followed any of the suggestions for ways of starting this unit (above), you should go straight into this listening activity. If you did not, you could consider one or more of the ideas now.

1 a You could pre-teach these words: *pregnant, accessible, emergency.*
- As you play **8.1** for the first time, students listen for how many of the speakers have a mobile phone.
- Check answer.

8.1

Speaker 1 I don't have a mobile phone, but I would like one so that I could call home when I was on the train, late home on the train.
Speaker 2 No, I don't have a mobile phone.
Would you like one?
I sometimes think it would be useful to have one on a motorway on a journey on my own just in case the car broke down and I was on my own with the children.
Speaker 3 I have got a mobile phone because when I was pregnant we were worried that I might get stuck in a car somewhere and not be able to contact someone so it was for safety reasons really.
I don't use it very often erm just when I'm out and about.
Speaker 4 I've got a mobile phone but I mainly use it for phoning other people, er in my job I need to be available to er my staff.
Speaker 5 Erm, I can't think of any really really good reason why I should have a mobile phone. Erm – It means that you're accessible 24 hours a day if you've got a mobile phone …
Speaker 6 Yes, very recently. I've never used it however. I don't know how to use it yet.
But why have you got one?
Essentially for the for the car again it's that – as this car although it's a wonderful car of course it has broken down on a number of occasions and a mobile is very very useful for for for getting emergency help in the middle of nowhere and that's the main reason.
Speaker 7 I don't have a mobile phone. I considered buying one erm because I was doing a lot of motorway travelling and I thought it would be very useful, erm just in case I broke down because you never know when you you know where a motorway phone might be …

Answer
Three of the speakers have mobile phones: Speakers 3, 4 and 6.

b Students read through the True / False statements. They could try to answer the questions from memory before you play the recording again.

- Play **8.1** again.
- Check answers.

Answers
1 False. Only one speaker (1) would definitely like a mobile phone.
2 True. Four out of seven speakers mentioned cars. (2, 3, 6, 7)
3 False. Only one speaker (4) uses a mobile phone in their job.
4 True. Speaker 6 says: *I've never used it …*

2 a Give students a minute or two to predict some of the things that annoy people about mobile phones.
- Elicit ideas about what speakers will say they find irritating about mobile phones, and note ideas on the board. This can be used as a checklist later.
b Students listen to **8.2** and check their predictions.
- Check answers and tick any that are listed on the board.

8.2

Speaker 1 I think they're a real pain in the neck – I find it really annoying when I'm on a train or I'm out for a walk and somebody's got a mobile phone in a shop or – I just think it's silly and it's unnecessary – erm I think people can be contacted at home and there should be some time and space where they don't have mobile phones.
Speaker 2 I get annoyed when mobile phones go off in church and erm when people are having a quiet time …
Speaker 3 It annoys me on public transport when people are talking on their mobile phones and in public places when the phones ring especially when they've got silly tunes – I find it very annoying.
Speaker 4 The most annoying thing about mobile phones is when they ring on trains and when people talk really loudly on their phones to let everybody else know they've got one.
Speaker 5 What really most annoys me about mobile phones is, as I've just said, that people have to answer them when they go off. You can't … You're talking to someone, their mobile phone goes off and they have no option but to answer it.
Speaker 6 I also find them very annoying especially when people are sitting in restaurants or on buses and their phones are going constantly and you have to overhear people's private conversations – they don't seem to have any er respect of either your privacy or their privacy funnily enough.
Speaker 7 I'm fairly resistant to the idea of mobile phones as fashion accessories which they obviously are for a lot of people because there's absolutely no reason to walk around with one clipped to your belt and the fact that some people do is, is purely to advertise the fact they've got a mobile phone …

Answers
The speakers find the following things annoying:
When people use them in public (on trains / in shops, etc.).
(Speaker 1)
Mobile phones ringing in church. (Speaker 2)
Mobile phones used on public transport. / Phones with silly tunes. (Speaker 3)
Mobile phones on trains when people speak very loudly. (Speaker 4)
People feel they have to answer mobile phones when they ring. (Speaker 5)
Overhearing private conversations in restaurants, on buses, etc. (Speaker 6)
Mobile phones as fashion accessories / worn to show off. (Speaker 7)

Vocabulary

1 • Students could work in the same pairs to guess the meanings of the expressions. You could refer them to the **Tapescript** on p.145 to help them with the context.

Answers

a	*get stuck*	be unable to move / trapped
b	*out and about*	travelling around / away from home
c	*in the middle of nowhere*	somewhere remote or isolated
d	*a pain in the neck*	annoying or boring thing or person
e	*funnily enough*	an expression of surprise at something that might not have been expected

2a–c Students exchange experiences and ideas in pairs.
 • Monitor their conversations, listening for the correct use of the expressions.
 • Elicit a few answers to question **c**. Encourage students to use relative clauses in their answers, e.g. *people who smoke in public / people who drive too slowly on motorways.*

Have your say

1–2 These statements could be the basis of a class discussion. Alternatively, you could choose one of the topics and have a quick class debate.

Grammar review – Reported speech (1)

This revises the main differences between direct and reported speech. The next grammar section, Reported speech (2) on p.77, focuses on Reported questions.
 • Before students look at the book, write up these two sentences on the board: *Mobile phones are fantastic. She said mobile phones were fantastic.*
 • Ask: *What is the main difference between these two sentences?*
 • Establish the idea of reported speech and the terms *direct* and *reported speech.*

1a–b Students work individually or in pairs through these tasks. Remind them about the **Language commentary** on p.133.
 • Check their answers.

Answers

a 1 *She said <u>she didn't</u> have a mobile phone.*
  2 *He said <u>he had</u> never used <u>his</u> mobile phone.*
  3 *She said <u>she would</u> get <u>herself</u> a mobile phone <u>the following week</u>.*
b • In reported speech verbs are often moved backwards in time.
   will becomes *would.*
  • Pronouns change.
   I → he / she; me → him / her
   We → they
   You → me, etc.
  • Time references
   next week → the following week, etc.
   today → that day, etc.

2a–b It may be better to do this task with the whole class. It is very common for students to learn the 'rules' of reported speech without recognizing that there are variations, depending on when we are reporting the statement and on our 'distance' from the statement. This exercise shows that there is more than one way to report a sentence. Ask students to read the three sentences in **a**. Ask them to find the exact differences between the two reported speech sentences (they could underline them). Check answers, then ask why one uses *the day before* and one *yesterday*. Elicit what this tells them.

Answer

In the second sentence only the pronoun has changed. The verb and the time reference remain the same as in direct speech.
She said she'd used her phone the day before.
This refers to a conversation that took place in the past before today and yesterday.
She said she used her phone yesterday.
The conversation took place *today* – i.e. on the same day as the reporting of the conversation.

 • Now let them work out the differences in meaning between the pair of reported speech sentences in **b**.
 • Check answers.

Answer

Again, in the second sentence only the pronoun has changed. The verb and the time reference remain the same as in direct speech.
She said she'd phone me the next day.
The conversation took place some time in the past.
She says she'll phone me tomorrow.
This conversation took place earlier today – the same day as the reporting of the conversation.

Check

3 • Elicit answers to **a** as an example, then let students work individually through **b–f**.
 • Check answers.

Answers

a I prefer to write an ordinary letter.
b I phoned you two or three times yesterday.
c I think e-mail is fantastic.
d I'll send you a postcard next week.
e We won't be home late this evening.
f I'm buying a new computer later this week.

4 • This time students could compare answers in pairs before you check them as a class.

Answers

a She said she thought they were a real pain in the neck.
b She said she got annoyed when mobile phones went off in church.
c He said he'd see me the next / following day.
d She said she couldn't pay me. She'd lost all her money.
e He said he was starting his new job that day.
f He said he'd finished his exams the day before / the previous day.

5
a This is a personalized practice activity.
- You could demonstrate the idea by whispering some information to one of the students and getting another student to ask what you said.
- Divide the class into groups of four.
- Students think of three ideas, then whisper them to the student on their left.

b The student who hears the information 'translates' it into reported speech and passes it on to the student on their left.
- Monitor carefully, correcting any reported speech errors you hear.

▶ **Photocopiable activity 15 p.169**

— p. 76 —

Listening

The theme now moves on to consider the difficulty shy people have making contact with others and what sufferers can do to overcome this problem. The recordings provide examples of reported questions.

■ In your experience ■

Students will hear two recordings: someone talking about what it's like to be shy, and an expert talking about what can be done to help shy people.

1 • Divide the class into pairs or groups, and give them a few minutes to discuss the question. Elicit ideas.

Possible answers

When?	In unusual situations with other people / when meeting people for the first time / at parties / when they have to do something new or difficult in front of people they don't know.
Why?	They think people are looking at them. / They think people find them stupid in some way.

2 • Check that everyone understands the words and phrases in the list, especially *butterflies in the stomach*, *stammering*.
- Students can think about which of these symptoms they have suffered from. Don't push them to tell other students if this would be embarrassing.

■ Listen ■

1 • Ask students to look at the list in *In your experience* **2** while they listen to the speaker, and cross off topics as he mentions them.
- Play **8.3**.
- Check answers.

8.3

It used to be terrible. Now I'm usually OK. I suppose it's worst in new situations especially if there are lots of people I don't know. Like at parties – I start feeling tense even before I get there – a sort of nervousness – I suppose you'd call it butterflies in the stomach. By the time I arrive my hands are sweaty and my throat's dry. I normally make straight for a friend, but if I can't see anyone I know, I just stand around feeling uncomfortable. If someone I don't know talks to me, I blush and sometimes I stammer when I talk. If I see someone I know a bit, I might try to start a conversation – sometimes it's OK, but not always. I went to an office party a couple of weeks ago and I started talking to a young woman I thought I knew. Anyway, I went up to her and asked her very politely if we'd met somewhere before. She said she didn't think we had. So I asked her where she worked. She said she didn't work. When I asked her if she knew anyone else in the room, she said, 'Yes'. So I asked her if she could introduce me to someone. But just then she saw a friend and she walked off. I found out later she was my boss's wife.

Answers
Inability to speak and shaky knees are not mentioned.

2 • Let students discuss their ideas in pairs.
- Elicit a few suggestions. You could write these on the board and then they can check if any of their ideas are mentioned by the expert.

3a–b Play **8.4**. Ask students to make very brief notes – key words – to remind them of the best advice they hear.
- Referring to their notes, students discuss what they think is the best advice.
- Monitor conversations.
- Elicit their ideas. Is there a consensus about the best advice?

8.4

Of course it's hard being shy, especially if you're single. But I should say right at the start that almost everyone has certain situations when they feel tense or shy. In the end most people learn to cope with these feelings – keep them under control and not let them ruin their lives. If you're naturally a very shy person, this can be quite a long process – it may take years – in fact you may never get over it completely – but I hope that following some of my suggestions will help you, especially if you want to form positive relationships with other people.
OK, rule number one – stop yourself worrying what other people are thinking about you – especially in social situations. Do anything you can to take your mind off yourself.
Number two – focus on other people. If you're at a party and there's someone you'd like to talk to, focus on that person. As you walk towards them, say their name or look for something you like about them – it could be the colour of their eyes or what they're wearing.
Number three – think about successful past experiences. Remember times when you were not shy and enjoyed meeting other people.
Number four – improve your small talk. Have something interesting to talk about apart from your dog, your job or your past relationships.
Five – use well-practised lines if you suddenly feel shy, 'Hello, my name's whatever' or ask the person you're talking to whether they know anyone in the room, that kind of thing.
Number six – imagine the worst thing that could happen. If the very worst thing that you can possibly imagine happens, how will you handle it? You think, 'Well, I might feel so shy that I'd run out of the room.' So, what if you do run out of the room! That's not so bad, is it?
Seven – try talking about something that embarrasses you, such as blushing. Bringing a fear out in the open takes away its power to worry you.
Eight – relax your muscles and breathe deeply both before and during the situation.
Number nine – smile, smile, and smile some more. Everyone loves a smile.
And finally number ten – think of yourself climbing a ladder – overcoming shyness can be like that. You go up two steps, slide back down one, you go up two or three more steps, then just hold on and persuade yourself you can climb higher.

Well, that's it. It's up to you now. Good luck and whatever you do, don't give up hope.

Understanding ideas

- Before they listen, ask students to read through the list of suggestions the speaker made, then play **8.4** again. You might want to pause after each of the pieces of advice in the list to give students time to note any ideas.
- In pairs, students try to explain the advice.
- Elicit ideas.

Possible answers
a Focusing on other people will help the shy person to stop thinking about themself.
b It may help to make the shy person feel confident if they think back to an occasion not spoiled by their shyness.
c It helps to visualize and then confront fears. It is fear of the unknown that is most frightening.
d Deep breathing helps the body to relax.

Vocabulary

1 • You could go through this activity with the class, or let students work in pairs.
- Monitor conversations, but do not interrupt.
- Having checked their understanding of the words and phrases in bold, elicit a few possible answers to the questions in small type.

Answers
a *ruin their lives* – *ruin* means spoil
b *social situations* – occasions on which they have to be with and interact with other people; for example parties
c *focus on* – think about / concentrate your attention on
d *small talk* – light topics of conversation that everyone can talk about
e *well-practised lines* – things people say that they have often said before

Possible answers
a Being shy could *ruin someone's life* if it meant that they had no friends and never went anywhere in case they met people, etc.
b–e Students will have their own personal answers to these questions.

2 • Suggest that students brainstorm alternative words in pairs or groups and then check their ideas in a dictionary.
- Check answers.

Answers
a *tense* – stressed / nervous / worried / slightly frightened
b *uncomfortable* – embarrassed / awkward / uneasy
c *hard* – difficult / tough / not easy / cruel
d *positive* – happy / satisfactory / successful

Have your say

- Students discuss these questions in pairs or groups.
- Monitor conversations, but do not interrupt.
- Round off this section with a class discussion, eliciting any personal experiences students are prepared to share with their classmates.

Grammar – Reported speech (2): questions — p. 77 —

Exploring concepts

Most of the differences between Direct and Reported speech have already been covered in the *Preview*, so let students work through this section independently.

1–2 Students can work individually or in pairs through these tasks. Remind them to check their ideas in the **Language commentary** on p.133.
- Check answers to 1 before they move on to 2, so you can clarify if necessary.

Answers

1 Differences between direct and reported questions:
  - The verb tense may move into the past, as in reported statements.
  - Pronouns change, as in reported statements.
  - Question words remain the same.
  - Word order is 'normal' – the subject precedes the verb.

2 *Yes / No* questions:
  a *whether* or *if* are needed before the question (**b, c, d, f**).
  b The auxiliary verbs *do / did*, etc. are not used in Reported questions (**c, f**). This ties in with normal word order.

Exploitation

1a–b Explain this two-part task by reading through the instructions and the examples with the class. They will need to make an accurate note of the questions they hear.
- Play **8.5**.
- Play the recording again, pausing after each question to give students time to write. Let them check answers in pairs.
- Students now change the direct questions into reported speech.
- Suggest that students only refer to the **Language commentary** to check their answers.
- Check answers.

8.5

A   What's your name, please?
TA Anderson. Thomas Anderson.
A   And where do you live please, Mr Anderson?
TA Yeah, it's 2678 Fairview Crescent, Vancouver, BC.
A   And what's your postcode?
TA V6T 2BP.
A   How do you want to pay for your order?
TA By credit card, if that's OK.
A   That's fine. Can you give me your number, please?
TA 5543 5654 7869 4239.
A   Thank you. And when is the expiry date?
TA September this year.
A   Thank you. And do you want our Fastpost service?
TA Yes, please.
A   OK, Mr Anderson. That should be with you some time tomorrow.
TA Thanks. Goodbye.

Answers
- She asked him what his name was.
- She asked him where he lived.
- She asked him what his postcode was.
- She asked him how he wanted to pay for his order.
- She asked him if he could give her his number.
- She asked him when the expiry date was.
- She asked him if / whether he wanted the / their Fastpost service.

2 a Elicit students' ideas about what is happening in the illustrations.

Possible answers
- Passenger at check-in wants to change her seat.
- They are discussing which place to visit next.
- One car has just driven into the back of the other.

- In pairs, students role play the conversations. These should be kept short and fairly simple. Give a time limit of about one minute for each conversation, then ask students to move on to the next topic. For each new topic, they could work with a new partner.
- Monitor, but only interrupt to move students on to the next topic.

b When all the situations have been role played, students should work individually, writing reports of two of the conversations using only reported speech.
- Be on hand to give help at this stage and remind students to refer to the **Language commentary** if they need to check the rules.

c Finally, students exchange reports with someone they did the role play with and compare ideas.
- They could correct any reported speech errors they come across.

■ Role play

3 a This is intended to simulate an everyday situation where people meet for the first time and try to find out about each other.
- Divide the class into groups, preferably of four or six students and get them to imagine the situation: they are the first arrivals at a party and don't know each other.
- Students choose one of the roles which are listed on p.158, then make up questions they might ask someone they had never met before.
- In their groups, students imagine they have just arrived at the party and start conversations with each other. The activity will work best if students talk in pairs to start with. As they become more confident in their roles, they might move on to three- or four-way conversations.
- Monitor, but do not interrupt. Allow conversations to continue for as long as they are interesting and enjoyable.

b Finally, students pair up with a partner from another group and tell each other about the people they 'met' at their 'parties'.

- This stage may naturally involve the use of Reported speech, but do not force this unnaturally. It will be interesting for you to listen to their use of Reported speech in what is primarily a fluency activity.

— p. 78 —

Skills

The new topic is bilingualism. The questionnaire provides a suitable lead-in to the subject, so go straight into this.

■ Write and speak

1–2 Ask students to complete the questionnaire individually, then compare answers with a partner.
- You could round off this introductory stage with a quick class survey: *Who can speak more than one language fluently?* (Don't count English!) *Are any students bilingual? What do they understand by* **bilingual**?
- If only a minority of the class are bilingual, get a few individuals to tell the rest of the class what it is like, what the pros and cons of being bilingual are. If bilingualism is commonplace, move straight on to the next stage.

■ Speak and read

1 • Explain that students are going to read an article about children and bilingualism, and that they should first work through the questions.
- Students work through the list in pairs, discussing then trying to agree on answers to the questions.
- Elicit possible answers if you wish, but don't tell students the actual answers. They will find them when they read the article.

2 • Explain that the article which follows was originally written in a question-and-answer format. The questions have been omitted, and they will have to fill them in.
- As they read, they should find the answers to questions **1a–f**, and write the question number above the correct answer.
- Check answers.

Answers
Paragraphs / Questions: 1   d   2   f   3   a   4   e
                    5   c   6   b

Additional activity

If there are students who are bilingual in the class, ask them how accurate they think the advice and information in the article is.
If there are enough bilingual students, others could interview them to find out about their experiences and opinions on the subject.

■ Understanding ideas   p. 79 ■

1–4 Remind students that not all the questions are answered directly by the text – sometimes they will have to use their

imagination. In this exercise only question 1 has
a definite answer.

- Students work individually or in pairs through
  the questions.
- Elicit answers.

Possible answers

1 – Children should start learning the second language as early as
possible / before they are taught to read.
  – Parents should only use their own language with the child.

2 – Children use the language appropriate to each side of the
family – with grandparents, for example.
  – It may be that a particular language is 'official' and is used in
school, etc. and that the other language is the one they use
with their family and close friends.

3 – When children start to read a language, they start to link
sounds with letters (the spoken and the written forms). Before
this, language is just a collection of sounds. There is no need
for them to differentiate between the two languages.
  – There is also the general point that children should learn
languages as early as possible. Reading comes at a relatively
late stage in their development.

4 It is well-known that for most children being seen as different
from their peers is the worst thing that can happen to them. This
applies to how they speak and sound (accent) as well as to their
appearance (e.g. clothes).

■ Have your say ■

- These two questions look at the more political / social
aspects of bilingualism. If the first question is not relevant
in your teaching situation, get students to think about
countries where bilingualism is the norm rather than the
exception. For example: countries with significant ethnic
minority populations (Australia / USA), countries which
were once occupied by colonial powers (India), countries
with two or more official languages (Switzerland /
Malaysia), amalgamations of originally separate countries
(Belgium / United Kingdom), border regions where
countries meet.

■ Listen ■

1–2 Read through the two while-reading questions with
the class.
- Play **8.6** for the first time. This listening is fairly long;
make sure that students know that the first time they
listen they should just try to get a general idea of what the
speakers say.
- Check answers.

8.6

Speaker 1
P When did you start learning your second language?
A My first second language, as it were, I started learning when I was
four and a half and that was Portuguese and I was very fluent in it
and then after a couple of years we moved to Argentina from
Brazil and I had to learn Spanish and I became very fluent in that.
Subsequently more or less forgot it but then started learning French
in a a French-speaking environment when I was about eleven,
twelve, and I was in that environment, it was in Geneva, for many
years, for ten, twelve years and I basically erm thought and wrote

and spoke in French as if I was French and everybody still thinks I'm
French when I speak French.
P Did you realize that you had … that this was a special thing?
A I suppose I did because erm I noticed that other people couldn't do
it and at the same time I didn't necessarily think of it as very special
because my father spoke so many languages, I mean he could
speak about seventeen languages, so erm it didn't seem unusual to
me – it seemed very obvious.
P Do you feel more comfortable in English?
A No, funnily enough I don't actually. In some ways and for … in
some subjects … if I'm talking about erm feelings and philosophy
and things like that I'm more comfortable in French than I am in
English. I also have noticed that I gesticulate more when I'm
speaking French and I also use a wider range of expressions – facial
expressions and bodily expressions and so on.
P Were you ever confused about the languages?
A Not at all – not the least little bit, no.
P And have you found any disadvantages?
A Not that I can think of. I think it's always been a plus actually and
part of the plus is knowing that I can erm communicate in lots of
different languages and that other people don't necessarily know it,
so I very often walk behind somebody talking Chinese on the
street, for example, and I know what they're talking about and
they don't know that I know what they're talking about.

Speaker 2
P When did you learn your second language?
L When I was … I started learning it when I was three – in Argentina.
P And when did you first realize that you could speak more than
one language?
L Erm I think when I was four and a half, because I learnt to say the
time in English before I learnt it in Spanish and suddenly I realized
that some people couldn't understand it.
P And how did you … why did you become bilingual?
L Well that's a family story, it's because my parents didn't want me to
go to the state system, so I had to go to a private school and as
I was going to a private school, they thought it was better if I learnt
another language, so my father wanted me to learn English
because it was a useful language and my mother wanted to learn,
me to learn French because it was a nicer language, so I had to
learn both.
P And do you feel, or did you ever or have … do you feel now more
comfortable in one language than another?
L Yes, I always feel much more comfortable in Spanish, because you
can … there is a certain nuance in your language and feelings
feelings you can always say certain things in your own language,
you know.
P So you feel very strongly that Spanish is your first language?
L Absolutely, yes, yeah.
P And were you ever confused?
L I don't remember being confused – I don't know, but I don't think
I ever was, no.
P And have you ever found any disadvantages to being bilingual?
L Not really, no. I think it's quite a great advantage, I … My son is
also bilingual and I think it's a great advantage.
P And how … in what way have you brought him up?
L Well, because he, he was born here in England so he … his first
language is English, but at home we speak Spanish and when we
lived in Holland he also had to speak Dutch so there was a routine
by which he knew which language to speak when, so he knew that
when we were the three of us alone he would speak Spanish,
when he was alone with me, because we were living in Holland, to
keep his English we would speak in English and when he was at
school or with friends or whatever he would speak Dutch.

1 Both speakers feel positive about being bilingual.

2 Speaker 1: Her first two languages were English and Portuguese, but she also learned Spanish, French and Chinese.
Speaker 2: Her first two languages were English and Spanish (and French at school). Her son speaks English, Spanish and Dutch.

■ Understanding ideas

This time the questions require more careful listening and thought.

1–2 Read through the questions with the class.
• Play the recording again, this time pausing after the first speaker to let students answer the questions about her.
• Repeat the procedure for the second speaker.
• Check answers.

Answers

1 **Speaker 1**
 – She was four and a half years old when she learned her second language.
 – She seems to have learned her languages by living in environments where the languages were spoken.
 Speaker 2
 – She was three when she learned her second language.
 – She seems to have learned at school.

2 **Speaker 1**
 – She took the ability for granted / she didn't think it was unusual: *I didn't think of it as very special.*
 – She thinks of it as a great advantage: *It's always been a plus.*
 Speaker 2
 – She is more comfortable in one language than the other. She feels that Spanish is her real / first language.
 – She has found no disadvantages: *I think it's quite a great advantage.*

■ Have your say

1–2 Organize students into groups and let them discuss the questions for about three to four minutes each. They should note down any generally agreed answers or points.
• Monitor, but do not interrupt.
• A member of each group should report back the main conclusions of their discussions.

■ Speak and write

1a–d Divide the class into pairs whose first language is the same. This may not be possible in some mixed nationality classes. In this case students will have to work alone.
• Read through steps **a–d** with the class, clarifying any areas of difficulty. Stress that students should limit what they plan to teach by sticking to the suggested vocabulary items and expressions. Discourage them from being too ambitious and from trying to teach grammar.
• You could elicit a few ideas for interesting, useful classroom activities. (You could find the kind of activities your students choose are a real eye-opener!)

• Set a time limit, then monitor all discussions carefully, making constructive suggestions. Make sure pairs make a note of the key points so they can present them to the rest of the class in 2.

2 • Pairs take turns to present their ideas to the rest of the class. They could work through steps **a–d** explaining what and how they would teach.
• If there is sufficient time and there are students of different nationalities in the class, get a few volunteer pairs to teach a part of their lessons.

▶ Photocopiable activity 16 p.170

— p. 80 —

Grammar extra

Expressing quantities

• Lead in to the new theme, answerphones and people's attitudes to them, with a general class discussion. You could ask these questions: *How many of you have answerphones at home? When your telephone rings, do you pick it up or let the answerphone answer it? Do you listen to the message and interrupt if it is someone you want to talk to? Do you find it easy to leave messages on other people's answerphones? Do you know anyone who finds it difficult?*

■ Exploring concepts

1 • Explain that the article on answerphones contains 12 quantity words and phrases (including the underlined example).
• Before students work on their own, ask them to find the second quantity word in the text (*few*). They can then work individually or in pairs to read the text and find the quantity expressions.
• Check answers.

Answers

• Although lots of adults talk regularly to answerphones, few people actually feel comfortable doing it.
• Many people say they feel stupid talking to machines and a few callers even blush or stammer when they leave messages.
• It is quite common for people to spend some time preparing a message if they think there is likely to be an answerphone.
• Plenty of children seem quite happy to talk to answerphones, even those who don't have much experience of telephones.
• What annoys some callers is the thought that the people they are phoning are actually listening to their message instead of picking up the phone.
• A lot of elderly people are afraid they won't have much time to speak. In fact there is always plenty of time for messages.
• In spite of these worries, there is little evidence that sales of answerphones are decreasing.

• If you already discussed the questions about attitudes to answerphones, you could check at this stage how many of the ideas in the text are the same. Alternatively, ask students how many of the points in the text they have read they agree / disagree with.

2 • Before students do the task, check that they understand the terms *countable* and *uncountable* nouns. Elicit a few examples of each type.

a–b Students now work through a and b individually or in pairs.

• Check answers.

Answers
a 1 *few / many / a few* are followed by *plural countable nouns.*
2 *much / little* are followed by *uncountable nouns.*
3 *some / a lot of / lots of* are followed by either *plural countable nouns* or *uncountable nouns.*
b Negative verbs are used before *much.*
Remind students that *much* is used only on its own in negative statements and questions. In general affirmative statements, *a lot of* is more usual. It is of course also used in other phrases like *as much as / much more,* etc. in affirmative statements.

3–4 Give students a few minutes to work through these tasks, or elicit answers from the class. You could ask them to check their ideas in the **Language commentary** on p.134 before confirming answers with the class.

• Check answers.

Answers
3 The first sentence in each case sounds more negative.
little / few = not much / not many
a little / a few = some
4 a *Plenty of* can be followed by *plural countable nouns* or *uncountable nouns.*
b It means *lots* or *as much / many as you need.*

■ Exploitation

1 • Ask students to read the table, then look at the example which shows how the topics can be combined.
• Elicit one or two more examples of sentences from the chart to demonstrate that people and subjects can be matched in any way.
• Encourage students to use the full range of quantity words and phrases.
• This exercise could be done in writing in the first instance, then students could compare sentences with a partner.
• You could round off the activity by eliciting one sentence from each student in the class. Nobody should repeat a sentence someone else has said.

2 • This could be done in groups or as a class activity.

Possible answers
There are a few people in the office.
There's plenty of water in the dispenser.
There are lots of plants in the office.
There are a few pens on the desk.
There are lots of files on the desk.
There isn't much space on the desk.

Exploring words

Telephone language; *say, speak, tell*; adjectives

1 a Give students time to read and react to the answerphone message in the cartoon, then let them tell each other or the class about messages they have heard.
b Read through definitions 1–5 of the words and phrases students listen for when they hear the recording.
• Play **8.7**, twice if necessary.
c Students compare answers, then check with the **Tapescript** on p.146.
• Check answers.

8.7

Message 1 Hi, I'm not here right now but my answerphone is, so you can talk to it instead. Wait for the bleep.
Message 2 Hi! Jenny's answering machine is broken. This is her fridge. Please speak slowly after the tone and I'll keep your message fresh for Jenny.
Message 3 There's nobody here at the moment to take your call, but if you leave your name and phone number after the long tone, I'll get back to you as soon as I can.
Message 4 Hi. I am here, but I'm just avoiding someone I don't like. Leave a message, and if I don't call back, it's you.
Message 5 If you are a burglar, then we're probably here cleaning our guns and can't get to the phone. So please hang up. If you aren't a burglar, we probably aren't here, so it's safe to leave us a message.

Answers
1 bleep 1 / tone 2, 3
2 hang up 5
3 I'll get back to you 3 / call back 4
4 answering machine 2
5 leave a message 4, 5

d In pairs, students make up their own answerphone messages. Encourage humour and originality as well as the use of some of the common answerphone phrases.
• Ask some students to read out their messages. If you have the time and the equipment, get students to record their messages and play them back to the class.

2 • If you think your students will already know these phrasal verbs, let them go straight on to the gap-fill exercise.
• If not, read through the gapped sentences and elicit the meaning of the verb that is missing. So, in a, students might say *contact, get, reach.* When you have elicited the meanings, let them choose one of the phrasal verbs from the list.
• Check answers.

Answers
a get through   c put you through   e were cut off
b rang off   d pick up   f hold on

3 a Read through the example with the students. Don't try to explain differences in meaning between the three verbs at this stage – let students try to match the verbs with nouns. They can do this exercise on their own or in pairs.

• Check answers. Again, it is worth pointing out that it is best to learn these as complete phrases.

Answers

say   goodbye to someone   a prayer   Thank you
speak your mind   Russian
tell someone's fortune   a joke   a lie   someone a secret   someone a story   someone the truth

b Get students to work in pairs to fill the gaps and then discuss the questions.

• Monitor conversations. Listen for the correct collocations, but do not interrupt or correct at this stage.

• If one of the questions arouses interest or argument, it could be developed into a class discussion.

Answers

1	tell, tell	**4**	told, teller
2	speak	**5**	say, say
3	tell		

4 • Ask students to read through the sentences and complete them using one of the common adjectives in the list.

• Check answers, asking further questions to check that students understand the phrases.

Answers

a *public transport*
How many different kinds of *public transport* do you know?

b *mobile home*
What is a *mobile home* like? – It has wheels and can be moved.

c *quiet voice*
What is the opposite of a *quiet voice*?   A *loud* voice.

d *public opinion*
How can *public opinion* be expressed?   At elections / polls or surveys / through letters and phone calls to the media.

e *mobile phone*

f *small talk*
What are some common subjects of small talk?   The weather / the neighbours / holidays / work / children / health.

g *quiet weekend*
What is the opposite of a *quiet weekend*?   A busy / hectic weekend.

h *small businesses*
Give some examples of *small businesses* you know. Would you rather work for a *small business* or a large corporation?

Additional activity: Game

Students work in groups of four or five. One person in each group should be the referee / time-keeper and will need a watch with a second hand.

Each student chooses one of the five subjects below and tries to talk about it for one minute. If the student talking hesitates, another member of the group continues on the same subject for the remainder of the minute. The student talking at the end of the minute wins a point.

Subjects
• Life in a mobile home
• My favourite subject of small talk
• Public transport in my town
• Why I hate quiet weekends
• Why I like quiet weekends

— p. 82 —

Writing

E-mails

The writing section continues the theme by giving students practice in reading and writing e-mails. The main features of e-mails focused on here are their brevity and their tendency to be less formal than traditional letters. There is no need for a special introduction as e-mails were discussed at length in the *Preview*.

▌Read ▌

1 • Students read the three e-mails and decide what their purpose is.

• Check answers, and ask students which words or phrases helped them to decide.

Answers

A reply – 1.
Informal style: *Hi Paul*; verb contractions; *Bye for now*.
Content: *Thanks for the e-mail*.
A reminder – 3.
Informal style: *Dad*; XXXXXX – kisses; spelling mistakes
Content: *Subject: Your daughter*; Greeting: *Dad*; *Don't foget to fone*
A request – 2.
More formal style: *Dear Paul / Best wishes*; No verb contractions
Content: *go to conferences*

2 • Let students work in pairs to find the mistakes in e-mail 3.

• Check answers.

Answers

i	should be *I*
hour	should be *hours*
rivise	should be *revise*
foget	should be *forget*
fone	should be *phone*

• You could open up these final questions for class discussion.
• Elicit ideas.

Possible reasons for mistakes
The writer is in a hurry. She is not concentrating. She is not a good typist.

Reasons for not correcting mistakes
It isn't important because she doesn't need to impress her father.
Personal e-mails don't need to be accurate.
She hasn't got time.
The mistakes don't interfere with what the writer wants to say.

■ Read

- Students read both texts (an e-mail and an advertisement). You could ask them to think why the reply to **b** should be an e-mail.

Possible answers

One possible reason is that only an e-mail address is given. Other reasons could be that the company wants information quickly and that it suits their 'style'.

■ Preparation

- Give students a few minutes to think about the three points, then elicit their ideas. Don't spend more than five minutes on this.

Possible ideas

	e-mail	request to readers
Style	Very informal, conversational language – this is to an old friend.	Semi-formal – this is a reporting of something seen or read.
Content	The writer should tell Charlie what has happened to them over the last three years.	The writer will set the context, then report. Example: *In my Sunday paper there was a story about … It said …*
Length	100–120 words	50–75 words

- Read through the **Reminder** points with the class.

■ Write

The instructions for this writing activity encourage students to write their e-mail replies as they would in their own language. Speed and effective communication are the key features. This should be thought of as a fluency writing activity.

1–3 Set a time limit for writing the first draft replies.
- Students exchange e-mails, then read each other's replies. Ask them to think of the points you discussed in *Preparation* in order to suggest any improvements.
- Monitor these discussions and give help and advice if necessary.

4 • Finally, students write an improved version of one of their replies. As this should be done fairly quickly, you might prefer to ask them to do this in class, rather than for homework.

▶ **Writing model 8 (photocopiable) TB p.132**

— p. 83 —

Language in action

On the telephone

This lesson gives students an opportunity to identify, then practise, using common telephone expressions.

■ Introduction

1a–b Tell students they are going to hear people making phone calls in response to the two advertisements.
- Students read the advertisements and answer the questions.
- Check their answers and ideas. Do a quick survey to find out which advert students find more interesting.

Answers

a Mediterranean holidays
This is advertising an exclusive selection of package holidays with different kinds of accommodation. People who choose one of these holidays are looking for unusual destinations.

Original Daily Newspapers
This is advertising newspapers from the past which can be given as presents. Typically you might buy someone a newspaper which came out on the day they were born, or got married, etc.

2 a Play **8.8** for the first time. Students answer the questions, then compare their answers in pairs.
- Check answers.

8.8

1
A Hello, Mediterranean Holidays. Can I help you?
B Yes, hello. Could I speak to someone about self-catering holidays, please?
A Yes, certainly. Who's calling, please?
B My name's Kirkby.
A Just one moment, Mr Kirkby, I'll put you through to one of our assistants.
C Hello, I'm sorry to keep you waiting. I understand you're interested in self-catering holidays.
B That's right. I've just seen your ad in the paper. Could you send me a brochure, please?
C I'm afraid next year's brochure isn't out yet, but if you give me your name and address, we'll put one in the post to you as soon as they're available.
B Thanks very much. My address is 72, West Street …

2
A Hello, Olden Days News, Jeremy speaking. How can I help?
B Hello. Erm. Yes, I'd like to order one of your original newspapers.
A Yes, of course. Just hold on a minute. OK, first of all, which newspaper and what date are you interested in?
B Sorry, could you speak up, please. It's a terrible line.
A Yes, which newspaper and what date are you interested in?
B Sorry, it's no good. I can't hear what you're saying. I'll ring back in a couple of minutes.

3
A Hello.
B Oh, hello. Is that Olden Days News?
A No, sorry. You've got the wrong number.
B Oh, I'm sorry.

4
A Hello, Olden Days News, newspaper department.
B Hello, I'd like one of your newspapers, please.
A Certainly, can I ask the newspaper and the date you're interested in?
B Well, I really need to know how much they cost.
A Between £10 and £200, depending on the newspaper and the date.
B I see. Could you send me a sample newspaper?
A No, I'm afraid not, but we could send you a photocopy of the front page.
B That'd be fine.
A OK. I'll put one in the post to you today.

B Thanks very much.
A Not at all. Thank you for calling.
5
A Hello, Mediterranean Holidays. Can I help you?
B Yes, this is Mrs Forest here. Could you put me through to your self-catering holidays department?
A I'm afraid all the lines are busy at the moment. Would you like to hold?
B Yes, thank you.
A The lines are still engaged. Do you still want to hold?
B No, thanks. I'll try again later.
A Can I take a message or get someone to phone you back?
B Yes, please. I'd like some information about holidays in May. The name's Forest and my number's 453879.
A Thanks for your call, Mrs Forest, I'll pass on your message.

Answers
Conversation 3: the caller phones the wrong number.
Conversation 1: the caller wants to be sent a Greek holiday brochure.
Conversation 2: the caller wants to order an original newspaper.
Conversation 4: the caller wants to know the prices of the newspapers and a sample newspaper.
Conversation 5: the caller wants information about holidays in May.

b Students listen again and note down the telephone language used. Check that students know what kind of language they are listening for, by eliciting a few examples.
• Play **8.8** again, pausing from time to time to let students write down the expressions. You may need to play the recording a few times.
c Students help each other to compile complete lists of expressions. Finally, they add any other telephone expressions they know.
• Check their lists.

Expressions used by the people making calls
1 Hello. Could I speak to someone about ...?
   My name's (Kirkby).

2 Sorry, could you speak up, please?
   It's a terrible line.
   I'll ring back ...

3 Is that (name)?

5 ... this is (Mrs Forest) here.
   Could you put me through to ...
   I'll try again later.
   The name's (Forest) and my number's ...

Other expressions
Could you call me back?
Can I leave a message for ...?
I'd like to speak to ...
Is (Mr X) in?

Expressions used by the people answering calls
1 Hello, can I help you?
   Who's calling, please?
   Just one moment, I'll put you through to ...

2 Hello, (Jeremy) speaking. How can I help?
   Just hold on a minute.

3 You've got the wrong number.

4 Thank you for calling.

5 All the lines are busy.
   Would you like to hold?
   The lines are still engaged.
   Do you still want to hold?
   Can I take a message?
   Can I get someone to phone you back?
   Thanks for your call.
   I'll pass on your message.
Other expressions
Could I ask who's calling?

■ Pronunciation ■■■■■■■■■■■■■■■ p. 152 ■■

This section looks at the strong and weak forms of prepositions and sentence stress.

1 a Tell students that some prepositions have two forms – a strong form and a weak form. You could write these on the board before students hear the tape.

at	/æt/	/ət/	to	/tuː/	/tə/
for	/fɔː/	/fə/	of	/ɒv/	/əv/
from	/frɒm/	/frəm/			

• Play **8.9** so that students can hear the different pronunciations of the strong and weak forms of these prepositions.

8.9
(The strong form is said first.)
at   at
for   for
from   from
to   to
of   of

b Students can do the exercise in pairs or you can elicit ideas from the whole class. Don't confirm whether students' ideas are right or wrong.
c Play **8.10** so that students can check their ideas. Then check answers.

8.10
1 Thank you **for** calling. **W**
2 What type of holiday are you looking **for**? **S**
3 Who would you like to speak **to**? **S**
4 I'd like **to** speak to the manager please. **W**
5 I'm afraid Miss Smith is **at** a conference today. **W**
6 What's he looking **at**? **S**
7 Where did you get our number **from**? **S**
8 I got it **from** Yellow Pages. **W**
9 How many copies **of** our brochure would you like? **W**
10 What does the accommodation consist **of**? **S**

Answers
See Tapescript **8.10**.

d Allow students a moment or two to work out the rules of pronunciation for strong and weak forms of prepositions. Then check answers.

Answers
1 A   2 B

Note When people speak slowly and carefully, they will sometimes use strong forms. However, weak forms are the usual forms for natural speech and it is important that students are aware of them and use them.

2 a Tell students that they are going to hear eight expressions and that they have to identify the word they hear stressed most in each one. You could either ask them to write down these words (you will probably need to pause the tape between each expression), and go through the answers at the end. Or you could ask students to tell you what they heard after each one.
  • Play **8.11**. Check answers. If students don't get the answers right, tell them not to worry. Some native speakers also have problems hearing stress.

8.11

1 Can I **help** you?
2 Who's **calling**, / **please**?
3 I'll put you **through**.
4 Just a **moment**.
5 Let me take your **details**.
6 I didn't quite **catch** that.
7 Shall I **send** it to you?
8 I'll put one in the post to you **today**.

Answers
See Tapescript **8.11**.

b Play **8.11** again. Pause after each expression and drill.

■ **Practice** ■■■■■■■■■■■■■■■■■■■■■■■■■■■■ **p. 83** ■

  • Divide the class into pairs. Check they understand the task: they are going to phone each other to ask for information connected with more advertisements. They each have a situation where they need to get information, and an advertisement to use to give information. Student A has to ask for information about a holiday company, and give information about the Globe arts centre; Student B has to ask for information about the Globe arts centre and give information about the World of Adventure holiday company.
  • Allow students four to five minutes to prepare for the phone calls. You could put them into AA BB pairs to prepare the task. Tell them to think of questions to ask. They should also make sure they are familiar with 'their' advertisement, which they can refer to when their partner asks them questions.
  • Get pairs to sit back to back to make the situations more like real telephone conversations.
  • Remind students to incorporate some of the telephone expressions from their lists.
  • Monitor their conversations, but do not interrupt.

■ **Language check** ■■■■■■■■■■■■■■■■■■■■■■■■■

Follow the usual procedure.

9 Laws

Theme

The overall theme of this unit is laws.
Preview Cases of people suing individuals or companies for damages
Listening Noise and the law
Skills Murphy's Law
Grammar extra Laws of nature
Writing Whistle-blowing

Grammar

- Review of Conditional structures (1): zero and first conditional
- Conditional structures (2): second conditional
- Expressing purpose and reason

Vocabulary

- Crimes
- Crime and the law: people and verbs

Writing

- Writing a personal letter to a friend

Functional language

- Asking for and giving reasons

Pronunciation

- *Wh-* questions and strong and weak forms

Workbook

- Grammar and functional language as above
- Topic vocabulary: crime; noises; *good* and *bad*
- Extract from newspaper stories

Preview

The unit starts with newspaper stories about people who have sued individuals or companies for legal damages. The texts and recordings provide situations which can be discussed using Conditional structures. These are the subject of the Grammar review.

▌Your thoughts ▌   p. 84 ▌

- If there is a recent well-known case of this kind of legal action that students may have heard of, start by reminding the class of this and eliciting any details they can remember. This will set the scene for the stories.

1 •   You could start by pre-teaching these expressions: *to sue someone*, *to win damages*.
- Ask students to read the four stories and decide which is the craziest.
- Elicit their opinions and reasons.

2a–b Students can discuss the questions in pairs, in groups or as a whole class.
- Monitor conversations, but do not interrupt. It is possible that students will use *if* clauses when they are speculating in **2a**. Conditionals are revised and practised later in the unit, so don't correct them yet – simply listen out for how accurately students use them here.
- This could be broadened into a class discussion if students have strong opinions or interesting first-hand experiences to talk about with the class.

▌Read and listen ▌

1 •   Check students' understanding of these words: *minister*, *resign*, *star*.
- Divide students into pairs to predict news stories from the newspaper headlines and the photographs.
- Elicit a few ideas from the class, but do not say yet whether they are right or wrong.

2 •   Play **9.1** . Students listen and match the news reports they hear with three of the headlines.
- Check answers.

9.1

1 Last night, John Steele, who is appearing in the latest Spielberg film, appealed to his ex-wife Matilda to return his three children. Mrs Steele took the children as they came out of school last Monday. Steele is considering suing his wife, but is not happy at the thought of his children appearing in court.

2 Friends of Jeremy Carlton claim that they do not know where he was last weekend. They say they do not believe he has done anything wrong and see no reason why he should resign. It is thought that the Prime Minister is trying to persuade Mr Carlton to explain where he was on the two days in question and to deny rumours that he was with Hollywood actress, Marlene Shaw.

3 The London train was full of passengers. The injured man, Paul Lewis, was standing near a door when the attack occurred. 'I was reading the paper when two men approached me. One asked me the time, and as I looked at my watch, the other one hit me in the stomach and stole my wallet. They both had knives. There were people all around me. I can't believe no one has given the police a full description of the men.'

Answers

Report 1 – Star may not fight for kids
Report 2 – Lost weekend …
Report 3 – They asked me the time …
There is no news report with Red card for footballer …

3 • Explain that the answers to the questions are not given in the reports. Students must come up with their own ideas.
   • Students discuss ideas in pairs or groups. These are primarily discussion questions, not practice of first conditional sentences, so again, don't correct here. Use it as an opportunity to assess students' knowledge of conditionals.
   • Elicit a few possible answers.

Possible answers

1 a His children will / may have to appear in court – which Steele wants to avoid.
   b He may not see them again. / He'll lose touch with them.
2 a Newspaper reporters will look into the story. / People won't believe him.
   b Interest in the story may / will die down.
3 a The attack happened so quickly that witnesses didn't get a clear image of the attacker. / The witnesses may be afraid of the attackers' revenge.
   b People in the area won't feel safe. / The attackers may attack again.

■ **Vocabulary** ■ ━━━━━━━━━━━━━━━━━ **p. 85** ■

1–2 Let students work through questions 1 and 2 individually or in pairs. Before they begin to compile their lists in 2, warn them that some words could go in both lists.
   • You could either check answers to **1** and deal with any vocabulary queries before they move on, or let them work through both questions before checking answers.

Answers

1 a arson   **b** burglary   **c** mugging   **d** kidnapping
2 Crimes against people
   assault   blackmail   hijacking   kidnapping   mugging
   murder   robbery   theft
Crimes against property
   arson   burglary   fraud   hijacking   robbery
   shoplifting   theft

Additional activity

You could develop this vocabulary section one stage further by eliciting the words for the people who commit the crimes.

Crime	Criminal
arson	*arsonist*
assault	*assailant*
blackmail	*blackmailer*
burglary	*burglar*
forgery	*forger*
fraud	*fraudster*
hijacking	*hijacker*
kidnapping	*kidnapper*
mugging	*mugger*
murder	*murderer*
robbery	*robber*
shoplifting	*shoplifter*
theft	*thief*

■ **Have your say** ■

1–2 This should start as pairwork, but it might develop into a class discussion. If students do not know enough about one particular crime, they could talk about the penalties for crimes in general. Use these prompt questions: *Are judges too harsh, too lenient? What penalties should be imposed on, for example, murderers or kidnappers?* If there are recent interesting cases, uses these as a focus of attention.

▶ **Photocopiable activity 17 p.171**

━ Grammar review ━ Conditional sentences (1) ━

This section revises zero and first conditional structures. The next grammar section on p.87 moves on to the second conditional.

1–3 Students work individually or in pairs through this section. Remind them to check their ideas in the **Language commentary** on p.134.
   • Monitor and give help where necessary.
   • Check answers.

Answers

1 Type **a** – something that is possible in the future
   2 *Steele's children will have to appear in court …*
   3 *If he doesn't try to get his children back, he'll …*
   5 *Everyone will think Jeremy Carlton is guilty if he says…*
   6 *If he denies the rumours, people will…*
   Type **b** – something that normally happens
   1 *If you drive dangerously, you lose…*
   4 *You go to jail for life if you are found…*

2 a 1 the future (first conditional) 2, 3, 5, 6
       2 any / all time (zero conditional) 1, 4

   b First conditional: If + Present simple, → *will* OR *will* → If + Present simple
       Zero conditional: *If* + Present simple, → Present simple OR Present simple → *If* + Present simple

3 a The first sentence is more certain.
   b The second sentence is more certain.
       Make sure that students realize that *will* in the main clause conveys a greater degree of certainty than *may*.

4 • Point out that students must first decide whether the sentences they have to complete are first or zero conditional and then choose a suitable verb.

 • Students work through the exercise individually, then compare their ideas in pairs.

 • Check answers.

Answers

a If I *pass* my driving test tomorrow, I*'ll buy* a car at the weekend.

b If I *watch* TV late at night, I usually *fall asleep* in the armchair.

c If you *play* that computer game much longer, you*'ll get* a headache.

d Water *freezes* if the temperature *falls* below zero.

e That coffee's really hot. If you *drink* it now, you*'ll burn* your mouth.

f Everyone knows that if you *smoke* too much, you *get* a cough.

5a–b Students work through these personalized questions, writing note-form answers. These will form the basis of the stage where students compare answers with a partner. They need not be full conditional sentences at this stage.

 • Before they begin, elicit a couple of answers from the class, or supply your own ideas, to check that students understand that sentences in **a** should be in the zero conditional, and in **b** in the first conditional.

 • Monitor all the stages of this activity.

 • Finally, elicit a few sample answers to each question.

— p. 86 —

Listening

The theme of this section is noise and the law.

■ **In your experience** ■■■■■■■■■■

1a–b These personal questions prepare students for the new subject: noise and the law. They could exchange personal experiences and opinions in pairs or small groups.

 • Monitor conversations, listening for any particularly interesting stories which students could share with the rest of the class.

2 a Before students do the ranking task, check that they understand the vocabulary, particularly: *barking*, *building sites*, *car alarms*.

 • Ask individuals to rank the ten noises from the most to the least annoying, before they compare their order with other students.

 • Do a quick class survey to find out if there is a general consensus on the subject.

 b Before they look at the results of the survey on p.159 of their books, students could predict which noise British people found most annoying.

 • Discuss how the results of a similar survey might be different if it were done in students' own country or countries.

1–2 Set the listening task: as they listen to the radio programme, students should tick any of the noises in the list which are mentioned by the speakers. They should also note any other noises mentioned.

 • Play **9.2** only once for this first stage. Students should be used to this procedure by now; the first listening task is for them to get a general idea; they will have the opportunity to listen for more detail later.

 • Check answers.

9.2

PO   Are you the owner of this house, sir?

M   Yes, I am.

PO   Then I have to tell you, sir, that you are breaking the new Night Noise Law and I am now officially asking you to end this party.

M   But it's only eleven o'clock. Would it be OK if we turned the music down?

PO   I'm sorry, sir, but under new laws we have to uphold complaints from members of the public who complain about late night noise.

M   Look, officer, we've got all our friends here now. We can't just send them home.

PO   I'm sorry, sir, but you have no choice.

P   Yes, you're right – that wasn't a real life scene, but there are countries with strict anti-noise laws. In Switzerland, for example, neighbours can complain about any type of noise after ten o'clock at night. This law can cover everything from flushing toilets to crying babies and televisions. Here's Monica Greentree who lives in Switzerland.

MG   When we arrived, we heard a story about a foreign couple who decided to have a party.

P   Did you hear this from the couple themselves?

MG   No, but apparently all foreigners are told this story as soon as they arrive in Switzerland. Anyway, this couple were warned about the Swiss attitude to noise so they invited their neighbours to their party, thinking, you know, 'If we invite the neighbours, they won't complain.' How wrong can you be? The neighbours accepted the invitation, drank lots of wine and left promptly at midnight. As soon as they got home they phoned the police to complain about the noise. The police arrived within minutes and put an end to the celebrations.

P   That's incredible!

MG   It is, isn't it?

P   A Dutch person living in Geneva says that it is not the law, but the people who enforce the law who are to blame.

D   In Holland we have similar laws, but people are tolerant and the police would laugh if someone complained about a party.

P   Noise, it seems, is a cause of intense irritation for many people. Here in Britain, noise and badly-behaved children are the most common causes of arguments between neighbours. Complaints about neighbourhood noise in general have been rising steadily since the early 1980s. There is actually a very serious side to the subject. Here's a Chief Inspector of Police.

CI   We are seeing more and more cases of violence associated with noise – sort of 'noise rage' if you like. People have actually died as a result of attacks by irate neighbours. There was a particularly strange case recently when a man was jailed for life for killing a neighbour who had complained about the volume of his music.

P   What powers do the British police have in this area?

CI   Well, it depends where you are. In Scotland, for instance, the police could actually arrest you if you refused to stop making a disturbing noise. In England this job is left to environmental health officers. They cannot arrest people but they can remove the cause of noise.

P   In fact there was a famous case only last year, wasn't there?

CI That's right, a 16-year-old girl had her stereo taken away because she refused to turn down her music when her mother asked her to. Alarms are another area of growing concern for us – burglar alarms on houses and shops have been with us for a long time, but more and more people now have car alarms and it can be very disturbing if these go off at night, particularly if the car is parked some distance away from where the driver lives.

P Thank you, Chief Inspector. Well, that's about it for today. I'll say goodbye now and hope to have the pleasure of your company next week.

Answers

These noises from the list are mentioned: noisy parties, noisy neighbours, car alarms.
Other noises mentioned are: flushing toilets, crying babies, televisions, noisy children, stereos, burglar alarms.

■ Understanding ideas

1–5 Remind the class that they will have to use their imagination to answer some of these questions.
- Give students time to read through the questions and ask for clarification of anything they don't understand.
- Play **9.2** again.
- Students could discuss possible answers in pairs.
- Check answers.

Answers / Possible answers

1 It could be a serious warning or an *urban myth* (one of those surprising stories that you always hear from someone else, never from the person it is supposed to have happened to).

Anyone who meets them soon after they arrive in Switzerland. / Their new neighbours. / Colleagues at work.

2 Because those neighbours had actually been to her party – she had invited them deliberately so they would not be able to complain.

3 The Dutch police would not enforce the law and would laugh at anyone who complained about noise from a party; ordinary Dutch people are more tolerant – they would not complain in the first place.

4 In Scotland the police can arrest people who refuse to stop making a noise. In England it is the job of *environmental health officers* (these are local government employees) who cannot arrest people but can take away the cause of the noise.

5 Maybe the environment is actually getting noisier – more traffic, planes, alarms, more loud music in public places. Maybe people are at the same time becoming less tolerant, or are more aware of their rights. It may be a kind of *noise rage*.

■ Vocabulary

1 • Explain the task: students should complete the sentences with words related to the word in italics. You could demonstrate with the first sentence. Ask students to read the sentence and ask what kind of word is needed to fill the gap (a verb). Then ask them what the verb would be from the word in italics (*complain*), and ask what tense the verb should be (Past simple). They can then work on their own or in pairs to fill the gaps.
- Check their answers.

Answers

a	complained	d	invitation
b	neighbouring	e	irritates
c	foreign	f	violent

2–3 Students now think of their own endings to the sentences. Encourage them to use interesting or unusual ideas.
- Finally, they compare sentences with a partner and discuss any of the ideas that interest them.
- Elicit a few complete sentences to round off the activity.

■ Have your say

1–2 Students discuss these questions in the normal way.
- Monitor, but do not interrupt.

—Grammar – Conditional sentences (2) — p. 87 —

This section focuses on the second conditional. Unless this is a new structure for your students, remind them about the **Language commentary** on p.135, and let them work through 1–2 independently. You could start with a brief reference back to the zero and first conditional structures which were reviewed earlier in the unit.

■ Exploring concepts

1–3 Students start by identifying the verbs in sentences a–e, then move on to the concept questions. It is probably best to check their answers after they have completed 2 and before they move on to 3.
- If students are working in pairs, monitor their conversations. If they ask questions, prompt them, rather than giving direct answers.
- Check answers.

Answers

Note Where appropriate, you could point out the contrast between the first and second conditional.

1 a would complain; didn't invite
   b would laugh; complained
   c could arrest; refused   (also stop making)
   d were younger; (I)'d go and work
   e told; might help   (also look)

2 a It is unlikely that they won't invite the neighbours.
   b No.
   c No.
   d Because the speaker cannot be younger than he / she is – it's an impossibility.
   e Probably not. It's possible, but not certain that the police will help.

3 a 1a / b / c / e all refer to improbable future events or situations. 1d refers to an impossible present situation.
   b The second conditional:
   If + Past simple → would / *might* / *could*   OR
   would / *might* / *could* → *If* + Past simple

■ Exploitation

1a–c This task practises the 'improbable-future-event-or-situation' use of the second conditional.
- Students think about the situation shown in the cartoon and make up a chain of conditional events.
- Individually, each student thinks up a continuation of *If Nick went to the party, …*
- Elicit one or two suggestions from the class, then get students to continue the chain in pairs.
- Monitor and correct any second conditional errors you hear.
- You could set a time limit of say, five minutes. Pairs could compete to make up the longest chain.

Sample chain

If Nick went to the party, Sara would be very angry.
If Sara was very angry, she might throw him out of their home.
If she threw him out of their home, he wouldn't have anywhere to live.
If he didn't have anywhere to live, he might lose his job.
If he lost his job, he'd have no money.
If he had no money, he wouldn't be able to afford a home of his own.
If he couldn't afford a home of his own, he might go to live with his parents.
If he went to live with his parents, he'd get bored.
If he got bored, he might go out and find a job.

d Students make up another chain based on the second cartoon.
- If class time is short, this chain could be done orally around the class, or alternatively set for homework.

2a–c This exercise practises the 'impossible-present-situation' meaning of the second conditional.
- Ask students to write their own answers to **a1–4**, then turn them into questions to ask their partner.
- They should then ask their questions and note down their partner's answers.
- Ask them to mingle to find people with similar answers to theirs.
- Again, monitor and correct.

■ Free speech

3a–c Divide the class into pairs or groups to discuss situations **a–c**.
- Tell them to consider one situation at a time, list the likely problems and then think of possible solutions.
- Give them a little time to think about the first situation, then elicit a few ideas before they start discussing.
- Monitor, but do not correct. This is primarily a fluency activity which might naturally involve the use of conditional structures. You could make a note of any conditional errors you hear and deal with them at a later stage.
- Round off this section of the unit with a few of the best ideas from the groups.

Skills

The theme of this section is *Murphy's Law* – also known as *Sod's Law* – commonly used terms for the tendency of things to go wrong by chance.
Don't tell the class any of this or explain the term *Murphy's Law*. *Listen and Speak* introduces them to the idea.

■ Listen and speak

1
- Ask students to describe what is happening in the four illustrations. Can they think of anything that they have in common? Don't confirm or deny suggestions, but tell them they will find out the answer when they listen to the recording.

2
- Play **9.3** once. Students check their ideas.
- Check answers.

9.3

Speaker 1   Well again, connected to trains, erm I always find that the train never leaves on time – it's always four, five minutes late, maybe more, but the very day you arrive four or five minutes late, the train has just pulled out.

Speaker 2   … when I was very small and I was putting jam on my toast in the morning and I was standing up to have my breakfast and I dropped the piece of bread and it landed with the jam side down to the floor so of course picking up all the horrible bits off the floor …

Speaker 3   … you're in a supermarket or a bank or at the post office and you're standing in a queue waiting to pay and you notice that the queue next to you is moving faster, so you move into that queue and immediately it slows down and the queue you were in before starts moving faster …

Speaker 4   When I'm cycling in to work in the morning I try to…, not to carry too much on my bike because I have loads of bags to take because of the children's things, and er so if I think it's not going to rain, I won't bother to take my waterproofs but you can guarantee that if I don't take my waterproof in the morning, it'll be raining by the time I have to cycle home in the evening and then you know vice versa – if I, if I do take it, it's beautiful weather and by the time I cycle home, I'm just carrying four times too many coats and bags and things that I didn't need.

3a–b Before you play the recording again, get students to discuss the two questions in pairs. They will probably be able to remember the answer to **a**, but may need to listen again to describe it in detail.
- Elicit their ideas. If they still can't say what the four situations have in common, play the recording again.
- Check answers.

Answers

a 1 The train is always late but the one occasion on which you arrive late, it leaves on time.

2 If bread or toast falls off your plate it almost always falls with the butter or jam side downwards which probably means you can't eat it.

3 At the supermarket, bank or post office where there is a choice of queues to stand in you always seem to choose the slowest queue. The queues on both sides seem to move faster.

4 If you take waterproof clothes in case it rains, it doesn't rain. If you decide not to take them, it rains.

b All the speakers are describing ironic situations in which things go wrong – it's as if there is some supernatural power making these bad things happen to people who have done nothing to deserve punishment. These are all examples of Murphy's Law.

• If students have something interesting to say in reaction to what they have heard, e.g. their own examples of Murphy's Law, give them a few minutes to talk now. They will have an opportunity in *Have your say* to express their own thoughts on the subject.

■ Read

1a–b Students now read the five laws and say whether they think they are generally true or not.

• When they compare ideas in pairs, they could give their own examples of any they think are true.

• Round off with a quick class survey. Which of the five 'laws' do most students think are true?

2 The article provides 'scientific' explanations of two of the cases they have heard about.

• Students read the text and match the two cases with one or more of the five laws listed in **1**. This is a gist reading task, so set a time limit of three to four minutes for the first reading.

• Check answers.

Answers

Both cases illustrate Law 3. The queue case could also illustrate Law 2.

■ Understanding ideas ▬▬▬▬▬ p. 89 ■

1 • In pairs, students should each choose one of the two cases and take turns to explain to each other why these things happen. In the first instance they should do this with their books closed, so that they cannot refer to the article.

• If they find the explanation impossible, they could discuss it with their partner and if necessary look back at the article.

• Monitor this activity to check how much students have understood.

2–3 Let students read the text again if they want before they answer these questions. They can work on the questions individually or in pairs.

• Elicit ideas.

Possible answers

2 a If you stay in bed, nothing bad can happen to you.

b Because they think these things go wrong simply as a matter of chance – there is no scientific explanation for them. They are *old wives' tales* based on irrational superstition.

c Start with the book face down on the table.

d This is not an absolute law. If a very tall person was carrying the toast on a plate, it would fall from a higher point and might turn over twice.

3 a *looks* = seems (or appears)   **c** *Take* = think of as an example

b *in no time* = quickly

■ Have your say

1–3 Divide the class into pairs or small groups to discuss these questions.

• Monitor, listening for interesting examples and ideas.

• Individuals could tell the rest of the class about any particularly 'good' examples of Murphy's Law that have happened to them.

• You could elicit ideas about the sort of people who believe in Murphy's Law (pessimists; fatalists).

■ Speak and write

1 • You could read through and discuss these four 'modern laws' with the class, or let students discuss them in pairs. (*Parkinson's Law* is very well-known.)

• Find out if students know any other 'laws' like this.

2a–b Students now write their own laws following the style of those in their books. Laws like these are generalizations and therefore often use the Present simple. They may also be written using conditional structures (like some of Murphy's Laws).

• Students read each other's laws and, if necessary, ask for clarification.

• To round off the activity, ask some students to read out the final versions of their laws. Others could be displayed in the classroom.

──────────────────────────── p. 90 ──

Grammar extra

Expressing purpose and reason

The theme moves on to laws of animal behaviour. The title of the text, *The law of the jungle*, is a phrase often used with reference to human behaviour, which means the survival or success of the strongest or those with the least regard for others. The text contains six examples of purpose and reason expressions.

■ Read

- Ask students to read the text for general understanding, then choose the sentence which best summarizes the text.
- Check their answer.

Answer
Giraffes follow rules when they fight each other. (The last sentence of the text explains this.)

- Ask students to give any more examples of animal behaviour which shows they are obeying rules or laws.

■ Exploring concepts

1–3 If they are going to answer these questions independently, remind students to check ideas in the **Language commentary** on p.135. It is a good idea to check their answers to 1 before they move on.

- Check answers.

Answers

1 Students should have underlined the following words and phrases:
- feet **in order to** injure
- they can **to** frighten each
- **As** neither giraffe is frightened
- swings it back **so that** the short horns
- move their front legs outwards **so as not to** fall over
- **because** it is against the rules

2 • As / so that / because are followed by clauses with main verbs.
  • In order to / to / so as not to are followed by the infinitive.

3 a Because can be followed by a clause (2) or by of + noun (1).
  b As here is a time conjunction meaning at the same time as.

■ Exploitation

1a–b Elicit a few sample answers to the first question to establish the sentence patterns you expect students to use, then let them work individually through questions 1–6.

- Encourage students to think of unusual or humorous answers as well as the obvious, more serious ones.
- Students should compare answers in pairs or groups and choose the best (i.e. the most unusual or the funniest) answer for each question.
- Elicit some of these best answers for the class to hear.

■ Free speech

2 • Working in groups, students discuss what is going on in the photographs and think of explanations.
  • Monitor conversations, but this is primarily a fluency activity, so do not insist on the use of purpose and reason expressions.
  • Finish with a brief class discussion of each photograph.

Exploring words

Crime and the law

1 a Set a time limit of about five minutes for this first exercise which introduces collocations related to crime and the law, then let students compare sentences in pairs. Remind them that there several possible answers starting with each subject.
  • Check answers before going on to **b**.

Possible answers
Criminals break the law, commit crimes / offences, can win cases
Judges sentence criminals / the accused, question suspects / the accused
Police officers arrest criminals / suspects
The police catch criminals, enforce laws, prosecute suspects, question suspects / criminals
Solicitors defend the accused / their clients / criminals / suspects, prosecute criminals / suspects / defendants, win cases
Victims of crime give evidence
Witnesses give evidence

b Students now use the correct form of the verbs from column B to complete sentences 1–6.
  • Check answers.

Answers
1 won
2 arrested (for tells you that arrest is correct.)
3 committed
4 are enforcing / have been enforcing
5 questioned
6 are breaking

c In groups, students talk about two or three of these questions with reference to their own countries. Encourage them to talk about real cases if they can.
  • Monitor conversations, making a note of mistakes involving crime vocabulary. Deal with these after the discussions. Any of the questions which arouse particular interest could be a whole class discussion.
  • If your class includes students of different nationalities, spend some time at the end comparing the situation in their countries.

2 a Ask students to describe what is happening in each frame of the picture story. Emphasize the subject matter here; don't expect students to use phrasal verbs yet.
  • Students now read the text and put the six pictures into the correct order. As they do this, they will come across the six phrasal verbs in context.
  • Check answers.

Answers
1 f 2 e 3 a 4 b 5 c 6 d

b Elicit the meanings of the phrasal verbs in the text in students' own words, then ask them to choose the appropriate meaning from the list.

- Check answers.

Answers

to tip someone off	inform
to pick someone up	arrest
to take someone in (for questioning)	accompany to the police station
to give yourself up	allow yourself to be arrested
to break in	enter (a building) illegally and by force
to make off	leave quickly

3 a Introduce the idea of a *minor* crime and elicit one or two examples from the class, e.g. *motoring offences / shop-lifting / tax avoidance / not having a TV licence*, etc.
- Working in pairs, students should write down a minor crime. They then need to agree on a suitable punishment for that crime and write it down, too.

b Pairs exchange notes, discuss the crimes and punishments, then put a tick or a cross to show that they agree or disagree.
- The papers can then be passed on round the class, until everyone has read everyone else's ideas.
- To round off the activity, you could ask for a couple of cases where there has been disagreement and get the class to discuss them.

— p. 92 —

Writing

A personal letter to a friend

The new theme is the dilemma facing someone who discovers that a colleague is involved in a dishonest or illegal activity. Should they inform the authorities or not? The personal letter students write will be connected with this dilemma. People who inform the authorities about the dishonest or illegal behaviour of colleagues are called *whistle-blowers*.

Discuss

1–2 In pairs or groups students discuss this hypothetical question. Ask them to think about the general question first, and then discuss whether their reaction would depend on who the colleague was. They may know of real cases which they can describe.
- Monitor discussions, but don't interrupt. You could listen for conditional sentences which students may use when discussing this hypothetical situation, but do not correct.
- Round off this introduction with a quick class survey: *Who would inform the authorities? Who would do nothing? Who would warn the offender? Who would react differently depending on who the offender was?*

Read

1 a Ask students to read the extract from a letter from an imaginary friend who is facing the dilemma they have just discussed, and to think about how she feels. To get a full answer students will have to think themselves into the letter writer's situation.
- Check answers.

Possible answers

The letter writer has mixed feelings: she is *disappointed* – she is enjoying the new job and she likes the colleague – now she feels let down; *frightened* – the colleague is the best friend of her boss's son; *angry* – she feels she has to do something to stop the colleague's dishonest behaviour; *confused* – she doesn't know what to do.

b Students compare instant reactions to the situation described in the letter, and discuss the dilemma for a few minutes. If you have already had a class discussion on this subject, there is no need for another here.

Brainstorm and notes

1 • Divide the class into small groups. They have already expressed their instinctive reactions to the situation, but attention is now focused on the details of the case.
- Ask them to discuss the list of points and decide what effect these details might have on their reaction.
- Elicit some ideas before students start discussing in groups. For example, ask them to think about the relationship between the letter writer and her colleague. *How close is it? Could it get closer in the future or does the colleague's crime rule out a closer relationship?*

2 • Groups should now try to summarize their discussions by deciding what they would actually say to their friend who has the problem.
- They should make a note of the main ideas in the form of instructions or advice which will be incorporated into their letter.

Write

1 • When they write their first draft, students should concentrate on incorporating the advice they have decided on into the framework of a friendly, informal letter.
- Draw students' attention to the **Reminder** points. Elicit ideas for how they could avoid sounding negative, e.g. offer constructive advice / point out the advantages of the advice you are giving, etc.
- Students now write their first draft. If this is done as classwork, set a time limit which encourages students to express their ideas fluently rather than agonizing over the accuracy of every word.

2a–c We have suggested that students exchange letters with a partner from a different group, so that they will be coming across ideas they are not already familiar with. Because of this they can react in a more natural way to the advice in the letter.

- Having read each other's letters, and considered their probable effects on the readers, students suggest improvements – particularly to the style and tone of the letter.
- Monitor their discussions and give advice where needed.
- The final rewriting is probably best done for homework. Remind students that as well as incorporating any improvements agreed with their partner, they should now also focus on the accuracy of their writing.

▶ **Writing model 9 (photocopiable) TB p.132**

— p. 93 —

Language in action

Asking for and giving reasons

To tie in with the overall theme of the unit, the language of asking for and giving reasons is presented in four situations, all involving rules or laws of some kind.

■ Introduction

1a–c Elicit very general ideas from the class about what is happening in the four illustrations by asking questions, e.g. *Who are these people? What is their relationship? Where are they? What are they doing? What are they talking about?* Don't confirm or deny these ideas at this stage.

- Ask students to work in pairs and imagine what the four pairs of people are saying to each other. They should then choose one of the situations and make up a short conversation between the two people. They could improvise this first, then write it down so that they can check what expressions they used.
- Finally, they make a note of expressions they used to ask for or give reasons. They may need to refer back to these notes later.

2 a Play **9.4** . Students listen to four conversations and match them with the appropriate illustrations. This is a straightforward listening task, but check their answers before playing the recording again.

9.4

1
T What's the matter? You were OK five minutes ago. Why are you crying?
P Because Ben took my sandwiches and ate them, and now I'm hungry.
T Come on, don't cry. I'll have a word with Ben. Have you any idea why Ben took your sandwiches?
P Dunno – maybe it was because I took his cake.

2
O Perhaps you could tell me why your uniform is in such a mess? You've had three days to get it clean and tidy.
S Because I've been ill in bed since the weekend, that's why.
O That's why what?
S That's why my uniform is in a mess.
O That's why your uniform is in a mess, what?
S That's why my uniform is in a mess, sir.

3
T Why on earth are you out of bed at this time of night?
M For the simple reason that it's three o'clock in the morning and we were worried about you.
T Why were you worried? I'm quite old enough to look after myself.

4
P So, is there a reason why you didn't stop at the traffic lights at the corner of the High Street?
D The main reason was that they were green, not red.
P Don't get funny with me, sir. The last set of traffic lights were definitely red.
D Were they? Oh! Sorry.
P Could you blow into this for me, please, sir?
D Why should I?
P Because I think you've probably had too much to drink.

Answers
1 a **2** c **3** d **4** b

b–c They are now going to listen to the recording again and note down the reason expressions used by the speakers.
- Allocate A / B roles and play the recording again, pausing from time to time to let students write down the functional language.
- Students tell each other the expressions they heard and both compile two lists. They should also add any different expressions they used in their own conversations.
- Check their lists.

Answers

Asking for reasons	Giving reasons
1 Why (are you crying)? Have you any idea why (Ben took …)?	Because (Ben took my sandwiches). … maybe it was because (I took his …)
2 Perhaps you could tell me why …	Because (I've been ill …), that's why.
3 Why on earth are you (out of bed) …? Why (were you worried)?	For the simple reason that …
4 Is there a reason why (you didn't) …? Why should I?	The main reason was that … Because I think …

Notes

1 Point out the indirect question word order in these expressions: *Have you any idea why …? / Perhaps you could explain why … / Is there a reason why …?*

2 Explain the addition of *on earth* in *Why **on earth** are you out of bed?* It adds emphasis and surprise to the question. You could give some more examples of the same construction: *Where **on earth** have you been? / What **on earth** are you doing?*

- Get students to practise saying these questions with the appropriate stress and intonation.

▓ Pronunciation ▓▓▓▓▓▓▓▓▓▓▓▓▓ p. 153 ▓

This section looks at intonation in *Wh-* questions and strong and weak forms of *that*.

1 a Play **9.5** . Ask students to identify the main stressed syllables. Check answers.

9.5

1 What's the <u>matt</u>er?
2 Why are you <u>cry</u>ing?
3 What are you doing out of bed at <u>this</u> time of night?
4 Why didn't you <u>tell</u> me you had problems?
5 Why aren't you in <u>bed</u>?
6 What on earth are you <u>do</u>ing?

Answers

See Tapescript **9.5** .

b Play **9.5** again. Ask students to complete the rule of intonation.

Answer

Intonation in *Wh-* questions usually goes down.

c Play **9.5** again and drill. Make sure students use the correct intonation.

2 a If you like, demonstrate the strong and weak pronunciations of *that*, /ðæt/ and /ðət/. Then play **9.6** . Students should say which sentence contains the strong form and which the weak form. Check answers. Ask students why the speaker uses the weak form in 1 and the strong form in 2.

9.6

1 The main reason was that they were green.
2 That isn't a good reason.

Answers

The speaker uses the weak form in **1** because *that* isn't an important word (here, it is a conjunction). The speaker uses the strong form in **2** because *that* is an important word (here, a determiner). It tells us which reason the speaker is referring to.

b Students can spend a few moments doing this exercise in pairs or you could elicit ideas from the class.
c Play **9.7** so that students can check their ideas. Check answers.

9.7

1 That's no excuse. **S**
2 Another reason was that I forgot. **W**
3 I lost the instructions that you gave me. **W**
4 That's why. **S**
5 Don't give me that old excuse. **S**

Answers

See Tapescript **9.7** .

- Play **9.7** again and drill. Insist on correct pronunciation of *that*.

▓ Practice ▓▓▓▓▓▓▓▓▓▓▓▓▓▓ p. 93 ▓

▓ Role play ▓▓▓▓▓▓▓▓

1–2 This activity again asks students to imagine what is happening in the situations illustrated. This could be done as a class brainstorm. Ask similar questions to those suggested in **1a** in *Introduction*.

- Allocate A / B roles and ask students to turn to the appropriate page of their books to find their role card.
- Students should spend four or five minutes preparing what they are going to say. Be on hand to help them with this and remind them to incorporate reason expressions into their conversations.
- This is primarily a fluency activity, so monitor conversations, but do not interrupt except to encourage and prompt. You could listen for the correct, appropriate use of reason language, but do not correct.
- If there is time, students could choose another situation and swap roles.
- Round off the activity by asking one or two pairs to perform their conversations for the rest of the class.

▓ Language check ▓▓▓▓▓▓▓▓▓▓▓▓

Follow the usual procedure.

10 A roof over your head

Theme

The overall theme for this unit is houses and homes.
Preview Home
Reading Living underground
Skills Modern architecture
Grammar extra Eviction; the Pompidou Centre
Writing Homelesssness

Grammar

- Review of passive and active verb forms
- Passive verb forms (2)
- Relative clauses (2): *which, who, whose, where, when, why*

Vocabulary

- Buildings and materials

Writing

- Opinion letters

Functional language

- Checking and correcting information

Pronunciation

- Emphatic stress

Workbook

- Grammar and functional language as above
- Topic vocabulary: shapes and materials; adjectives ending in -*y*; house and home idioms
- Extract from a newspaper article: *Home Thoughts*

Preview

This section introduces the overall theme of the unit – houses and homes. The recordings and reading text also contextualize the review language: passive and active verb forms.

■ Your thoughts ■ p. 94 ■

1 • You could begin by eliciting a few different types of homes and writing these on the board, for example, *house (detached, semi-detached), apartment, flat, villa*. Then ask students to think about what the word *home* means to them.
- When they have done this, divide the class into pairs or small groups of three or four students. Ask them to compare their ideas of home and then describe their own home: *What kind of building is it? How old is it? Which floor do you live on? How many rooms are there? Is there a garden?* etc.
- Students now say whether they would like to live in any of the places in the pictures. Tell them to give reasons for their answers. Elicit some ideas.

2 • Ask students to match the words to the photographs.
- Check answers.

Answers
apartment **d** bungalow **b** boat **g** converted coach **e**
cottage **a** hotel **b** hut **f** tent **c**

■ Read ■

- Students should read the text for general understanding, then put the three ideas in order of importance for them. They can compare ideas with their partner or group before you get feedback.
- Explain any vocabulary students want to know.

■ Listen ■ p. 95 ■

1 • Before you play **10.1**, tell students to listen for general understanding. As they listen, they should note down the number of the speaker who mentions any ideas which are similar to theirs.
- Play **10.1** straight through. Then check if there were any similarities.

10.1

Speaker 1 Home to me is a place that I feel safe and comfortable – it's a place where I can just be myself and a place where I'm accepted and until I moved here home was always in New York

State but over the past few months there are at least two different places here in Oxford that I consider home – friends' places and where I'm living now and it just feels like home because, as I said it's safe and comfortable and it's a place where I just be myself.

Speaker 2   Home means my house erm which I bought two years ago and which I love dearly because I did all the work on it – it was in a terrible state when I moved in and it needed complete redecoration and, because I did it myself, I feel more at home there than anywhere else, I think.

Speaker 3   To me it means the place I go home, shut the door, nobody can bother me, I can do what I like, erm – it also means the place where I was born where my parents live, so when I say I'm going home that's often what I mean is going to their their country house and relaxing. It's a lovely old house – it was built in 1780 – erm it's got four bedrooms erm it's very comfortable huge sofas and fireplace – the kind of place you can completely relax.

Speaker 4   Home … oh well … is two things. Home is, is next door where I live, I'm happy enough to, lucky enough to be living next, next to my workplace and of course it's where my Mum lives – that's in Paris and where my family and friends (live) – so erm, yeah, that's where I go back.

Speaker 5   Home, I always think of my parents' home – erm I think a lot of it is because I've moved around so much so I've never lived in one house for a very long time and I've always rented so, because of me moving around, so again I don't think you really, really think of it as your home until you actually buy all the furniture and do a bit of work on it maybe and stay there for quite a while.

Where is your parents' house?

Erm that's outside Manchester erm, and they still live in the old family house – they're talking about selling it now which will be quite sad and it's a, a, large house and it's from the end of the last century, so it's, it's old. It's got a very big garden with a summer house in it. It's, it's nice 'cos it's so spacious and so you can have lots of people to stay. I'm always taking people back there and my Mum and Dad enjoy it, so, so to me that's home really.

2 • Students are still listening for gist on the second hearing. Tell them to write the numbers of the speakers (1–5) next to questions **a–c** in their books as they listen. Play **10.1** again. Allow students a few moments to compare answers, then check.

Answers
a Speakers 1, 3 and 4
b Speaker 5
c Speakers 3 and 5

▩ Vocabulary

1 • Students can work on their own, then compare answers with a partner. Check answers to **1** before students do **2**.

Answers
a 3   **b** 5   **c** 1   **d** 2   **e** 4

2 • Students read through and discuss the questions in pairs.

▩ Have your say

• Check that students understand the meanings of *dream* and *nightmare* in this context: *dream home* (the home they would have if money wasn't a problem), *nightmare home* (the worst home they could imagine).
• Allow students a few minutes to exchange ideas in pairs or small groups then hear some examples.

─Grammar review ─ Passive and active verb forms

• If you are confident that your students will be able to answer the questions, let them work through 1–3 in pairs. Tell them to check their ideas in the **Language commentary** on p.136, then check the answers with the class. Alternatively, you could go through each question step by step with the whole class.

1 • Write these two sentences on the board.
1 *Millions of people watch baseball.*
2 *Baseball is watched by millions of people.*
Establish which sentence is in the active and which the passive. Circle the active form *watch* in Sentence 1, and underline the passive form *is watched* in Sentence 2.
• Ask students to do **a–e** (on their own or in pairs), then check answers.

Answers
1 a (It's) a place where I (can) just (be) myself and a place where I'm accepted.
b (It's) the place where I was born, where my parents (live.)
c (It's) a lovely old house – it was built in 1780 …
d My dad (worked) in the army, so we were often moved around.
e My house was decorated five years ago.

2 a Check answers.

Answers
a Present simple
b, c, d, e Past simple

b Ask students to look at what they have underlined if they are not clear about form at this stage.

Answer
We form the passive with a tense of the verb *be* + the past participle.

3 • Write this on the board.
The army often moved us around.
Try to get students to change this sentence into the passive form.
• Point out that we use the active form when we are more interested in who (or what) did an action (the subject of an active sentence), and we use the passive form when we are more interested in the person or thing affected by an action (the object of an active sentence). Then go through sentences 1a–e eliciting answers to questions 3a–c.

Answers
a a The action is *accept*.   b *I* am affected by the action.
   c *The people I live with* do the action.
b a The action is *give birth*.   b *I* am affected by the action.
   c *My mother* did the action.
c a The action is *build*.   b *The house* was affected by the action.
   c *Somebody or some people* did the action– we don't know who.

d a The action is *move around*. b *We* were affected by the action. c *The army* did the action.

e a The action is *decorate*. b *The house* was affected by the action. c *Somebody or some people* did the action – we don't know who.

Check

4 • Ask students to rewrite the sentences putting the verbs into the passive form. Do **1** with the class as an example. Point out that none of these sentences requires an agent when in the passive. (The use or non-use of the agent is dealt with in Passive verb forms (2) on p.97.)

• Monitor, pointing out any mistakes and asking students to try to correct them. Check answers.

Answers
a Many multi-storey apartment blocks were built in the 1960s.
b Letters are delivered to our house twice a day.
c The American President is elected every four years.
d I was brought up in a lonely country area.
e I was sent to a school in the city centre.
f The two men who broke into my house were arrested.

5 • This can be done as a competition with students working in small groups to try to answer the questions. Allow about five minutes, then stop the activity. Check answers. You could award points for correct or close answers.

Answers
Eiffel Tower, Paris, France. 1889 by Alexandre-Gustave Eiffel, a monument for the Centennial Exhibition. Now a tourist attraction.
Stonehenge, near Salisbury, England. Begun about 3100 BC, probably a place of worship. Now a tourist attraction.
Statue of Liberty, New York harbour, USA. Begun 1875, by Frédéric-Auguste Bartholdi, to commemorate friendship of peoples of US and France. Now a tourist attraction.
The Pyramids, Giza, Egypt. Built 2575–2465 BC by Khutu, Khafre and Menkaure, all kings of the 4th dynasty, as burial chambers.
Sydney Opera House, Australia. Opened 1973, designed by Jorn Utzon.
Taj Mahal, Agra, India. 1632–54, by Shah Jahan in memory of his wife, as a mausoleum.

▶ Photocopiable activity 18 p.172

— p. 96 —

Reading

The theme of this section is living underground.

In your experience

1a–b Check that students understand the meaning of the characteristics before they do the ranking activity. When they have done this they can compare their order and ideas with their partner.

• Hear some ideas.

Possible ideas
Proximity to other buildings, materials used to build it, age, how secure it is.

Read

1 • Students can work in pairs. Allow them a few minutes to think of some ideas and two or three questions to ask, then hear a selection of ideas and questions.

2 • Ask students to read the article quickly. As they read it, they can find the answers to any of their questions in **1**. You could set a time limit of about four minutes.

• Check answers to **a** and **b**.

Answers
a Depends on students' questions.
b The article focuses on the positive aspects of living underground.

Close up

Answers
– The usual plural form of nouns ending in *-f* is *-ves*, for example, calf / calves, leaf / leaves, shelf / shelves, thief / thieves, wolf / wolves, loaf / loaves, scarf / scarves.
You could also point out that singular nouns ending in *-fe* follow the same rule: knife / knives, wife / wives, life / lives.
– The other compass points and the adjectives related to them are: south (southern), east (eastern), west (western).
– An alternative to *run* here could be 'live in' or 'own'.
Some other meanings of *run* are:
  • move quickly. (*He ran 100 metres in under 10 seconds.*)
  • (for public transport) go backwards and forwards between two places. (*The buses don't run on Christmas Day.*)
  • manage a business. (*They run a small hotel on the coast.*)

Understanding ideas

• Tell students to read the text again more carefully this time, but without using dictionaries. They should try to guess the meanings of any words they don't know.

1 • Students can answer the questions on their own then compare answers with a partner.

2a–b Discourage students from using dictionaries. They should try to work out the meanings of these words from the context and supply alternative words, then think of their opposites.

Answers
1 a Ordinary houses may be built on green areas. Trees may have to be cut down, and areas of woodland cleared. Some animals may lose their natural habitats.
b They are easy and cheap to build because the basic structure is already there. You don't need to build walls or a roof.
c Repairs might be needed because of damp or cracks in walls or ceiling due to earth movements caused by tree roots, for example.
d Because you wouldn't hear your neighbour through even a thin wall made of rock, there is no need for gardens, etc.

2 a 1 insane, crazy
   2 *dark*: gloomy / badly lit; *miserable*: horrible / awful
   3 *quieter*: less noisy / more peaceful; *ordinary*: normal
   4 big, important
b 1 sensible   3 noisier; unusual
   2 light; pleasant   4 minor, small

■ Have your say

• Elicit ideas from the whole class. Ask students what they would and wouldn't like about living underground.

— Grammar – Passive verb forms (2) —— p. 97 —

■ Exploring concepts

• If you are confident that your students will be able to answer the questions, let them work through 1–4 in pairs. Tell them to check their ideas in the **Language commentary** on p.136, then check the answers with the class. Alternatively, you could go through each question step by step with the whole class.

• Remind students of what they studied in *Preview*. Ask them to put these active sentences into the passive and then tell you how the passive is formed.
   1 *They collect the rubbish every day.* (The rubbish is collected every day.)
   2 *They ate all the food.* (All the food was eaten.)
   The passive is formed with *be* in an appropriate tense + past participle of main verb.

1 • Elicit the names of the tenses in **1a–d** one by one and ask students how the passive of each tense is formed. Write these up on the board.

Answers

1 a Present perfect passive (*have* / *has been* + past participle)
   b Past simple passive (*was* / *were* + past participle)
   c Present continuous passive (*is* / *are being* + past participle)
   d Present simple passive (*is* / *are* + past participle)

2 • You could write up another sentence or two containing an infinitive then elicit the name of this form of the passive.
   1 *This medicine shouldn't be taken by children under five.*
   2 *I don't like to be told what to do.*

Answer

This is the infinitive. It is formed with *be* + Past participle.

3 • Students can discuss question 3 in pairs. Allow a few minutes for this then check answers.

Answers

a 1a The homes.
   1b The caves.
   1c The caves.
b How much space is needed.
c b (the masons)
d 1a We don't know or want to say who did the action; the person who did the action is unimportant or no one in particular.
   1c As 1a.

4 • Ask students to read through the two descriptions, then check their ideas.

Answer

Description **a** sounds more scientific. The writer is more interested in the thing affected by the action than who did the action so he or she uses the passive rather then the active form. Description **b** is personal.

■ Exploitation

1 • Check that students understand the vocabulary before they change the sentences into the passive form.
• Students can do the exercise on their own, then check with a partner. You could monitor, indicating mistakes and getting students to correct them.

Answers

a A man was killed by a falling tree as he was driving home.
b Old people are being moved from their homes and taken to public halls and schools.
c Ten men have been rescued from a boat in the North Sea (by lifeboats).
d The roofs have been blown off many houses in the area.
e Roads in several seaside towns have been closed because of high seas.
f The M25 motorway was blocked by an overturned lorry for several hours.
g A 20-storey office block in the centre of Leeds has been hit by lightning.

2 a Students can do this exercise on their own, then compare sentences with a partner. You may want to check that they understand the vocabulary first.

Answers

2 The instruments and voices are recorded.
3 The recorded sounds are mixed.
4 Effects are added.
5 The final mix is transferred to a master CD.
6 Copies are made from the master CD.

• You could extend the exercise by asking what they think happens next. Give prompts if necessary: *CD cover (design), copies of the CD to radio stations (send), CD on radio stations (play),* etc.
b Students do the activity in pairs. Tell them to choose one of the processes, and write the name of the process they are describing at the top of their paper. They should then write the first stage of the process. Help with any vocabulary they don't know, but don't help with ideas.
• When they have written Stage 1, they should pass their paper to the next pair who should write the next stage of the process. Tell students that if they disagree with what any of the previous pairs have written, they can change it before writing the next stage and passing it on. Continue until most of the processes have come to an end. Monitor, pointing out errors, and then round off the activity by reading out a couple of completed processes.

3a–b Students could continue to work in pairs or you could divide the class into groups of three or four students. Students could discuss how to improve the town or city where they live, or a town or city near where they live. If you think your students will need some ideas, write these topics on the board. Elicit a couple of examples before students start: *Cars, traffic and public transport*; *Housing, schools, hospitals*; *Green areas, sports facilities*; *Shops and shopping*; *Noise, pollution, litter*.

- This is a free speaking activity so don't insist that students use passive forms. Monitor, but don't correct. When students have run out of ideas or time runs out, stop the activity and hear some examples.

— p. 98 —

Skills

The theme of this section is modern architecture – in particular the work of painter and architect Friedensreich Hundertwasser.

Background information

Born Austria 1928. Hundertwasser's paintings follow in the abstract Art Nouveau tradition. In his works everything (people, buildings, objects) is transformed into spirals, with gold, silver, phosphorescent red and green his preferred colours.

■ Speak ■

- Divide the class into pairs.

1–2 Ask students to look at the photographs in their books and discuss the questions. Elicit some opinions.

Possible answers

1 a Brightly coloured walls / rectangular shapes are broken up by colour. They look more interesting / less regimented / brighter. They look fun to live in – not oppressive.
  b Students merely have to guess. Actually they are: flats, a health resort, a waste incinerator plant.

■ Listen ■

1 • See how much of this task students can do in pairs before you go through the list with the whole class.

Answers

amazing (P), unusual (Neut), a real breath of fresh air (P), cool (P), brilliant (P), dull (Neg), grey and boring (Neg), colourful (Neut), dreadful (Neg), OK (Neut), gimmicky (Neg), fun to look at (P), they brighten the place up (P), artistic (P / Neut), cosy (P), they don't do anything for me (Neg)

2a–b Play **10.2**. You could pause the tape briefly between each conversation to give students time to note down their ideas, but don't check answers yet. After you have played all five conversations, allow students a few moments to compare their ideas with a partner before you check answers.

10.2

Conversation 1

A Have you seen these buildings? They're amazing!
K Let's have a look. Wow! They're really unusual. But what exactly are they?
A Well, that's a block of flats in the middle of Vienna, that's an incinerator and this one's a health resort, apparently.
K An incinerator?
A Yeah, you know, where they burn the city's rubbish. So, what do you think of them?
K They're fantastic! I mean, I think they're a real breath of fresh air – I'd love to live somewhere like that.

Conversation 2

T I think they're absolutely dreadful – I could design better buildings than that myself. I think they should knock them down and start again.
J They're OK, but they're not as wonderful as some people say – I mean they're fun to look at and they brighten the place up a bit, but they don't do anything for me.

Conversation 3

M Cool! They're brilliant – I'm fed up with modern buildings, they're all grey and dull – I mean, why do they always have to use such boring colours? Why can't we have more bright, colourful buildings like this?
W Oh that's not fair. Not all modern buildings are grey and boring. You're thinking of those typical 1960s office blocks – things have moved on you know – it's not just concrete these days – they can do amazing things with glass and steel. I must admit these places look like kids' playgrounds to me. I certainly wouldn't like to live in one – or even near one for that matter.

Conversation 4

R If you ask me, the bloke who designed them is a genius. I'd love a few colourful buildings like those where I live. I think they're really artistic.
E Me too, all those round shapes are sort of cosy – not hard and sharp like most things you get in modern cities, you know, all built by macho middle-aged architects trying to be different.

Conversation 5

E I really like them, but they're not as different as all that. I mean, they're the same as all the others inside – they're only different on the outside.
G Yeah, I expect people will get fed up with the colours in a year or two. They'll get dirty and messy and – and eventually nobody will want to live in them. I wouldn't be surprised if they end up knocking them down and replacing them with something less gimmicky.

Answers

a Conversation 1, 4, 5
b Conversation 2: the woman, Conversation 3: the man

3a–b Play **10.2** again. Students make brief notes of any opinions they hear that they especially agree with. Ask them to compare their ideas with a partner, then elicit opinions from the class.

■ Read ■

- Ask students to read the article to get a general idea and note the answers to the questions.
- Check answers when most students have finished reading. Students who finish first could go on to *Understanding ideas*.

Answers

- Ordinary people love his work: *People queue up for the chance to live in his buildings* (l.5), *Hundertwasser's architecture is popular with ordinary people* (l.33)
- Tourists love his work: *his fantastic housing projects are tourist attractions* (l.6)
- Other architects don't like his work: *many other architects dislike it …* (l.34)

▓ Understanding ideas ▓▓▓▓▓▓▓▓▓ p. 99 ▓

1–2 Students can discuss their ideas to both exercises in pairs. Students need only refer to the relevant part of the article to answer these questions, unless you feel they need to read the text again.

Answers

1 a By a *humane* building Hundertwasser probably means a building which makes people feel good, one which is not oppressive.
b A *sick* building is one which makes the people who live and work in it ill. They can be cured by getting rid of straight lines, growing grass and trees on balconies and roofs, painting them bright colours.
c Hundertwasser dislikes straight lines because he thinks they give people headaches and make them feel unwell and violent.
d A habitable work of art is one that people can live in.
e They don't think it is complex enough. You get bored with it after two minutes.

2 a *then* refers to the time when he was a young artist.
b *This* refers to the Hundertwasserhaus.
c *It* refers to modern architecture (with its straight lines).
d *this* refers to Hundertwasser's belief that ground removed to build a building should be replaced on top of that building.
e *it* refers to Hundertwasser's architecture.

▓ Have your say ▓▓▓▓▓▓▓▓▓▓▓▓▓▓▓▓

1–2 You could either do this brief discussion with the whole class or students could spend a few moments discussing the questions before you get some feedback.

▓ Speak ▓▓▓▓▓▓▓▓▓▓▓▓▓▓▓▓▓▓▓▓▓▓

▓ Role play ▓▓▓▓▓▓▓▓▓▓▓▓▓▓▓▓▓▓▓

1 • Divide the class into groups of three or four students. Tell them to decide which town or city the new building is going to be in. It could be where they live or where they study. They should then agree on the type of building to be built. There are some examples in their books. You could elicit more ideas, e.g. a college, a leisure centre, a post office.

2 • Once these decisions have been taken, go through the instructions.

3–4 Stop the activity after about five minutes and give students a few more minutes to prepare their presentation to the class. They will need to say what their new building will be, possibly where it will be, and which architect they have chosen and why. One person from each group should make the brief presentation.

Grammar extra

Relative clauses (2)

▓ Read ▓▓▓▓▓▓▓▓▓▓▓▓▓▓▓▓▓▓▓▓▓▓▓▓

1–2 Ask students to read the text and answer the questions.
• Check answers.

Answers

1 Miss Barton must leave her house because the council have said it is not fit to live in, and because she can't afford to pay for the necessary repairs to make it fit to live in.

2 She feels angry about having to move. The previous owners had promised to pay for the repairs before she moved in, but didn't.

▓ Exploring concepts ▓▓▓▓▓▓▓▓▓▓▓▓▓▓

1–3 This grammar section is an extension of Relative clauses (1) in Unit 7. If your students did this unit some time ago, you could remind them of what they studied there.
• You could write these two sentences from the text on the board and ask these questions.
1 *Miss Barton, who is 72 years old, lives alone.*
2 *'They promised to pay for any repairs which were needed before I moved in,' she says.*
Which are the relative clauses? (Underline these on the board.) *Which relative clause gives non-essential information and which gives essential information?* (Sentence 1: non-essential information; Sentence 2: essential information.) You could ask for / give the names of each type of clause: non-defining, defining.
• Students can now do question **1** in pairs. Check answers before they go on to **2** and **3**. They can check their ideas in the **Language commentary** on p.136 before you do a final check. Alternatively, you could work through the questions with the class.

Answers

1–2 The cottage ⟨where⟩ she has lived happily for the last 20 years is … (essential information)
Now, at a time ⟨when⟩ Miss Barton simply wants to live a quiet life, the council says … (essential information)
The inspector ⟨whose⟩ report led to the council's decision said … (essential information)
It is unlikely that Miss Barton will be able to afford the necessary repairs, ⟨which⟩ could cost as much as £20,000. (non-essential information)
Miss Barton, ⟨who⟩ has three months to find a new home, blames … (non-essential information)
They promised to pay for any repairs ⟨which⟩ were needed before I moved in … (essential information)
This is the reason ⟨why⟩ I am so angry now. (essential information)
Miss Barton is not the kind of woman ⟨who⟩ accepts help easily. (essential information)

3 a *who* refers to people, *which* refers to things.
Both pronouns can be replaced by *that* in defining clauses, but not in non-defining clauses.
b whose **c** where **d** why **e** when

Exploitation

1 • Check answers before students talk in pairs. Tell them to give reasons for **a** and **b**.

Answers
a where   **b** whose   **c** why

• Hear some ideas.

2 • Ask students to read the text and the sentences which follow. Deal with any new vocabulary.
 • Explain the activity to the class. As students do the exercise on their own, monitor, indicating mistakes and getting students to correct them. Finally, check answers.

Answers
2 a famous art and culture museum in Paris, where visitors can see permanent and temporary exhibitions of all kinds of art.
3 The Centre, which was finished in 1978, is located
4 first thought of the idea in 1969, when he became the President of France.
5 by Renzo Piano, who is Italian, and
6 Richard Rogers, whose other designs include the Lloyds building in London.
7 The lifts, which are painted red,
8 the escalators, which are in clear plastic tunnels,
9 giant tubes, which carry water, electricity and air all around the Centre, are
10 its ultra-modern style, which they thought was too industrial.
11 the Centre, which attracts 26,000 visitors a day, has been

3 a You could demonstrate the activity by building up an example on the board of, e.g. an important building: *(Name)_____ art gallery, which is situated in the centre of (Name of city) _____, has several famous paintings by Picasso which used to be in private collections.*
 • Students then write short descriptions.
 • Monitor the activity, helping and indicating mistakes.
 b Ask students to exchange descriptions with a partner and choose the description they think is the most interesting. Ask students to read some out.

— p. 101 —

Exploring words

Buildings and materials

1 a In pairs, students match the words to the parts of the buildings. They will know some but not all of these words. You could either explain the words they don't know, or use this as an opportunity for dictionary work.

Answers
aerial **d**   arch **f**   attic **i**   balcony **e**   basement **k**   chimney **d**
doorway **a**   roof **h**   shutters **g**   tiles **b**   wall **l**   window **j**

 b Check the meaning of the words in the list before they start. When most pairs have finished, check answers.

Possible answers
The balconies are probably made of wood.
The walls are made of bricks or concrete.
The windows are made of glass.
The castle roof is made of metal.
The castle is made of stone.

 c Students can work in pairs to make their lists or you could elicit ideas from the class. Get them to give examples as you go through.

Possible answers
1 Precious metals: gold, silver, platinum
  Non-precious metals: tin, iron, copper, brass, lead, aluminium
2 Cutlery is made of steel.
  The back of my watch is made of steel.
  My ring is made of gold / platinum.
  My necklace is made of silver.
  The bottom of a saucepan is made of copper.
  Pipes are made of copper or lead.
  Saucepans are made of aluminium.
  The door handle is made of brass.

2 • As before, students can use dictionaries to check the meanings of words they don't know, or you can explain words to them. The easiest way to do this is by drawing the shapes on the board. Check answers.

Possible answers
The arch is curved.
The tower is pointed and round; the other walls are flat and straight.
The apartment building is probably rectangular.
The roofs are sloping.

3 • Divide the class into groups of three or four students. Demonstrate the activity with the class first. Tell them that the object can be in their classroom, in a house or flat, or in another kind of building. To make the game easier they could give their group this information first. Make sure they realize they can't ask questions like: *What shape is it?* but must ask *Is it round? Is it made of steel?* etc. The student who guesses correctly then thinks of an object.

— p. 102 —

Writing

A letter expressing opinions

Discuss

1–2 Students could spend a few minutes discussing the ideas in small groups or you could elicit ideas from the whole class. You could ask some of these questions: *What is the level of unemployment in their country? Which age group is most affected? What happens to young people who have no jobs? Are there a lot of homeless people in their country? How many are young people? Why are they homeless? Where do they sleep? How does the public feel about homeless people?*

Possible answers

2 The government should
   – encourage people to stay on at school to get qualifications.
   – pay companies to employ young people.
   – provide more houses or hostels especially for young people.
   – encourage young people to stay at home with their parents.

▬ Read ▬

- Before you ask students to read the text and answer the questions, check *resident*, *refuge* and *council*.
- After students have read the text, elicit some ideas and deal with any vocabulary queries.

Possible answers

   – A resident of Oak Street would probably be worried. They would expect young people to cause problems. (Noise, theft)
   – An unemployed homeless young person would probably be pleased, as it would give them somewhere to live.
   – Someone who lived five kilometres from Oak Street might think it was a good idea. It wouldn't really affect them.

▬ Brainstorm and notes ▬

1 • Divide the class into small groups. Allow groups about five minutes to think of ideas for and against the refuge. Elicit ideas and write these on the board in note form.

Possible reasons

For	Building has been empty for two years. Will provide temporary accommodation for 30–40 young people.
Against	No work for young people in that part of the town. Young people will not feel welcome there – residents against the idea.

2 • Monitor and help as students make notes.

▬ Write ▬

1 • Before students start writing, check the **Reminder** box.
   • Students write the first draft of their letter.

2 • Students exchange letters with someone whose opinions they don't know. As they read the draft letter they should keep in mind the questions on layout, content, etc.

3 • Students hand back their letters and make one or two suggestions for improvement.

4 • Set the final version of the letter for homework.

▶ **Writing model 10 (photocopiable) TB p.133**

Language in action

Checking and correcting

▬ Introduction ▬

1 • Before you play **10.3**, ask students to read the questions in their books.
   • Play the recording and check answers.

10.3

B Oh, hello, is that Mr Smith?
S It's pronounced Smythe actually.
B I'm sorry, Mr Smythe. This is the Sports Club here. We're just ringing to check that the information we have on our members' files is still correct. We've had a few problems recently with our new computer system – that's why we're contacting all our members. Have you got a few minutes to spare?
S Yes, that's fine.
B Thank you – it shouldn't take too long. OK, I'd just like to check your name again. It's Smythe – and that's S-M-Y-T-H-E. Is that right?
S No, it isn't actually. In fact, there's no E on the end.
B OK, thank you. And your first names, Mr Smyth. We have Michael, Stuart, Humphrey. Is that correct?
S No, I'm afraid that's completely wrong. It should be Glen, Edward – I've only got two names.
B Oh dear, we're not doing very well, are we?
S No, are you sure you've got the right person?
B I certainly hope so, let me just check your address. Is it 33, Salisbury Avenue? Have we got that right?
S Yes, that's correct.
R And the postcode is CO3 3FG.
S No, I'm afraid that's not right. In fact, it isn't CO anything. It's CM5 6RD.
B Oh no. That's a different town. I'm so sorry. Let me just check again on the computer. I won't keep you a moment.
   Hello, Mr Smyth, I can't find your details anywhere on the computer.
S That's strange, I've been a member of the tennis club for more than 15 years now.
B This is not the tennis club, Mr Smyth, it's the squash club. I'm so sorry to have troubled you.

Answers

a The speakers are: Mr Smyth and someone who works for the Sports Club.
b She is telephoning Mr Smyth to check that the information on his file is still correct.
c The caller makes four mistakes. (Five, if you count the fact that she has the wrong person altogether.) (Wrong pronunciation of name, wrong spelling of name, wrong first names, wrong postcode.)

2 • Play **10.3** again. This time students correct the wrong information. Check answers.

Answers

Smyth	Glen Edward	CM5 6RD

3 a Students could either work in pairs to list the expressions they remember or you could elicit ideas from the class and write them on the board.

b When students can't think of any more expressions, they should look at Tapescript **10.3** on p.147 and add any new ones there (or any others that they know) to their lists.

- Check ideas. Write all the expressions on the board and make sure students note them down. You could leave the list on the board for students to refer to during *Practice*.

Answers

Checking information	Correcting information
Is that (Mr Smith)?	No, it isn't actually.
I'd just like to check …	No, I'm afraid that's completely wrong.
Is that right?	No, I'm afraid that's not right.
Is that correct?	There's (no 'e' on the end).
Let me just check …	It should be …
Have (we) got that right?	It isn't … It's …

■ Pronunciation ■■■■■■■■■■■■■■■■■■■■■■■■■■■■ p. 153 ■

This section looks at emphatic stress.

1 a Ask students to read the conversations and in pairs to decide which syllables they think will be especially stressed in B's responses.
- You could elicit ideas but don't confirm whether students are right or wrong.

b Play **10.4** so that students can check their ideas.
- Check answers.

10.4

1 A So you're going to Italy. Lucky you!
 B I'm not going for a holiday! I'm going there on business!
2 A Is that the Grand Hotel?
 B No. This isn't the Grand Hotel. It's the Hilton Hotel.

Answers
See stress marked above. The speakers use strong stress on these syllables to point out that A's information is wrong, and to correct the wrong information.

c Play **10.4** again. Ask students to repeat B's replies.

2 a Ask students to read the information in their books and listen to the first example exchange.
- Play **10.5**. Pause after each sentence where marked * and nominate a student to correct the information. Remind them to stress the information which is wrong and the information which is correct. There are many possible answers.

10.5

Your surname is Smith. Is that right?
No, it isn't Smith. It's Kennedy.

Sorry. You live at 60, Smith Avenue?*
And that's in Black Hill?*
Oh, dear. We're not doing very well here are we? I'd better check where that is. It's in Tasmania, isn't it?*

I'm so sorry. Can I check your postcode? 3134?*
Oh well, almost right that time. Telephone number 9577 5291.*
Oh well, let's hope that's the last mistake. Finally, your date of birth. The 14th of April 1980.*
I'm terribly sorry. We've been having a lot of problems recently with the computers. I can't apologize enough.

b Play **10.6**, which is the whole conversation. Students simply listen. Point out that this is one possible version.

10.6

A Your surname is Smith. Is that right?
B No, it isn't Smith. It's Kennedy.
A Sorry. You live at 60, Smith Avenue?
B No, it isn't 60, it's 16.
A And that's in Black Hill?
B No, it isn't in Black Hill. It's in Forest Hill.
A Oh, dear. We're not doing very well here, are we? I'd better check where that is. It's in Tasmania, isn't it?
B No, it isn't in Tasmania. It's in Victoria.
A I'm so sorry. Can I check your postcode? 3134?
B No, it isn't 3134. It's 3131.
A Oh well, almost right that time. Telephone number 9577 5291.
B No, it isn't 9577 5291. It's 9877 5291.
A Oh well, let's hope that's the last mistake. Finally, your date of birth. The 14th of April 1980.
A No, it isn't the 14th of April. It's the 14th of January.
B I'm terribly sorry. We've been having a lot of problems recently with the computers. I can't apologize enough.

■ Practice ■■■■■■■■■■■■■■■■■■■■■■■■■■■■■■■ p. 103 ■

1 a Divide the class into pairs. Tell each student to write down any facts they know about their partner. This should include the facts on the page. They could also include age, job or occupation, hobbies.

b Students should take turns to 'phone' each other to check their information. This is most effective when students sit back to back or opposite each other. They should have similar conversations to the one they heard in *Introduction*.
- Monitor, correcting any wrong expressions or incorrect intonation. Don't worry about other mistakes you hear.

■ Role play ■■■■■■■■■■■■■■■■■■■■■■■■■■■■■■■■■

2 • Students can do the role plays in the same pairs. Decide who is A and who is B. Ask them to turn to the appropriate page in their books and read the instructions. Check that there are no problems with vocabulary and that students understand who starts each conversation. You could demonstrate how to begin **Situation 1**. Tell students to change any wrong information in their books.
- Monitor, but don't interrupt as students work through both role play situations. Round off the lesson with feedback on any points you noted during monitoring.

■ **Language check** ■■■■■■■■■■■■■■■■■■■■■■■■■■■■

Follow the usual procedure.

11 Fashions

Theme

The overall theme for this unit is fashions.
Preview Eating styles
Listening Body adornments
Skills Tastes in music
Grammar extra Fashion models
Writing Films, books and music

Grammar

- Review of *have* and *get*
- *have something done*
- *so* and *such*

Vocabulary

- Adjectival suffixes
- The Arts

Writing

- Writing a film, album, book review

Functional language

- Apologizing: preparing someone for an apology, apologizing, accepting an apology

Pronunciation

- Pitch and emphatic stress

Workbook

- Grammar and functional language as above
- Topic vocabulary: the arts; idioms with *play*
- Extracts from newspaper articles on music

Preview

This section looks at the theme of changing eating styles. The reading text and the recording also contextualize the review language: *have* and *get*.

▨ Your thoughts ▨▨▨▨▨▨▨▨▨▨▨▨▨▨ p. 104 ▨

- You could introduce the theme by asking students to describe what they can see in the pictures.

1 • Divide the class into pairs or groups of three or four students to discuss the question. You could start by giving examples about yourself.

2 • You could ask students to think about the following: *Who cooks? How much time is spent on cooking and preparing food? How is food cooked? Do people eat the same foods? Do people eat out more? Do people buy ready-made meals? Do people still eat all together as a family?*
- Monitor, listening to students' ideas, then elicit a variety of opinions / information.

▨ Read ▨▨▨▨▨▨▨▨▨▨▨▨▨▨▨▨▨▨▨▨▨▨

1a–b Before students read the article they should quickly answer questions **a** and **b**. You could elicit ideas and write them on the board to use as a checklist while they read.

2 • Ask students to read the article to check their ideas. Check the answers to **a** and **b** according to the text.

Ideas from text
a hot dogs, hamburgers, fried chicken, pizza.
b It's easier – you don't have to spend time making the food; you don't need to do much, if any, washing up afterwards; Americans work harder then they did thirty years ago so they don't have time; fewer women are full-time housewives; eating is regarded as something you do while you are doing something else.

▨ Vocabulary ▨▨▨▨▨▨▨▨▨▨▨▨▨▨▨ p. 105 ▨

- Give students a few minutes to do the exercise on their own or in pairs, then check answers. They can refer back to the text if they like.

Answers
a not really surprising
b similar kind (of fast food restaurant)
c put quickly (informal)
d to spend a long time working hard (like a slave) in unpleasant working conditions
e the extra advantage

- Explain any other important vocabulary which students want to know.

Listen

1 • Play **11.1**. Check the answer to the question.

11.1

I   You've lived in Spain for some time now.
M   Yes, about twelve years.
I   And have you noticed any changes in people's eating habits in that time?
M   Oh yes.
I   What kind of changes have you seen?
M   Well, I suppose the biggest change is that women are spending less time in the kitchen than before. A lot of women, particularly in the cities, go out to work nowadays and, of course, have very busy lives. And it seems that they're less prepared to spend the free time they do have preparing elaborate meals.
I   So they don't spend as much time cooking?
M   That's right. They still cook but it tends to be fairly quick things.
I   What about ready-cooked meals?
M   Yes, they're getting more popular but they're still not nearly as popular as they are in Canada and the States.
I   Do people have microwaves?
M   Yes, they do. More and more people are getting microwaves.
I   Hmm. Any other changes?
M   Yes, lunch is changing. People used to spend a long time over lunch. Some still do, of course, but now a lot of people just have a sandwich for lunch. I'm talking about during the week, of course, not weekends.
I   That's still the big family meal?
M   On the whole, yes.
I   What about young people? Have their eating habits changed?
M   That's where I notice most of the changes. Fast food is very popular – McDonald's, Burger King, that sort of thing. Young people nowadays tend to prefer to eat hamburgers than the traditional Spanish 'tapas'.
I   The snacks they serve in the bars?
M   Yes. But of course, it's a fashion and like all fashions it could change tomorrow.
I   Can I just ask you one last question?
M   Sure.
I   Have you got a microwave?
M   I'm afraid I have to admit that I do. I got it for Christmas. It was a present from my mom – but it's still in its box.

Answer

A lot of women go out to work and have very busy lives. (Article: fewer women are full-time housewives.)

2 • Ask students to read statements **a–f**. Play **11.1** again then check answers.

Answers

a   True
b   False (They are quite popular.)
c   False (Most people don't.)
d   True
e   True
f   False (She hasn't used it yet.)

Have your say

1–2   Students can discuss these questions in pairs or small groups. Check that they understand the comment 'Fast food will be the death of us' before they start. ('Fast food is very bad for us.' Literally – 'Fast food will kill us'.)
   • Allow a few minutes for students to exchange opinions then elicit ideas.

Possible answers

1   Fast food usually contains a lot of fat – too much fat in one's diet is bad for you. It can lead to heart attacks. It contains a lot of calories. If you eat a lot of fast food you could become overweight – obesity leads to health problems.

A little fast food probably doesn't do you any harm but eating only fast food can't be good for you. A diet needs to be varied.

2   **What** – You should eat a varied diet: lots of fresh fruit and vegetables, and carbohydrates to give you energy. You should limit the amount of fat you eat in your diet and not eat too much red meat. You should drink lots of water; you shouldn't drink too much alcohol.
   When – You should eat when you are hungry. You should make sure you eat a proper breakfast and not eat a heavy meal just before you go to bed.
   How – You should sit down to eat and take your time eating.
   How often – You should eat three main meals a day and try not to snack between meals. If you do need a snack you should eat a piece of fruit and not a packet of crisps or a bar of chocolate.

— Review – *have* and *get* —————————

This section is not a grammar review, but looks at the different meanings and forms of *have* and *get*.

1–3   Students can do these exercises on their own, check ideas with a partner, then check with the **Language commentary** on p.137. Finally, check answers.

Answers

1 a   2   b   3   c   5   d   1   e   4
   – When *have* means *take, eat or drink* or *experience* you can use both the simple and continuous forms.

2 a   You can use *have got* in sentence **1b**: *Have people got microwaves?* and *have got to* in sentence **1c**: *You haven't got to do much washing up afterwards*.
   b   The past tense of *have got* is the same as the past tense of *have*: *had*.

3 a   2   b   3   c   1

Check

4 • Allow students a few minutes to do the exercise. They could compare answers with a partner before you go through them.

Answers

a   I have a mobile phone.
b   Both alternatives are possible.
c   Both alternatives are possible.
d   Ivan had a beard when he was at university.
e   Both alternatives are possible.
f   You don't have to apologize.

5 •   Students discuss the questions in pairs. Tell them to choose four questions that they have something to say about. If there is time, they could discuss more than four. Make it clear that they are not supposed to give one word answers.

•   You could round off the lesson by hearing one or two answers to each of the questions.

— p. 106 —

Listening

The theme of this section is the fashion of ear- and nose-piercing and tattoos. The recordings also contextualize the grammatical structure: *have (get) something done*.

■ In your experience

1–2   Discuss these questions in pairs, small groups or as a whole class. Deal sensitively with this topic.

•   Elicit students' opinions. Don't worry if students use the *have something done* structure incorrectly at this point.

■ Listen

1 a   This activity gives students practice in listening for specific information. Tell students that they are going to hear five people talking about ear- and nose-piercing and tattoos. The first time they listen they should complete the table in their books with short answers.

•   Play **11.2** through without stopping. Then check answers.

11.2

Speaker 1   I had my ears pierced first when I was 16. Erm, I think it was a birthday present from my parents, that's the reason that I originally had it done, and then I had a second earring put in probably about three years later just because it was fashionable.

Speaker 2   I had my left ear pierced oh back at the end of the 1970s erm and I had a gold small gold ring in my ear for a long time and I occasionally would vary that but I stopped wearing it when I got a proper job 'cos I was told it looked unprofessional but I still put it in from time to time.

Speaker 3   I've taken them out recently erm because I don't know I've got too old, I've got too old for wearing them. They looked OK on me when I was young but now they look a bit daft so I've got rid of them.
When did you have it done?
When I was about 16.

Speaker 4   About two months ago I had my nose pierced with a silver stud. I'd been wanting to get it done for a long time but my mum told me that my nose was too big so I decided that I wanted to get it done anyway and I think it suits me but my mum didn't like it.

Speaker 5   I had my left ear lobe pierced about two or three years ago and I was goaded into it by my teenage daughters – and they quite liked the idea of their father approaching middle age with still a little rebellion left in him.

Answers

1   Speaker 1 ears, Speaker 2 ear, Speaker 3 ears, Speaker 4 nose, Speaker 5 ear.

2   Speaker 1 between 16 and 19, Speaker 2 end of 1970s, Speaker 3 at 16, Speaker 4 two months ago, Speaker 5 two or three years ago.

b   Play **11.2** again. Check answers.

Answers

–   Speaker 2 doesn't wear his earring any more because he was told it didn't look professional. Speaker 3 doesn't wear his earrings any more because he thinks he's too old to wear earrings now. He thinks they look stupid on someone his age.

2a–b   Elicit ideas to the questions from the whole class or ask students to discuss their ideas in pairs for a few minutes first.

Possible answers

a   – By *a proper job* Speaker 2 probably means a permanent full-time professional post. He probably had a series of temporary jobs before.

b   – Wearing an earring shows a little rebellion because it is still considered unacceptable by some more traditional people for men to wear earrings.
– Other ways of showing rebellion are having long hair (men), having a shaved head, having brightly coloured hair, having a very unusual hair style, having lots of tattoos, wearing unconventional clothes.

3   •   Ask students to read questions a–c. If you like you could predict possible answers to the questions before you play the tape. Ask students to take notes in answer to the questions as they listen.

•   Play **11.3** . Allow students a few moments to compare answers with a partner. If necessary play the tape again, then check answers.

11.3

My first tattoos were the ones were ones on my hands done, done at school with a few mates – Indian ink – and they're probably the ones I hate the most now and they kind of grew. A friend of mine became a tattooist and I had an old tattoo on my right arm, which I didn't like. It was a skull and a snake and he covered it up quite nicely with a pattern and er then he showed me some more, so I had another on the inside of my arm then I moved over to my left arm and had a few on there to balance things up a little, erm, all of which I regret today. I wish I'd listened to dad who said, 'You'll regret those.' I didn't finish there. I had one on my leg as well but fortunately then I moved away from my friend who was quite good at giving me free tattoos – they didn't cost any money. I suppose these ones would cost quite a lot of money but no, I'd like to be free of tattoos and listen to dad. I wish I had …

Answers

a   His hands, both arms, one of his legs.
b   He moved away from the friend who did the tattoos free.
c   He wishes he didn't have tattoos.

■ Have your say

1–2   Students can discuss these questions in pairs or small groups.

■ Vocabulary

1–2   Students could discuss their ideas to 1 in pairs and check their answers with you before they do 2. Alternatively, you could do 1 with the whole class and 2 in pairs. Do the first one as an example.

- Check answers to 1. You could write these up on the board in a table.

Answers

a	-al
	emotional

-ant	-ent	-able	-ive	-ful
important	confident	comfortable	attractive	careful
significant	intelligent	fashionable	effective	powerful
	patient	reasonable	expensive	successful
		protective	useful	

b The adjectives which don't form the negative with *un-* are: *(in)significant, (im)patient, (in)effective, (in)expensive, careful (careless), powerful (powerless), useful (useless)*. Students could add the negative forms to their tables.

- Elicit some example answers to 2 if you have time.

— Grammar – *have something done* —— p. 107 —

■ Exploring concepts ■

1–3 Students can answer the questions in pairs and then check their ideas in the **Language commentary** on p.137 before you go through answers with them.

Answers

1 1 The speaker did the action herself in **b** and **c**.
  2 Another person did the action for her in **a**.

2 a The structure *have something done* is formed with *have* (in all tenses) + object + Past participle.
  b In the *have something done* structure the object comes between *have* and the Past participle. In the Past perfect tense the object comes after the Past participle.

3 • We can only use *get* in imperatives.
  • We can only use *have* in the Present perfect.

■ Exploitation ■

1 • Students can do this exercise on their own, then compare answers with a partner.

Answers

a She can't decide whether to get her ears pierced.
b I had to get my glasses fixed because they were broken.
c Have you had the window repaired yet?
d She is going to get her skirt shortened.
e I had the flowers delivered to her house.

2a–b Divide the class into A / B pairs. Elicit or provide a couple of example dialogues and practise them with the class before students do the dialogues on their own.
  Student A *Do you cut your own hair?*
  Student B *No, I don't.*

Student A *When was the last time you had it cut?*
Student B *Last month.*
- Tell Students A to ask all the questions and B to respond, then change over. Monitor, getting students to correct any mistakes you hear them make. Ask a few students to give information about their partner.

3 • Students can continue to work with the same partner. Allow students three to five minutes to do the activity, then elicit ideas. You can either provide vocabulary as students do the exercise or during the elicitation stage.

Possible answers

- At the hairdresser's
  You can have your hair cut / trimmed / permed / tinted / bleached.
  You can have highlights / lowlights done.
  In some salons you can have your eyelashes and eyebrows tinted, and you can have a manicure. (Note: We don't use the *have something done* structure for *manicure*.)
- At the dentist's
  You can have your teeth checked / cleaned / x-rayed / filled / crowned.
- At a garage
  You can have your car repaired / fixed / mended / resprayed.
  You can have the oil checked / changed.

4 • Students can stay in the same pairs to do this freer speaking activity. Give an example: *I'd have my house painted bright yellow. Then I'd buy lots of new furniture …*
- Monitor, but don't correct. Use this as an opportunity to see how well students can use the *have something done* structure. Elicit a few examples to round the lesson off.

▶ **Photocopiable activity 19 p.173**

—— p. 108 —

Skills

The theme of this section is tastes in popular music.

■ Speak and write ■

1 • Divide the class into pairs. Ask students to read through the music questionnaire and add two more questions of their own. Monitor, helping with vocabulary where necessary. Check each pair's ideas.

2 • Redivide the class into pairs so that students are not working with their original partner. They interview their new partner and write down their partner's answers on their questionnaire.

3 • Students should give a brief resumé of their partner's tastes in music. With a large class you could ask each student to choose one piece of information about their partner.

■ Read ■

- You might like to introduce the reading text by checking what students know about the Beatles.

Background information

The Beatles, (John Lennon and Paul McCartney – who wrote most of the songs – George Harrison and Ringo Starr) were all born in Liverpool, in England. They were most popular in the 1960s and 1970s although they are still popular. They split up in 1970. John Lennon made some albums with his second wife, Yoko Ono. He went to live in the United States and was assassinated outside his New York apartment in 1980. Paul McCartney formed the group *Wings* with his American wife Linda and had many hit records with them. George Harrison went solo for a while and then set up his own film production company. Ringo Starr, the drummer, went to live in Hollywood and appeared in a couple of Hollywood films.

- Ask students to read through the article and answer the question. You could pre-teach the following: *survey*, *album*, *the charts*, *idol*.

Answer

The Beatles are still popular with teenagers in Britain today because they grew up hearing Beatles songs (they are part of their childhood) and because the groups and singers of today don't last, whereas the Beatles' music has.

■ Guessing meanings ■■■■■■■■■■ p. 109 ■

1–2 Students can answer these questions in pairs.
- Check answers.

Answers

1 a consider to be (on a scale of importance)
      You would rate it 3.
   b complete
      A comprehensive guide to New York tells you everything you want to know about New York.
   c interest which doesn't get less
      Last means to go on for a long time. If something *appeals* to you, you like it.
   d take in
      If you put a paper tissue on top of some liquid, the tissue absorbs the liquid.
   e Intended to be thrown away when you've finished with them – they are not meant to last forever.
      You throw them away.

2 a *Being into* means being interested in; *uncool* means unfashionable.
   b *it's not my scene* means it's not the type of thing I like.

■ Understanding ideas ■■■■■■■■■■

1–4 Ask the students to read the text again and ask any questions about vocabulary. You will probably want to limit this to six to eight words. Allow enough time for students to answer the questions in pairs. Then check answers.

Possible answers

1 It was a comprehensive survey so they would have had to ask people of all ages. They possibly asked people aged between 10 and 60 or 65.

2 *disbelieving* and *supposed* on lines 22 and 23.

3 *This* refers to the fact that young people nowadays have their own CD players and spend a lot of money on music.

4 Possibly because young people get tired of things easily and want something different; possibly because the artists are nothing extraordinary. They can easily be replaced by another group or singer because they are all so similar.

■ Listen ■■■■■■■■■■■■■■■■■■■■■

1 - You could introduce this section by asking students to look at the illustration and see how many of the singers and groups they can name.

Answers

The photographs are of George Michael, Joan Baez, Madonna, Elvis, the Spice Girls, U2, the Supremes, Mick Jagger (the Rolling Stones).

- Before you play the tape, ask students to complete the sentences with one of the periods of time given. They can do this on their own or with a partner. Tell them that they do not need to use all the periods. Before you play the tape you could check their ideas, but if you do, don't confirm whether these are correct or not.

2 - Play **11.4** once. Tell students to correct any wrong answers as they listen.
   - Check answers.

11.4

I   … and who better to tell us than record producer Rod Wallace. Thanks for coming on the programme, Rod.
R   My pleasure.
I   My first question has to be 'Has popular music always existed?'
R   Well, pop music, as we know it today, only goes back to the 1950s, when teenagers in the USA began to dance to the rock and roll of singers like Little Richard and Elvis Presley. For the older generation in America at that time, rock and roll was the music of the devil. It was considered immoral as well as being too noisy.
I   A criticism made by many parents even today.
R   Oh, yeah. Pop music has continued to upset parents throughout its history.
I   So rock and roll was very much an American thing?
R   Yes, but it soon crossed the Atlantic, and in the 1960s Britain returned the compliment with dozens of British groups making it in the States. The most important of these were of course, the Beatles and the Rolling Stones.
I   Uhmmm. But pop music was changing, wasn't it?
R   Very much so. The 60s saw the rise of singer-songwriter-poets like Bob Dylan, Joan Baez and Paul Simon, many of whose songs criticized the war in Vietnam and American society at that time, which they saw as totally materialistic. They attracted an audience of young people who were dissatisfied with their parents' values. But there … there were a lot of different musical styles around in the 60s and 70s. There were black groups like The Supremes and The Jackson Family, and black solo artists like Otis Redding and Aretha Franklin. There was glam rock, folk rock, country rock, hard rock, punk rock, and groups like Pink Floyd and Genesis, who

wrote longer compositions called progressive rock. Oh, and two that got everyone dancing again in the 70s – disco with the Bee Gees, and reggae with Bob Marley.

I   I remember that! The whole world was dancing!

R   Yes. By the 80s pop music was a truly international industry and top acts like U2, George Michael, Elton John, Michael Jackson, Bruce Springsteen and Madonna were household names around the world. There were new musical styles too, like rap and new age. But good marketing came to be more important than musical talent in the success of some 90s groups like the Spice Girls or the Back Street Boys.

I   And what about the future? What will change?

R   The format in which we buy music has changed from the three-minute single, to the record album, to the cassette, to video and CD. I believe that in the future we'll buy music from the Internet. Songs will frequently be sung in English – wherever the singer's from – and pop music will still upset parents. You can guarantee that!

Answers

a	1950s	d	1970s
b	1960s	e	1990s
c	1960s		

3 • Give students time to read through the questions before playing the tape again for them to find the answers.

• Check answers. You could ask whether students agree with Rod Wallace's predictions and whether they can add any of their own.

Answers

a   American parents thought Rock and Roll was immoral and too noisy.

b   Bob Dylan was popular with some young people because he wrote songs which criticized the war in Vietnam and American society, his values and theirs were different from their parents'.

c   The decades which had the most different styles of pop music were the 60s and 70s.

d   Rod Wallace makes the following predictions about pop music: We'll buy music through the Internet; songs will frequently be sung in English wherever the singer is from; pop music will still upset parents.

■ Have your say

1–2 Divide the class into groups of three or four students. Check that students understand the quotations.

• Groups discuss the questions. Get a quick summary of ideas from each group.

• Allow a few minutes for each group to write their own controversial statement about music. These can be passed round the groups or you could read them out to the class. The class could vote on the one they like best.

▶ **Photocopiable activity 20 p.174**

Grammar extra

so and *such*

• You could introduce the topic of this section – fashion modelling– by asking students: *Would you like to be a fashion model? Why / Why not? What are the advantages and disadvantages of modelling as a career?* Use the photograph to pre-teach the words *fashion show* and *catwalk*.

■ Listen

• Ask students to read the questions first and take notes as they listen.

• Play **11.5**. Allow students a few moments to compare ideas with a partner then check answers. If necessary play again, then check.

11.5

I   Beatrice, you run your own modelling agency now?

B   Yes. I have done for quite a few years now.

I   And you were, of course, a successful model yourself in the 70s.

B   Thank you.

I   How would you say the modelling business has changed since you were a model?

B   I can probably sum that up in one word – money. Top models earn so much money nowadays that they can choose who they work for, when they work. Really, there's no comparison.

I   How did you get into modelling? Had you always wanted to be a model?

B   I was lucky. Someone approached me at a fashion show and asked me if I'd like to be a model. I'd had no experience at all, but modelling had always looked so glamorous on TV and I thought it would be exciting so I said 'Yes, please.'

I   And was it exciting and glamorous?

B   Yes, but I suppose I was a bit naive really. I had no idea that modelling was such hard work and that I'd have to work such long hours.

I   What were the most memorable moments of your career?

B   The most exciting was my first Paris Fashion Show. The most embarrassing was when I fell.

I   On the catwalk?

B   Yes. You remember the shoes that were fashionable in the 70s? At one show the heels I had to wear were so high that I fell over. It was rather embarrassing.

I   I bet it was. Would you recommend modelling as a career to young girls?

B   Yes, I would. The only problem is that not everyone is successful. So many young girls don't make it to the top. It really is such a difficult career to break into, but certainly it's a very exciting career if you're one of the lucky ones.

Answers

a   She thought it would be exciting.

b   She was surprised that modelling was such hard work and that she had to work such long hours.

c   Her most embarrassing experience was falling over on the catwalk during a fashion show.

d   The main problem is that not everyone is successful.

Exploring concepts

1–2 Either allow students a few minutes to do the exercise on their own or in pairs, then check their ideas in the **Language commentary** on p.138, or work through the exercises with the whole class. You could ask students to find all the examples of *so* and *such* in the **Tapescript** on p.148 before they do **1** and **2**.

Answers

1 • Use *such* before *a / an* + adjective + singular countable noun, etc.
   • Use *so* before an adjective without a noun.

2 *So / such* expressions + *that* express a result / consequence. (The consequence of the heels being so high was that she fell over.)

Exploitation

1a–b Students can do **a** on their own and **b** with a partner. Tell them to use each ending once only. Check answers to **a** before students do **b**.

Answers / possible answers

a 1 d **2** b **3** f **4** a **5** c **6** e
b 1 … she made herself ill.
   2 … she has no privacy.
   3 … she lost her job.
   4 … everyone wants her to model their clothes.
   5 … she never has time to go out.
   6 … she makes friends very easily.

2 • Students can do the exercise in pairs or on their own. Monitor, indicating errors.
   • Check ideas.

Possible answers

a Andy likes clothes **so** much that … (he spends most of his salary on them.)
b Designer clothes are **so** expensive that … (most people can't afford to buy them.)
c There were **so** many people in the shop that … (I decided to come back later.)
d The jacket was **such a** good bargain that … (he bought it immediately.)
e Paul has **such** big feet that … (he can't find shoes to fit him.)
f We spend **so** much time shopping that … (we don't have time for other things.)

3 a Ask students to write down notes on the topics in their books. Give an example: name of actor (*Brad Pitt*), why you like him (*good-looking, good actor*), etc. Make sure that students only write notes at this stage.
   b Ask students to tell their partner what they like or dislike using *so / such* structures. Tell them they can refer to their notes as they do so.
   • Monitor, but don't correct. Use this as an opportunity to see how well students are able to use the structures. Finally, hear some examples. Get students to correct any mistakes they make.

Exploring words

The arts

• Use the photographs to introduce the topic.

1 • Students can discuss the questions in pairs. Tell them they should say as much as they can about each topic. Allow a few minutes for this then ask a couple of students to tell you about their partners.

2 a Ask students to read through the exercise and check they understand all the words, then allow some time for pair discussions.
   b This exercise gives an opportunity for dictionary work. Students can work in pairs. Tell them they may need to look up key words, for example *live* in sentence 1 but should only look up as many key words as necessary.
   • Check answers. Then check the following words – *live, set, stage, props, lighting, works, gallery, chapter, screen.* Students should make a note of these.

Answers

1 A live concert.
2 A play.
3 An exhibition (paintings, sculpture).
4 A novel.
5 A film.

3 • Students can continue to work in pairs or in small groups, again looking up words they don't know.
   • Check answers. Then ask students to add the words from exercise **2b** to their lists (in italics below).

Answers

Cinema	Music	Theatre
director	album	cast
acting	conductor	director
cast	*live*	performance
performance	lyrics	play
plot	orchestra	playwright
screen	performance	plot
script	recording	title role
story	track	set
title role		*stage*
		props
		lighting

Books	Art
author	artist
autobiography	landscape
biography	portrait
fiction	*works*
non-fiction	*gallery*
novelist	
pen-name	
plot	
story	
chapter	

4 a Elicit ideas from the whole class. If your students are all from the same country the titles needn't be in English.

Possible answers
thriller: Alfred Hitchcock's *Psycho*
cartoon: *The Lion King*
war film: *The Killing Fields*
western: *The Magnificent Seven*
historical film: *Elizabeth*
horror film: *Nightmare on Elm Street*
disaster movie: *Titanic*
comedy: *National Lampoon*
romantic comedy: *Sleepless in Seattle*
science-fiction: *Star Wars*
musical: *Grease*

b Students discuss the type of films they like and dislike with a partner. Get feedback.

c You could discuss this question with the class.

5 a Divide the class into groups of three or four students. Check that they understand the following words before they start: *blockbuster, setting, time period.*
  • Set a time limit. Tell them that an outline of the story will be enough.

b Groups could either appoint a spokesperson to present their ideas or share the presentation. Then take a vote on which film will be successful.

— p. 112 —

Writing

Reviews

▌Read ▌

1 • Ask students to read the reviews. Check they understand that they have to decide what the reviewer's opinion is in order to give a star rating. They decide on a star rating.
  • Check ideas. You could ask students what words in the review made them decide.
  • Explain any important words which students want to know.

Possible answers
The Voyage of the Narwhal: excellent
Taming the Tiger: average or good
Elizabeth: excellent
Smile of the Shark: good

2a–b Students could spend a few moments discussing these questions in pairs before you hear their opinions. Alternatively, you could elicit opinions from the class directly. They should give reasons for their answers.

▌Brainstorm and notes ▌

  • Before you divide the class into pairs or small groups you could ask students to think of a film, video, book, TV programme and album they could write a review about. Then pair or group students according to their answers and preferences.
  • Students should discuss their answers to the checklist questions for their review and write these down in note form. (They can choose to have different opinions.) They will all need to take notes. Help with any vocabulary students need, as you monitor the discussion.

▌Write ▌

1 • Students should write the first draft of their review on their own.

2a–b Stop the activity at the end of the allotted time. Ask students to exchange reviews with someone from a different pair or group and consider the points in **b**. They should make a couple of suggestions for improvement, then hand back the review and discuss their ideas.

  c The final draft can be written for homework.

▶ **Writing model 11 (photocopiable) TB p.133**

— p. 113 —

Language in action

Apologizing

▌Introduction ▌

1a–b Divide the class into pairs. Ask students to look at the illustrations at the top of the page. For each of the four situations they should discuss what they think has happened, decide on the possible explanation a person apologizing would give, and make a note of their ideas. You could do the first one with them as an example. Elicit ideas and write them on the board in note form, but don't tell them if their ideas are right or wrong.
  • Monitor, helping with vocabulary where necessary.
  • Elicit some ideas but don't confirm any guesses.

2 a Play **11.6** once only. Students listen to see how many of their ideas were correct.
  • Check answers.

11.6

1
A Debbie?
D Yeah?
A You know that tape you lent me?
D Mm? What about it?
A Er, well, I'm afraid there's been a bit of an accident.
D What have you done?
A Well, actually, it wasn't me. It was my kid brother. He started playing with it and it got a bit tangled.
D Tangled?

A Yeah. It's more or less OK but I'm afraid it jumps a bit on one of the tracks.
D Which track?
A The title track.
D Oh, no, that's my favourite.
A I'm really sorry. I'll buy you another one.
D No, I don't want you to buy me another one, honest. It doesn't matter. It's not the end of the world.
A Well, thanks for being so nice about it.

2
A Ed, there's something I've got to tell you.
E What?
A You know your blue jacket?
E The one I lent you?
A Yes. I'm ever so sorry but I got tomato sauce all over it.
E What? How on earth did that happen?
A Sally and I had a bit of an argument and, well, she threw a plateful of spaghetti bolognese all over me.
E In the restaurant?
A Yes.
E In front of everyone?
A Yes! I tried to wash it out but, well, you can still see the stain quite clearly.
E Oh well, it can't be helped.
A I'm really sorry.
E Oh, don't worry about it. It really doesn't matter.

3
M I really don't know how to tell you this.
B Tell me what?
M Your car. I can't tell you how sorry I am.
B What's happened?
M There's been a bit of an accident.
B An accident? Are you all right?
M Yes, I'm fine, but the front headlamp's smashed and the wing mirror on the same side. It's all my fault. This car stopped suddenly in front of me and I crashed into him.
B Look, you're all right, aren't you?
M Yes, but …
B Well, that's all that matters. The insurance will cover the damage.
M But I feel really bad about it. You've only had it a few months.
B Matthew. Forget it! It's only a car!

4
B Christopher? It's Brian here. Look, I'm afraid I won't be able to come on Saturday. I've got to attend a conference in Prague.
C Oh well, never mind. It can't be helped.

Answers

Conversation 1 The tape has got tangled. Her younger brother started playing with it.
Conversation 2 The jacket has a tomato sauce stain. His girlfriend got angry with him and threw a plateful of spaghetti at him.
Conversation 3 The car has been damaged. The front headlamp and the wing mirror are smashed.
Conversation 4 The person can't go to dinner. They have to go to a conference instead.

b Play **11.6** again. Student A and Student B should each note down the language they are listening for. Remind them that they don't need to write down whole sentences. You could pause at the end of the first conversation and check that students are on the right track. At the end of the recording allow them a few minutes to tell each other the expressions they heard and note them down.

• Check answers before doing c. Elicit ideas and write them on the board under the headings.

Answers
Apologizing
1 / 2 I'm really sorry.
2 I'm ever so sorry but …
3 I can't tell you how sorry I am.
   I feel really bad about it.
4 I'm afraid I …

Accepting an apology
1 It doesn't matter.
   It's not the end of the world.
2 Don't worry about it.
   It really doesn't matter.
3 Forget it!
4 Oh well, never mind.
   It can't be helped.

c–d Before you play the tape again ask these questions: *When isn't it necessary to prepare someone for an apology and when is it necessary?* (It isn't necessary when it is something small or relatively unimportant. It is necessary when it is something important and / or the speaker thinks the other person will be very upset.) Play the tape again. This time you could stop at the end of each conversation and elicit the language used for preparing someone for an apology from the whole class. Write this up on the board.

Answers
Preparing someone for an apology
1 You know that (tape you lent me)?
1 / 3 (I'm afraid) there's been a bit of an accident.
2 You know your (blue jacket)?
3 I really don't know how to tell you this.

■ Pronunciation ▬▬▬▬▬▬▬▬▬▬ p. 153 ■

This section looks at pitch and emphatic stress.

1 a Ask students to read sentences 1–3 and continuations **a** and **b**. Tell them to listen to the tape and decide what they think the speaker will go on to say, sentence **a** or sentence **b**.
   • Play **11.7**. Pause for a moment after each speaker to allow students time to mark their answers.

11.7

1 There's something I've got to tell you.
2 You know that tape you lent me?
3 You know your new green shirt?

b Play **11.8** for students to check their answers.

11.8

1 There's something I've got to tell you. I'm getting married next month.
2 You know that tape you lent me? I've lost it.
3 You know your new green shirt? I'm afraid I burnt it while I was ironing it.

- Ask: *Does the speaker start high or low to give good news? What about bad news?* (The speaker starts high to give good news and low to give bad news.)
c Tell students that they are going to prepare their listener for bad news. Play **11.9**. Pause after each speaker and drill. Make sure students start low.

11.9

1 There's something I've got to tell you.
2 You know that tape you lent me?
3 You know your new green shirt?

2 a Ask students to read the expressions of apology and decide which syllables they think will be stressed and which will be the main stressed syllables.
b Play **11.10** so that they can check their ideas. Write up the answers on the board.

Note The main stress could also be on *really, sorry,* or *ever.*

11.10

1 I'm <u>really</u> <u>sorry</u>.
2 I'm <u>so</u> <u>sorry</u>.
3 I'm <u>ever</u> so <u>sorry</u>.

Answers
See Tapescript **11.10**.

c Tell students that they are going to hear two people apologizing. They have to decide which speaker sounds more sorry in each pair, **a** or **b**.
- Play **11.11** and check answers. Ask: *How does the speaker manage to sound extremely sorry?* (They give special stress to *really, so* and *ever* as well as *sorry* and speak in a lower tone.)

11.11

1 a I'm really sorry.
  b I'm really sorry.
2 a I'm so sorry.
  b I'm so sorry.
3 a I'm ever so sorry.
  b I'm ever so sorry.

Answers
1 a   2 b   3 b

d Play **11.11** again. Pause after each apology and drill.

▪ Practice ▪▪▪▪▪▪▪▪▪▪▪▪▪▪▪▪▪▪▪▪▪▪▪ p. 113 ▪

▪ Role play ▪▪▪▪▪▪▪▪▪▪▪▪▪▪▪▪▪▪▪▪▪▪▪▪▪

- Students could either stay in the same pairs for the role play or you could change pairings. If you think your students are likely to have problems thinking of explanations you could pair them up AA BB for an initial discussion and then divide them into A / B pairs.
- Tell Students A to read the instructions on the page and Students B to read the instructions on p.157. Check that they understand the situations and the vocabulary.

- Allow students a few moments to think of explanations. You can help with vocabulary if necessary but don't let them write down their ideas – they will end up reading a dialogue rather than doing a role play.
- When students are ready start the role plays. As this is a free activity don't correct any mistakes. You could round off the lesson by asking what the best or worst explanations were.

▪ Language check ▪▪▪▪▪▪▪▪▪▪▪▪▪▪▪▪▪▪▪▪▪

Follow the usual procedure.

12 Success

Theme

The overall theme for this unit is success.
Preview Personal ambitions
Reading Women's football
Skills How to be a success
Grammar extra Exams
Writing Winning the lottery

Grammar

- Review of advice language
- Third conditional
- *all, both, none, neither, either*

Vocabulary

- The language of money

Writing

- Writing an article

Functional language

- Review

Pronunciation

There is no pronunciation focus in this unit.

Workbook

- Grammar and functional language as above
- Topic vocabulary: money; British and American English; idioms with money
- Quotations about success

Preview

This section looks at the theme of personal ambitions. The reading and the recordings also contextualize the language of advice.

Your thoughts ▬▬▬▬▬▬▬▬▬▬ p. 114 ▬

1 • Ask students to write down three personal ambitions they have and when they would like to achieve them by. You could suggest the following topics: marriage, family, studies, job, flat / house, travel, retirement and give a few examples, e.g. *I'd like to have a family before I'm 30. I'd like to be a company director by the time I'm 40. I'd like to retire when I'm 50.*

2–3 Divide the class into pairs. Ask them to exchange information and briefly discuss whether they think it is important to have ambitions and why.

• Elicit any ambitions which pairs have in common and their ideas on question **3**.

Listen ▬▬▬▬▬▬▬▬▬▬▬▬▬

1 • Ask students to read the three radio programme extracts and predict what problems each of the speakers has. Students could first of all discuss this in pairs or you could elicit ideas directly from the whole class. Don't confirm whether their ideas are correct or not.

2 • Play **12.1**. Students check their ideas to **1** as they listen.
• Play the tape once (or twice if necessary). If you like you could stop and check after each speaker.

12.1

Speaker 1   My daughter Zoe is nine years old and wants to be a successful skater. She's at the ice-rink at six o'clock in the morning and again after school for a couple of hours. She comes home exhausted, has something to eat, spends half an hour on her homework and goes straight to bed. Weekends she's either doing more training or travelling the length and breadth of the country going in for competitions. I don't think that's any kind of life for a nine-year-old but it's one against two in our house. It seems I'm the only one who thinks there's something wrong with it. I think Zoe should be out with her friends and should be concentrating on her schoolwork, not spending her time chasing a dream. I'd like to know what you think.

Speaker 2   I'm phoning in for some advice. I'm twenty-five years old and I work for a large international company. The job's OK, the money's quite good – but it's not very exciting and quite honestly I can't really see myself here for the rest of my working life. What I'd really like to do is set up my own company. I've got one or two ideas and I think I'd be able to get a bank loan but it's a big decision and I don't know whether I could make a success of it or not. I'm in two minds about the whole thing.

Speaker 3   Hallo. I'm fourteen years old and my parents want me to be a professional musician. They're both musicians themselves. I've been having piano and violin lessons since I was five and I'm quite good, but not really good enough to make a career out of it. I've tried telling my parents that I'd rather have music as a hobby and do something else as a career but they won't take me seriously. I really don't know how to convince them.

Answers

Speaker 1 doesn't think that his daughter should be spending so much time on her skating. He thinks she should be out with her friends and concentrating on her schoolwork but his wife and his daughter disagree with him.
Speaker 2 doesn't know whether to stay in her present job or leave and set up her own company.
Speaker 3's parents want her to be a professional musician. She doesn't, but her parents won't listen to her.

- Students then spend a few moments in pairs discussing what advice they would give to each of the speakers. Elicit some ideas. Don't worry if students are not using advice structures correctly at this point.

3 • As students listen to █12.2█ they could take notes on the advice which the members of the panel give to Speaker 2.
 • Play the tape once (or twice if necessary), then check answers.

█12.2█

P You don't sound very confident, Nicole.
N No, I'm not really. I'm confident about the business – well, there is definitely a gap in the market for the product – but I've always worked for someone else before and the idea of being responsible for everything is quite scary.
P What do you think Nicole should do, James?
J Nicole?
N Yes?
J Is this what you really really want to do?
N Yes.
J Well, if you're absolutely positive that that's what you want to do, you should just do it, go for it, because if you don't, you might regret it later on.
P Professor Webb?
W It seems to me from what I've heard that Nicole is lacking in self-confidence but, don't take this as a criticism, Nicole, but are you?
N I am, yes.
W Well, I think you ought to consider doing a self-improvement course. Do you know the kind of thing I mean?
N Yes, I know what you're talking about, but I'm not sure that's really for me.
W Well, if you don't like the idea of doing a course, why don't you read one of the books there are on the subject? There are a lot about.
N Can you recommend one?
W 'Yes, You Can!' is very popular. 'How to Succeed in Business' is another. If I were you, Nicole, I would put your plans on hold for now. I wouldn't do anything until you yourself feel more confident that it's going to work. But that's just my advice.
P Has that been any help, Nicole?
N Yes, it has. Thank you.
P And so on to the next caller who is …

Answers
One speaker thinks that she should leave her present job and set up her own company if it's what she really wants to do, because if she doesn't, she might regret it later; Professor Webb thinks she should do a self-improvement course or read a book on the subject to help her become more confident. She suggests Nicole doesn't take any decisions until she feels more confident.

- Ask students whether they agree with the advice given or not. If they don't agree, get them to tell you what advice they would give. Check they understand *a self-improvement course.*

▌Vocabulary ▌

- Ask students to do the exercise in pairs. You could tell them that **a** and **b** relate to Speaker 1, **c** to Speaker 2, and **d**, **e** and **f** to Speaker 3. They could check the context with the **Tapescript** on p.149. Allow a maximum of five minutes for this.
- Check answers.

Answers
a all over (the country)
b trying to be something she will never be
c undecided; whether to leave and set up her own business or stay where she is – the problem
d listen / pay attention to what I'm telling them
e there is a need for the product and no one else is providing it at the moment
f wait, don't take any decisions yet

▌Read ▌   p. 115 ▌

1–2 Ask them to read the headings and answer any vocabulary queries. In pairs, they discuss which ideas would be useful to Nicole and question 2.
 • Check ideas.

Possible answers
The headings which might be useful to Nicole are:
 – Increase your self-esteem
 – Get organized
 – Avoid negative self-talk
 – Make better decisions
 – Reduce your worry
 – Feel more optimistic

▌Have your say ▌

1–2 Students can discuss these questions in pairs. You could add these extra questions to the ones in their books: *What other alternatives are there for people who need advice? What are the advantages and disadvantages of each one? Can you think of any other ways in which someone can increase their self-confidence?*
 • Elicit some ideas.

Review – Advice

1–3 Students can answer questions 1–3 on their own, check ideas with a partner and then check with the **Language commentary** on p.138. Follow this up with a whole class check.

Answers

1 The modal verbs *should* and *ought to*, and the phrases *Why don't you … ?* and *If I were you, I would …* are all followed by the infinitive without *to*.

2 The negative forms of the sentences are:
  a He *oughtn't to / ought not to* tell his boss
  b She *shouldn't* apologize.
  c I *don't think* you should go.

3 a means it's essential.
  b means it's a good idea.

Check

4 • Students can do these exercises on their own as written practice or in pairs as either written or spoken practice. If they are done orally students could take turns to give as many pieces of advice as they can for each situation using the words and phrases given.
  • Monitor, correcting any mistakes you hear or see.
  • Get feedback. You could write some of their ideas on the board.

Possible answers

You could use these ideas to elicit further examples.
  a *You shouldn't* wear that tie. *You shouldn't* ask if you can smoke during the interview.
  You ought to get that suit cleaned before the interview. *You ought to* find out as much about the company as you can before you go.
  If I were you, I would get my hair cut. *If I were you, I would* go to bed early the night before.
  b *Why don't you* get out more? *Why don't you* take up a sport?
  You oughtn't to / ought not to stay at home so much. *You oughtn't to / ought not to* watch so much TV.
  You should look for another job. *You should* take up a hobby like skydiving!
  c *I don't think you ought to* work so hard. *I don't think you ought to* work at weekends.
  You should relax more. *You should* get some exercise.
  If I were you, I would take a few days off. *If I were you, I would* get a life.

5 a Divide the class into pairs if they are not already in pairs.
  • Read through the instructions with the class and the examples.
  • Set a time limit for the letter writing.
  b Monitor during the writing stage. If there are mistakes in the advice language you could point these out and ask students to correct them, but don't worry about any other mistakes. Students will probably finish their pieces of writing at different times. Pass their letter on to any pair which is free to answer.

• If you have time at this stage in the lesson, you could make this a variation of Consequences. A number of pairs could read the original letter and write their advice, each time folding the paper so that only the letter can be seen by the next pair. At the end, the original writers can read the different advice and decide which is best.

— p. 116 —

Reading

The theme of this section is women's football, and the successful English women's football club Doncaster Belles. The text also contextualizes the language focus of the section, the third conditional.

In your experience

1–2 Divide the class into pairs or groups of three or four students.
  • Before students start the discussion check *spectator sports*. Elicit some examples of popular spectator sports, e.g. football, Formula 1, golf, basketball, horse-racing.
  • Allow students enough time to discuss the questions, then get feedback.

Read

1 • Ask students to read questions **a–e**. Check: *England* (The English national football team), *nowadays*, *split up*.

2 • Tell them that they have two minutes to find the answers to the questions. Remind them how to find information quickly – tell them not to read the whole article but to look for key words like *England*, *1920*, etc. Ask them to tell you when they have finished. (Good readers will take one minute or less.) Stop the activity after two minutes even if not all the students have finished.
  • Check answers.

Answers

  a Yes, several of the team play for England.
  b More than 50,000.
  c 500.
  d Lou Ryde.
  e She's a physiotherapist.

Close up

  • You could either give students a couple of minutes to answer the questions, or you could elicit ideas from the class directly.

Possible answers

  – *Prohibit* has a similar meaning. Other things which can be *banned* are: films, songs, plays, demonstrations. A person can also be *banned* from driving.
  – The verb is *succeed*, the adjective *(un)successful*, and the adverb *(un)successfully*.
  – *Classmate, room-mate, cell mate, flatmate.*

1–4 Ask students to read the text again, carefully, and then answer the questions either on their own or with a partner. Remind them that they will need to use their imagination to answer some of the questions.

- Check answers, then deal with any vocabulary queries.

Answers

1 *The cream* means the best. They are the best because they have won a large number of trophies and several of the team play for England.

2 Women's soccer was probably so popular during the First World War because there probably weren't any men's football teams then – all the men who were fit would have been away fighting. But people still wanted to watch football.
It was probably popular just after the war finished because there would have been a shortage of male footballers – a lot of men were killed or wounded during the war. Also by this time people would have got accustomed to watching women play.

3 They were probably banned because the people in charge of men's soccer didn't want the competition. Women's football had become too popular.
The ban meant that they had no proper place to play – they would have had to play in public parks. Not many people would have been able to watch them and they wouldn't have been able to charge them.

4 It means that they are also friends when they are not playing. They probably go out together socially, e.g. to the pub, for a meal.

■ **Have your say** ■■■■■■■■■■■■■■■■■■■■■■■■

- Students can discuss these questions in pairs or small groups. Before students start you could elicit some examples of sports where sportsmen are paid more than sportswomen, e.g. tennis, golf, boxing, horse-racing. Allow a few minutes for students to give their opinions, then get feedback.

─ Grammar – Conditional sentences (3) ───────

■ **Exploring concepts** ■■■■■■■■■■■■■■■■■■

1–3 Students can answer questions 1–3 on their own or with a partner, then check their ideas in the **Language commentary** on p.138 before a final teacher check.

Answers

1 The sentences refer to the past.

2 The third conditional is formed with *If* + Past perfect + *would* + *have* + Past participle.

3 The *if-* clause can come before or after the main clause. If the *if-* clause comes before the main clause, we put a comma at the end of it. If the *if-* clause comes after the main clause there is no punctuation.
Point out the weak pronunciation of *have* /həv/ or /əv/.

■ **Exploitation** ■■■■■■■■■■■■■■■■■■■■■■■■

1a–b Ask students to read the short text. Explain any vocabulary they don't know. Do the first sentence in **b** with them as an example. Warn them that some mistakes are of fact and some are of grammar.

- Monitor, indicating correct answers and mistakes.
- When students have corrected their mistakes, check answers with the class. Insist on correct pronunciation of weak forms.

Answers

Check whether students have found the correct sentences first. Sentences **2** and **8** are correct.

1 If Luke *hadn't* gone to Diana's party, he *would have gone* to bed earlier.

3 If he ~~wasn't~~ *hadn't been* so tired, he *would have remembered* to set his alarm clock.

4 He *wouldn't* ~~oversleep~~ *have overslept* if he *hadn't forgotten* to set his alarm clock.

5 He *wouldn't have woken up* if a colleague *hadn't phoned* him.

6 If a colleague *hadn't wondered* if he was ill, he ~~didn't phone~~ *wouldn't have phoned* him.

7 If he *hadn't* been on time, his boss *wouldn't have been* annoyed.

▶ **Photocopiable activity 21 p.175**

2 - Students can work in pairs and either do this as an oral or written exercise. You may need to pre-teach the following: *take a dog for a walk, put a dog on a leash (or lead), run after (chase), bite (bit, bitten), tear (tore, torn).*

- Monitor, getting students to correct any mistakes they make.
- Check ideas. You could write them on the board and use them for pronunciation practice.

Possible answers

– If the woman had put her dog on a leash (lead), it wouldn't have chased the other dog.

– If the woman's dog hadn't chased the man's dog, he wouldn't have got angry / wouldn't have shouted at her.

– If the dog had been on a lead, it wouldn't have torn the woman's coat.

– If they hadn't taken their dogs for a walk, nothing would have happened.

3 - If you did the previous exercise as a written exercise, do this as an oral pair exercise. It will give you the opportunity to see how well students are able to use the third conditional form.

- Monitor the activity. Correct as you monitor or at the feedback stage.
- Check ideas.

Possible answers
- I wouldn't have gone for a walk in the mountains in February.
- If I had gone for a walk, I would have told the people at the hotel where I was going.
- I would have worn proper clothes – an anorak, waterproof trousers, walking boots. I would have carried a small rucksack and taken chocolate and water with me. I wouldn't have taken chewing gum, crisps and cola.
- I wouldn't have decided to go on. I would have gone back as soon as it had started to snow.

Free speech

- Students can do this activity in pairs. Allow them a few minutes to think of two or three important events in their life and how the events affected them. Give them some examples: where they met a special person, what they studied at school or university and how this affected their future life, a holiday where something happened. You could give an example of your own, e.g. *I met my husband at a friend's wedding. If I hadn't gone to the wedding, I wouldn't have met him. If he hadn't been a friend of the groom*, etc.
- Students could report back on what their partner said.

— p. 118 —

Skills

Speak

1 • Students can either check the meaning of any words they don't know in their dictionaries, or with you.
  • Tell students they must limit themselves to three qualities.

2 • Allow time for students to compare ideas and add any other qualities they think are important, then elicit some ideas from the whole class.

3 • Students can do this exercise in pairs, then check their ideas in a dictionary. Alternatively, you could elicit ideas from the whole class.

Answers

ambitious	ambition
confident	confidence
dedicated	dedication
determined	determination
energetic	energy
enthusiastic	enthusiasm
intelligent	intelligence
motivated	motivation
talented	talent

Listen

1 • Play **12.3** once only. You could pause briefly after each speaker to give students time to tick the ideas they hear. Tell them they can tick several words more than once. Check answers after each speaker or at the end of the tape.

12.3
What kind of person do you think you have to be to be successful?

Speaker 1 Determined. Determined and ambitious. Erm, yes, you've got to have a single thing in your mind and you've got to be determined to go for it.

Speaker 2 I think you need to be confident, erm enthusiastic, and energetic.

Speaker 3 I think you have to be quite confident, and er perhaps quite lucky, too.

Speaker 4 I think you have to be very determined. Erm, you have to be confident. You have to not be afraid of disappointment. Erm, can't think of anything else.

Speaker 5 Flexible, and I think you need to be, have a sense of humour, erm I think you need to know exactly what you want to achieve, I think you need to have a sense of priorities.

Speaker 6 Hard-working, dedicated, erm, someone who can get on with people, yes, a good people manager, person manager, and focused, and that's about it.

Speaker 7 I think you need to be ambitious, you have to have a lot of belief in yourself, erm you have to do something that you enjoy, so you've got the enthusiasm for it, erm and that's about it.

Speaker 8 Single-minded, I think. You have to want it more than anything else, you have to want success in whatever field you're in. Erm, and I think you have to be obsessed and you have to stay obsessed. I think single-mindedness is the … is the most important thing.

Speaker 9 To be successful in anything, not any particular, not one particular business or field or anything …?
Erm oh my goodness! Erm very driven. Very motivated and very determined to succeed. Erm, I think you have to believe really passionately in whatever it is you're doing or whatever you're trying to succeed at … and you have to believe that it's going to work and you believe that you've got a really great idea, and just keep going, keep trying keep going. What else what else can I say?

Answers

ambitious ✓✓	good with people ✓
confident ✓✓✓	hard-working ✓
dedicated ✓	lucky ✓
determined ✓✓✓	motivated ✓
energetic ✓	single-minded ✓✓
enthusiastic ✓✓	self-belief ✓✓
flexible ✓	a sense of humour ✓
focused ✓	

2 • Do a quick class check to see which were the most popular ideas. Do not spend too long on this phase as you will return to this topic at the end of the lesson.

Read

1 • Ask students to decide whether they think the statements are True or False. Students could compare answers in pairs.

2 • Tell students to read the article to check their ideas and for general understanding.
  • Check answers.

Answers
a False **b** False **c** True **d** True

Guessing meanings p. 119

- Students can work on their own or in pairs. Allow about five minutes for this then check answers.

Answers

a *launch* means start.
Rockets are *launched* into space.

b A *short-cut* is a way of doing something more quickly.
The most direct route from A to B is in a straight line.

c An *incentive* is a stimulus, something which encourages you to do something.
Most people need something extra like a bonus to encourage them to work harder.

d *charm* is the special quality which some people have which attracts people to them. (It is a difficult quality to define so give some examples of people your students know who have or had this quality, for example Nelson Mandela, Princess Diana.)

Understanding ideas

1–4 Ask students to read the text again and deal with any vocabulary students want to know. You will probably want to limit this to six to eight words.

- Ask students to discuss the questions in pairs. Point out that *artists* (1) is used in the wider sense of the word and would include any creative person.
- Check answers.

Possible answers

1 Perhaps an unstable, insecure family background would make artists more creative. Poets and songwriters for example are often more creative when they are unhappy. It would also give novelists a wider experience of life which they could use in their writing.

2 Some examples of orthodox jobs are: mechanic, doctor, nurse, lawyer.
Some examples of unorthodox jobs are: night-club dancer, street artist, magician, stand-up comedian.

3 It means people might not see beyond your pretty looks; they might not take what you say seriously. A decorative ornament is something pretty which is put on display for people to look at and admire.

4 People would take their ideas more seriously.

Listen

1 • Check students understand the task, then play **12.4**, twice if necessary.
- Check answers.

12.4

Speaker 1   I suppose a big achievement for me personally was when I passed my maths GCSE. I didn't actually take the exam until I was forty and I'd always failed terribly at maths at school and been bottom of the class but when I when my children started secondary school I found that I couldn't help them with their maths so I decided to take the matter in hand and so I went to evening classes with my friend and passed my maths GCSE in a year, which I was very proud of.

Speaker 2   Something I found very hard to do originally was to stand up in front of lots of people, erm talk to them, in a in a comfortable way. Erm, it actually took me quite a long time to do that once I started my job. In the end I suppose it was really a matter of practising and doing it erm often enough, preparing myself for doing it. Erm, that took quite a long time to start with. I had to make sure that I had all my notes very carefully prepared and I rehearsed it. I used to stand in front of a mirror or record myself on video. And that was quite time-consuming but I think in the end it worked and … It doesn't it doesn't really worry me too much any more. I still feel a little bit nervous before I stand up in front of people but as soon as I'm there in front of them and I've started it feels quite natural and er I'm not unhappy about it any more.

Speaker 3   The thing I'm think I'm most proud of achieving is passing my driving test because I passed it when I was very young and I had to overcome a total loss of confidence in driving. That was because on my second test I had a very bad experience where the driving examiner grabbed the wheel from me and we almost collided with a bus. So when I eventually passed my test it was a really great sense of achievement because I felt that I had really been able to achieve something which I had thought I would never be able to achieve.

Answers / possible answers

Speaker 1 is proud of passing a maths exam. She is proud because she didn't take the exam until she was forty and because she had always been bad at maths when she was at school.
Speaker 2 is proud of being able to stand up and talk in front of people without feeling very uncomfortable. He is proud because it was something he found very hard to do originally.
Speaker 3 is proud of passing her driving test because she had to overcome a total loss of confidence in her driving abilities.

2 • Students can discuss their ideas in pairs.
- Check answers.

Answers

a to take control of the situation
b using too much time; had the desired effect
c fight against and defeat

Have your say

- Students can tell each other about their personal successes. Tell them that they can be small ones or big ones. Elicit a few examples from the class.

Speak

1 • Ask students to write down their own personal definition of success.

2 a Divide the class into groups of three or four students. Ask them to compare definitions and together agree on one. If they can't reach agreement they can simply choose one of them.

b They now have to draw up a five-point plan for being successful. Point out that their plan must relate to their definition of success.

c Each group should present their plan. The class can vote on the best plan.

— p. 120 —

Grammar extra

all, both, either, neither, none

▇ Read ▇

1 • Students exchange information in pairs. Hear a few opinions.

2 • Ask students to read the text. Explain any new vocabulary, then find out if anything like this has happened to anyone in the class.

▇ Exploring concepts ▇

1–3 Students can work on their own or in pairs, then check their ideas in the **Language commentary** on p.139. Check answers to 1 before they go on to 2 and 3. Follow this up with a whole-class check.

Answers

1 *all of the students I've known ..., none of them thought ..., Both of them were exceptionally bright, neither of them got an A grade, they both got Cs, They had both assumed ...*

2 a *All students hate exams.*
 b *all of the students I've known ...; none of them thought ...*
 c *Both of them were exceptionally bright; They both got Cs; They had both assumed ...*
 d *neither of them got an A grade*

3 • *neither* and *either* can be followed by a singular noun.
 • *both* is followed by a plural noun.
 • *none* is followed by *of the* + noun, or *of* + pronoun.

▇ Exploitation ▇

1 • Ask students to do the exercise and then check with a partner. Monitor, pointing out any mistakes.
 • Check answers.

Answers

a both **d** either
b Neither, both **e** all
c All, None

2a–c Give the class time to read through the instructions, then make groups of three. Elicit a couple of ideas from one student to demonstrate the task, then set a time limit before getting feedback on **b**. Set a time limit for **c**, then get feedback.

— p. 121 —

Exploring words

The language of money

1 a This is an opportunity for dictionary work. Students can do the exercise in pairs looking up any words and expressions they don't know.

• Check answers.

Answers

1 spends (*waste* means to use badly.)
2 borrow (The person who has sth *lends* it to another person.)
3 loan (A *mortgage* is money which the bank lends you to buy a house or flat.)
4 change (*cash* is money in coins or notes.)
5 a pension (An *inheritance* is money or property sb leaves you when they die.)
6 in the red (An account cannot be *bankrupt*, only a person. A person is *bankrupt* when they are legally unable to pay their debts.)
7 value (*cost* is the price of something. It is more usual as a verb.)
8 broke (*poor* is a permanent state of having very little money.)
9 well-off (*well-earned* does not mean rich. It is used with words like *rest, break, holiday, promotion, pay rise* and means that it is well deserved by the person who has or gets it.)

b Students could either continue to work in pairs or you could do this activity with the whole class, as 2 will involve more dictionary work.

Possible answers

1 You can *spend* money, a period of time (the weekend, the morning, the holiday). You can *waste* money, a period of time (the weekend, the morning, the holiday), food.

2 – *rich* colours are deep strong colours like dark red, purple, gold
 – *rich* in vitamins means it contains a lot of vitamins.
 – a *rich* and varied life is complex and interesting.
 – a *rich* chocolate cake contains a lot of fat, butter, eggs, etc.
 – *rich* soil contains a lot of minerals so it is good for growing plants.

3 a This means that you are overdrawn on your bank account.
 b This means she was wearing red clothes.
 c This means that they were indicating that traffic had to stop.

4 a took out
 b came into
 c went
 d set up

2 a Students can work in pairs. Before they do the exercise they should look up any words in the list they don't know in their dictionaries.

Answers

1 valuables **5** priceless
2 ✓ **6** expense
3 worthless **7** ✓
4 ✓

b Give students a few minutes to discuss the questions then elicit some answers.

▶ **Photocopiable activity 22 p.176**

3 a Divide the class into groups of three or four students. Go over the instructions with the class but don't give them any ideas. Give them a time limit to agree on their plan.
 b Ask one student in each group to present the group's ideas. Then take a vote on the best plan.

Possible ideas
- Knock down the house, sell the land to a building contractor, invest the money in stocks and shares, and property.
- Sell half the land, with the profit rebuild the house and make it into a luxury hotel with its own golf course.

— p. 122 —

Writing

Articles

- If your students come from different countries you could introduce the theme by asking them these questions: *Do you have a national lottery in your country? How does it work? What do you have to do to win?* If your students come from the same country ask: *Do you do the lottery? Why do / don't you do it? Have you ever won anything?*
- Divide students into pairs or groups of three or four students. Tell them to write down two or three advantages and two or three disadvantages of winning a large sum of money on the lottery.
- After about five minutes stop the discussion and elicit some ideas.

■ Read

- Tell students they are going to read a short magazine article about winning the lottery. As they read, they could check how many of their advantages and disadvantages are mentioned, and answer the question in their books.
- Find out which pair / group had the most ideas the same.
- Check the answer and explain any new vocabulary.

Answer
The writer mentions three advantages and only two disadvantages, but the general tone of the article is more negative than positive at the end.

■ Brainstorm and notes

1–2 Ask students to read the instructions in their books and choose a topic. Check that everyone has chosen a topic and allow time for them to think of two or three advantages and two or three disadvantages for their topic. If you want students to do the writing on their own they will all need to make a copy of their ideas.
- Monitor, helping with vocabulary if necessary but not giving ideas. If some groups don't have many ideas at the end of the allotted time, you might like to elicit ideas from the whole class and write these in note form on the board.

3 • If they need ideas, draw their attention to the way the article begins with four short statements:
Congratulations! You've just won £12,000,000! Great you think. All my worries are over.
You could also point out how it catches the reader's attention because it refers to the reader directly (*you, my*),

by the use of exclamation marks, by the reference to a large sum of money – most people dream of being rich.
- Allow a few minutes for pairs or groups to think of an interesting beginning. Even if they are not completely satisfied with their beginning at the end of the allotted time they should move on to the next stage.

4 • Draw their attention to the article on the page if necessary to help with ideas for this. The final summarizing sentence is a rhetorical question which tells us the writer thinks that possibly it would be better if we didn't win the lottery.
- Ask them to decide whether there are more advantages or disadvantages for their topic and to write a final sentence for their article.

■ Write

1 • As usual, students should write the first draft fairly quickly. Check the information in the **Reminder** box with them. Monitor the writing activity, but don't correct any grammatical errors.

2 • At the end of the time tell students to exchange articles with someone from another pair or group, preferably someone who has chosen a different topic. They should follow the normal procedure for suggesting and discussing improvements.
- The final version can be done for homework.

▶ **Writing model 12 (photocopiable) TB p.133**

— p. 123 —

Language in action

Review

Functional language from earlier units is reviewed, in particular, checking and correcting information, making (accepting, turning down) requests, asking for reasons.

■ Discuss

1 • Divide the class into groups of three or four students. Tell them that they are going to go into business together. First of all, they should decide what business to go into. Go over the three choices in their books.
(House / flat-sitting is being paid to live in someone's house or flat while they are away. It involves keeping the house / flat clean and sometimes looking after pets.)
- Elicit / give some more examples of services: *baby-sitting, sandwich delivery service, cleaning.*

2a–b Check that every group has decided on their business and explain stage 2. You could prompt them with some of the following questions.
Small company / service
1 Product or service: *What kind of business / service is it?*
2 Location: *Where will your business be based? What kind of building will you need? How big will it need to be?*

3 Advertising: *How will you advertise? In the newspaper? Put flyers through doors? Hand out flyers in the street? On the Internet? How much can you afford to spend on advertising?*

4 Furniture / equipment: *What have you already got? What do you need? How much will it cost?*

5 Employees needed: *What is each of you going to do in the business? Will you need any other employees? If so, how many?*

6 Capital needed: *How much capital will you need to cover all your costs? How much can you each afford to invest? How much will you need to borrow?*

Language school

As above but also

1 Languages: *What languages will the school offer?*

2 Number of students / nationalities: *How many students do you hope to have? What nationalities will they be?* (You will need to advertise in these countries.)

3 Class size / number of teachers: *What will be the maximum class size? How many teachers will you need to employ?*

· Ask all students to make a note of the decisions they take.

Role play

1 · Tell students that they are going to ask the bank manager for a loan. First, each person in the group has to fill in the loan application form. They can write this on a separate piece of paper if they like. The loan required will be the money they need to borrow to set up the business. Each person in the group should write in the same amount. Tell them to make three or four small mistakes on their form, for example, wrong first name, one digit wrong in the telephone number, wrong house number.

2 · Divide the class into pairs. Each student must do the role play with someone from a different group. If you have an extra student they can work as a pair with someone from their own group.

· Go through the instructions with the class. Allow students a few minutes to prepare what they are going to say about their business plans first.

· Tell students to exchange their application forms and demonstrate the activity with one student. Take the part of the bank manager first, and then the role of the loan applicant.

Follow up

1 · At the end of the role play students should go back to their original groups and exchange information. Were they offered a loan? What were the conditions of repayment? They should choose the best offer.

2 · Set a time limit for this writing phase, and display the advertisements in the classroom. You could also get groups to present their business plans to the rest of the class.

Language check

Follow the usual procedure.

Writing models

Describing leisure facilities — Unit 1

Important features

1 Link ideas by using
   - relative pronouns (like *which*)
   - conjunctions (like *although*).
2 Use opinion adjectives (like *amazing*) to make your writing personal and more interesting.
3 Avoid repeating nouns by using pronouns (like *it*).

Rock Palace is a live music club which is easy to get to by bus from the city centre. It's in an old warehouse on the outskirts of the town. They play an amazing variety of pop and rock music which appeals mainly to the under-25s. Most people dance but you can just listen if you like. Although they have got a very sophisticated sound system, it's not too expensive. There's a really exciting atmosphere. I'm sure you'll have a great time.

Describing a public event — Unit 2

Important features

1 Write each new topic in a separate paragraph.
2 Write in formal English – don't use contractions.
3 Give factual information – for this topic, the name of the festival, when it dates from, when and where it takes place, the main events.

The world wife-carrying championship takes place in July every year in the village of Sonkajarvi in Finland. It dates from the nineteenth century, when a robber called Ronkainen chose members for his gang by asking them to complete an obstacle course carrying a heavy weight.

Although it is a relatively new festival – it only started in 1991 – many people come to Sonkajarvi from all over the world to watch the annual event. The race, in which a man carries a woman on his back over an obstacle course, is run over 235 metres. The prize for the winners is the woman's weight in beer.

After the race, the spectators can enjoy themselves eating sausages and pancakes with honey, and drinking Finnish lager.

Letters and faxes — Unit 3

Important features

1 Present factual details – names, addresses, dates, etc. – in the right way for the type of writing.
2 Choose a formal or informal style depending on who you are writing to.

Formal letter

17, Beech Way
St Albans,
Hertfordshire HT2 3DY
Tel: 01306 572235
Fax: 01306 572237
17 May …

Clare Gordon,
Personnel Manager,
KKK Software,
Islington
London N12 5TG

Dear Ms Gordon,
   Thank you for taking the trouble to interview me in London yesterday. I realize that this was not very convenient for you.
   As I promised, I am now enclosing my full CV and two recent references.
   I look forward to hearing from you.

Yours sincerely,

Ian Harriman

Ian Harriman

Informal fax

FAX

Message for: Clare Gordon
From: Chris Griffiths
Tel: 0181 346 7640   Fax: 0181 346 8375
Date: 17 May …
No. of pages (including this one):   4

Message

Dear Clare
Here are my notes on the interviews. I thought Ian Harriman did well – and a couple of the others were OK. Sorry we didn't get a chance to talk yesterday.
Let me know if you have any queries

Chris

Describing an incident — Unit 4

Important features

1 Set the scene. Who were the main characters? Where and when did it take place?
2 Use adjectives and adverbs to describe the situation and people's feelings.
3 Use time clauses and sequence words and phrases to show the relation between events.

The taxi dropped us off at the airport. We paid the driver and got out. Then, my sister suddenly said, 'Oh no! I've left something cooking on the stove.' Our flight was due to leave in just over an hour.
'I'll go home and check,' I said to my sister, who was looking extremely worried. 'You go to the check-in desk and explain what's happened. I'll be as quick as I can.'
Fortunately it was Sunday morning, the streets were empty, and the taxi-driver enjoyed the challenge. We got home in under fifteen minutes.
When we arrived, I shouted to the driver, 'I won't be long,' feeling in my pockets for the key. The key? Where was it? 'Oh, no!' I said out loud. My sister had locked the door – she had the key!

Describing places — Unit 5

Important features

1 Select interesting features, and use interesting adjectives to help the reader imagine the scene.
2 Use prepositions and prepositional phrases to say where things are in relation to each other.

The mountains, which are over 3,500 metres high, are snow-capped all year round. However, their tops are sometimes hidden from view by mist and low-lying cloud.
In summer cattle graze on the lower slopes, which are covered in grass and wild flowers. In winter, when the slopes are covered in snow, the mountains are a favourite destination for skiers. Then, it looks like a magic wonderland. The pine trees are covered with snow, which sparkles in the bright winter sunlight. The sky is deep blue.

Personal letters — Unit 6

Important features

1 Begin the letter appropriately. Ask how the person is, say how you are, if necessary apologize for not writing sooner.
2 End the letter appropriately. Don't end abruptly. Sign off with Love or Best wishes.
3 Use informal language.

Dear Amy,
How are you? I'm fine. I really must apologize for not writing sooner. Life has just been hectic recently. Mostly, I've been doing boring things like sitting exams, but there have been one or two bright spots as well. Did I tell you that I had passed my driving test? Finally! On my third attempt! I'm now saving up for a second-hand car. Can't afford anything expensive, but hopefully the next time I write I'll be the proud owner of my own personal metal box on wheels!
Also I've got a summer job working as a tourist guide in London. Basically I have to give help and information to any tourists who need it. The money isn't brilliant but it should be fun. I'm going to stay at Ana's. She has a spare room in her flat which she says I can rent for a couple of months.
What about you? Have you finished your exams yet? Are you still going out with Thomas? Why don't you come down to London for a few days when I'm there? I can't offer you a bed but I'm sure Ana won't mind if you sleep on the sofa for a few days.
Well, I'd better sign off now. I'm supposed to be going out to a party in an hour's time and I haven't even washed my hair yet. Write soon. Regards to your mum and dad,
Love,
Hannah

Short stories   Unit 7

Important features

1 Use the right past tense verbs:
   - Past simple for the main events
   - Past continuous and Past perfect for the background.
2 Use time expressions (*First of all*, *after that*, etc.) to mark or link the different stages of your story.
3 Use dialogue to make your story come alive.

> *Last summer Jack and I went to a party.*
> *Afterwards we decided to get a taxi home.*
> *'London Road, please,' I said to the driver.*
> *Suddenly I realized I had no money.*
> *'What shall we do, Jack?' I whispered.*
> *He didn't reply.*
> *'Chest!' shouted Jack suddenly. 'Pain!'*
> *'He's ill. Can you take us to the hospital? Hurry!'*
> *'OK,' said the driver.*
> *I helped Jack out of the taxi.*
> *'Are you OK?' I asked.*
> *'Has the taxi gone?' asked Jack.*
> *'Yes,' I said. 'Why?'*
> *Jack laughed, 'I'm OK now.'*

A letter giving advice   Unit 9

Important features

1 This is a personal letter, so write in a friendly, conversational style.
2 Make your opinions clear – be direct.
3 Give honest but friendly advice.

> Thanks for your letter. It was great to hear from you. I was amazed by your story of the guy who's stealing from your customers. It puts you in a really tricky position, doesn't it?
>
> I think you should tell someone what's going on. If you don't want to phone the police, tell your department head. If you don't tell someone and the crime is discovered, people may think you're guilty too, especially if you've been going out with the guy.
>
> I'm sorry if this sounds hard – it probably isn't what you wanted to hear, but I think in the end it's the best for everyone. Give me a ring if you want to chat about it again.

E-mails   Unit 8

Important features

1 Present factual details, like names, addresses, dates, etc. in the correct way. (Most of these details are automatically included in e-mails.)
2 The style and tone of e-mails can be as formal or informal as other forms of writing. Often they are written quickly and without much planning or thought.
3 Do not use unnecessary language, especially in informal e-mails.

Informal e-mail

> Subject: Long time no see
>
> Charlie,
>
> Great to hear from you! That was a real coincidence – I was thinking about you last week. I decided I was going to try and find out where you were and make contact with you – where are you?
>
> I've got a new job based on the south coast – working for a small company producing computer software. I'm working on a new jazz music composition programme. It's great – a real change from London. How are things with you?
>
> I'm a bit busy right now, but I'll write to you with all my news at the weekend. Keep in touch.
>
> Luv
>
> Nicky

A letter expressing opinions — Unit 10

Important features

1 If you are writing a serious letter to someone you don't know personally, use formal language. Use opinion expressions, for example *It seems to me that …, My own opinion is that …*

2 Lay your letter out correctly.

3 Use the right conventions to start and end your letter.

> 46, Oak Street,
> Melbury,
> TO3 3BN
> 10 March …
>
> The Editor,
> The Melbury Echo,
> High Street,
> Melbury TO2 9TR
>
> Dear Sir / Madam,
>
> I have just read the story in the Echo about the plans for a refuge for homeless people in Oak Street. I am writing to say that I support this plan.
>
> My own view is that the town desperately needs somewhere like this. Whenever I am in Melbury at night, I am surprised by how many young people are sleeping in shop doorways.
>
> It also seems to me a good idea to use this old hotel to help people. The building is empty and looks terrible.
>
> Many people do not want this refuge, but I think your newspaper should try to persuade them that it is in everyone's interest to solve the problem of homelessness.
>
> Yours faithfully,
>
> *John Bunion*
>
> John Bunion

Reviews — Unit 11

Important features

1 Give relevant information. Say what the film, etc. is about, who the main actors are, etc.

2 Give your opinion or recommendation. Say what is good or bad.

> ### Amistad – Now out on video
>
> True account of the slaves captured in Africa for the American market in the 1830s, who mutinied en route and were recaptured and tried. With the help of a former U.S. President and an idealistic lawyer they challenged the justice system. Good performances by Anthony Hopkins and Matthew McConaughey in the starring roles under the direction of Stephen Spielberg.
>
> ***

Articles — Unit 12

Important features

1 Catch the reader's attention with an interesting title and opening sentence.

2 Use a personal, informal tone to involve the reader.

3 Write an interesting ending which summarizes what you have said.

> Simply the best!
> Wouldn't it be wonderful to be a world-class athlete?
>
> • Everyone would look up to you!
> • People would congratulate you and say how wonderful you were all the time!
> • You could make loads of money from sponsorship and advertising!
>
> But it wouldn't be roses all the way.
>
> • You'd have to train really hard. And I mean REALLY HARD. You'd have to watch what you ate and drank. No late nights or parties, either.
> • It would be stressful! There would always be someone waiting to take your place.
>
> Would it be worth it? I'm not so sure it would.

Test 1 (Units 1–2)

Grammar

Present simple and frequency expressions

1 Answer these questions using the frequency expression in brackets.

1 How often does Jim go sunbathing?

(never) ....

2 How often does Jim's father wash the car?

(every weekend) ....

3 How often does Jim's mother visit a museum?

(twice a month) ....

4 How often are Jim's friends late for school?

(often) ....

5 How often do Jim's parents have dinner in a restaurant?

(sometimes) .... | **5** |

Present perfect simple and adverbs

2 Complete the postcard with the Present perfect simple form of the verb in brackets, and put a suitable adverb from the list in the circles.

| so far   yet   just   already   still |

Dear Philippa,

I .... (**1**) .... **2** (arrive) in Beijing after a very long flight and I'm happy to be here. (**3**) I .... **4** (not have) any problems communicating as most people speak English. I (**5**) .... **6** (not see) a Chinese dragon although it's New Year but I'm sure we'll see one tonight when we go on our first guided tour. I .... (**7**) .... **8** (eat) my first Chinese meal: sweet and

sour chicken with rice, but I .... **9** (not try) any of the local specialities (**10**) – I'm saving that for tonight!

Love

John

| **10** |

Comparison

3 Make comparative or superlative sentences from the prompts.

Example
Aerobics / enjoyable / jogging
Aerobics is more enjoyable than jogging. ....

1 Rowing / tiring / sailing

....

2 Motor-racing / fast / sport

....

3 Volleyball / interesting / cricket

....

4 Most football players / short / most basketball players

....

5 A boxer / big / a cyclist

.... | **5** |

used to / Past simple

4 Complete the story with *used to* or the Past simple form of the verb in brackets.

Paul .... (be) **1** an accountant, but last year he .... (change) **2** his job and now he sings in a rock band. He .... (spend) **3** all day at work, but now he can work when he chooses to. Last month his band .... (make) **4** their first record and they .... (sell) **5** a thousand copies the first day.

| **5** |

Adjective order

5 Put these words in the correct order.

1 TABLE / RECTANGULAR / LARGE / A / WOODEN

....

2 EXPENSIVE / WATCH / SWISS / GOLD / AN

....

3 SMALL / SUITCASE / A / LEATHER / RED

....

4 BLUE AND WHITE / A / VASE / CHINA / BEAUTIFUL

....

5 PERSIAN / FAT / FOUR / CATS / BIG

....

☐ **5**

Present perfect simple and Past simple

6 Choose the correct verb form.

My sister *lived / has lived* **1** in London for over six years now. She first *went / has gone* **2** there when she *was / has been* **3** eighteen to study at the London School of Economics. She *had / has had* **4** four different jobs since she *left / has left* **5** university and now works for a merchant bank.

☐ **5**

Vocabulary

Holiday activities

7 Match the activity in the list to the correct definition.

sailing	sightseeing	snorkelling	sunbathing	surfing

1 When you lie in the sun to try and get brown.

....

2 When you visit the beautiful places in a city.

....

3 When you ride the waves on a special board.

....

4 When you swim under water to see fish.

....

5 When you take a boat out to enjoy the sea.

....

☐ **5**

Cooking verbs

8 Complete the recipe with words from the list.

decorate	peel	drain	add	boil

1 .... the potatoes and carrots before you chop them.

2 Put them in a saucepan of water and .... some salt.

3 .... them for about twenty minutes or until they are soft.

4 .... the water off the vegetables.

5 Purée them and .... with chopped parsley.

☐ **5**

Language in action

Personal questions, invitations

9 Complete the dialogues. Use one word in each space.

1 **Interviewer** Can I ask you a few questions?

Paul Yes, go ahead.

Interviewer How .... have you .... **1** for this company?

Paul About three years now.

Interviewer And how .... **2** do you earn?

Paul I'd .... not answer that, if you don't .... **3**.

2 **Suzie** Helen and I are going to a concert. Do you .... **4** coming?

Becky I'd .... **5**.

☐ **5**

TOTAL ☐ **50**

Test 2 (Units 3–4)

Grammar

Present perfect simple, Present perfect continuous

1 Choose the correct verb form.

Dear Marie,

You won't believe this but *I've won / I've been winning* **1** the lottery! I can't decide whether to spend the money or put it in the bank. *I've had / I've been having* **2** problems with my car recently so I could buy a new one – what do you think? *I've looked / I've been looking* **3** around car showrooms and *I've seen / I've been seeing* **4** about six cars I would like to buy, but I think that's too many, don't you? I'd also like to buy a house and *I've found / I've been finding* **5** the perfect place right in the centre of town – I can't wait to show it to you!

I haven't given up / I haven't been giving up **6** work. But *I've bought / I've been buying* **7** plane tickets for a long holiday – do you want to come? *I haven't told / I haven't been telling* **8** anyone else the news yet!

Let me know about the holiday soon

Love
Edward

`8`

Past simple, Past continuous, Past perfect

2 Complete the story with the verb in brackets in the appropriate form.

James had changed his job that summer and at 5 o'clock on Friday afternoon he .... (regret) **1** it. It .... (be) **2** a long week and there .... (be) **3** still a huge pile of papers on his desk. He .... (think) **4** about phoning his wife to say he was going to be late for the fifth time that week when suddenly his door .... (open) **5**. His new boss .... (walk) **6** slowly into the room and .... (look) **7** at the mess on the desk. 'Are you going to resign or do I have to sack you?' he .... (say) **8**. James .... (be) **9** shocked. 'You can't leave until you've finished all this, the boss .... (add) **10**, and then he .... (leave) **11** the room. James .... (pick up) **12** the

phone and .... (start) **13** to dial his wife's number. But the phone .... (not work) **14**. He went to find a colleague to ask about the phone but his boss .... (lock) **15** the door of his office and he couldn't get out. He .... (begin) **16** to feel a little nervous as he .... (hear) **17** stories of people being trapped in time before. Would he ever get out of this unbearable situation?

`17`

Adverb word order

3 Put the words in the correct order to make sentences. There is sometimes more than one possibility.

1 for over forty years / has worked / in the cinema / my uncle

    ....

    ....

2 a new film / in Australia / at the moment / he is directing

    ....

    ....

3 during the week / and at weekends / in Sydney / he works / to see his family / he goes back to Alice Springs

    ....

    ....

4 from 9.00 a.m. to midnight / on weekdays / he works

    ....

    ....

5 at his house in Alice / next summer / we're going to visit him

    ....

    ....

`5`

Landmark Intermediate © Oxford University Press **PHOTOCOPIABLE**

Vocabulary

Verbs and nouns to do with jobs

4 Complete the sentences with a word or expression from the list in the appropriate form.

earn	get promotion	apply for	salary	resign from

1 Doctors .... more than teachers.

2 James doesn't like his job so he's going to .... a different one.

3 I'm really pleased because my boss has told me I'm going to .... next month.

4 Sarah always complains about her low ....

5 He .... his job because he wanted a new career.

☐ 5

Airport vocabulary

5 Two of these sentences are correct. Tick the correct ones and correct the wrong ones.

1 The flight attendants walk up and down the runway serving you drinks.

....

2 When you get to the airport you go to the control tower to get a boarding pass.

....

3 You take your hand luggage on the plane with you.

....

4 The passengers sit in the hold.

....

5 On the plane you have to fasten your life-jacket.

....

6 After the flight, you find your baggage in the departure lounge.

....

7 The overhead locker is where you put your hand luggage.

....

8 You board your plane at the check-in desk.

....

☐ 8

Language in action

Agreeing and disagreeing; requests

6 Complete the dialogues. Use one word in each space.

1 A .... ¹ me. .... you .... ² opening the window?

   B .... ³.

   A Thanks.

2 A I'm really not keen on this music.

   B .... ⁴ I. I don't like it at all.

3 A I think it's a good idea to ban smoking in the workplace.

   B I .... ⁵. If people want to smoke, there should be a place for them.

4 A I .... if you .... ⁶ help me. This bag is too heavy.

   B Certainly.

5 A Could you lend me your car this evening?

   B I'm .... ⁷. I need it myself.

☐ 7

TOTAL ☐ 50

Test 3 (Units 5–6)

Grammar

Futures

1 Complete the text with a suitable future form of the verb in brackets: *will*, *going to* or the Present continuous.

My plans for the future? Well, next year I

.... (study) **1** medicine at Oxford because

my dream is to become a doctor. Before I go I have to pass

my exams, but I'm sure .... (get) **2** good

marks as I've been studying hard all year. In the summer I

.... (travel) **3** around Europe with my

boyfriend. We've always wanted to see Paris so that

.... (be) **4** our first stop. I suppose we

.... (visit) **5** the rest of France too but I'm

more interested in the big cities and the museums. We

.... (meet) **6** some friends in Rome

in August.

☐ **6**

2 Choose the correct alternative.

1 'Look at that waiter! He *will drop* / *is going to drop* those plates.'
2 'What would you like to drink?' '*I'll have* / *I'm going to have* a glass of wine, please.'
3 'Those bags look heavy. *I'll carry* / *I'm going to carry* one for you, if you like.'
4 '*I'll phone you* / *I'm going to phone you* as soon as I arrive at the hotel, OK?'
5 '*I'm meeting* / *I'll meet Frank* after work tonight.'
6 '*I won't come* / *I'm not coming* to class tomorrow as I've got a dentist's appointment.'

☐ **6**

Articles

3 Complete the text with *the*, *a*, *an* or *0* if you think no article is necessary.

My last holiday was in .... **1** India and I had **2**

great time. As soon as the plane touched down in

.... **3** airport in New Delhi, I knew I was going to enjoy

it. On .... **4** first day we just walked along the banks of

.... **5** River Ganges and saw .... **6** man being

taken to .... **7** hospital because he had fallen out of his

boat and nearly drowned. Later, we discovered that

.... **8** man who had been taken to hospital was a

British tourist. Then we visited the Taj Mahal – I could go on

forever but you must go and see for yourself how beautiful

it is.

☐ **8**

Permission, obligation, prohibition

4 Correct the following sentences. Choose from these words: *can*, *can't*, *must*, *mustn't*, *have to*, *don't have to*.

1 At weekends I have to stay out all night if I want to.

   ....

2 In Britain you can drive on the left.

   ....

3 You must smoke on a bus.

   ....

4 Laura mustn't get married yet because she's only 15.

   ....

5 Young people have to drink alcohol when they are 18.

   ....

6 You can carry your ID card with you wherever you go.

   ....

☐ **6**

Indefinite pronouns

5 Match the two halves of the sentences.

A
1 ☐ Would you like
2 ☐ We'll have to go shopping – there's
3 ☐ Where are my glasses? I know I put them here
4 ☐ I can't find my wallet! Perhaps
5 ☐ Sharon will do
6 ☐ I want to go out but there's

B
a anything to get her boyfriend back.
b something to drink?
c nothing in the fridge.
d somewhere.
e nowhere to go on a Sunday.
f someone has stolen it.

☐ **6**

Vocabulary

Opposites

6 Match the adjectives with their opposites.

A
1 ☐ crowded
2 ☐ deep
3 ☐ high
4 ☐ narrow
5 ☐ straight
6 ☐ pebbly

B
a wide
b shallow
c winding
d sandy
e deserted
f low

☐ **6**

Relationships: people words

7 Match the words in the list to the definitions.

father-in-law   groom   widow   fiancée   bride

1 The person someone is engaged to marry.

....

2 A man the day he gets married.

....

3 A woman whose husband has died.

....

4 A woman the day she gets married.

....

5 Your wife's / husband's father.

....

☐ **5**

Language in action

Opinions; permission

8 Complete the dialogues. Use one word in each space.

1 A What's .... **1** fox-hunting?

 B It's not something I've really thought about.

2 A Sara – I'm going to a party this evening. .... **2** leaving early today?

 B Sure. .... **3**.

3 A Excuse me. Is .... **4** take this chair?

 B .... **5**.

4 A .... **6** could possibly borrow your mini-disc recorder?

 B .... **7**. Last time I lent you something you broke it!

☐ **7**

TOTAL ☐ **50**

Test 4 (Units 7–8)

Grammar

can, could, may, might

1 Choose the correct alternative.

Dear Jim,
Thanks for your letter – I'm so glad you *may / could* **1** find
time to write! I'm thinking of coming to visit you next month
– I *might / could* **2** be able to get a few extra days off work
but I'll have to ask my boss. How about the holiday
weekend? *Might / Could* **3** I come and stay then? We *could /
may* **4** spend the first day sightseeing as I've never been to
Prague before, but you'll have to help me out as you know I
can't / couldn't **5** speak any Czech.
Looking forward to seeing you next month. Write soon.
Catherine

5

Reported speech

2 Re-write this phone conversation in Reported speech.

1 **Jill** What time can you meet me tonight?

Jill asked ....

....

2 **Ben** I'm not going out tonight.

Ben replied ....

....

3 **Jill** But there's an important concert on in the Town Hall.

Jill said ....

....

4 **Ben** Well, I can't go.

Ben said ....

....

5 **Jill** But I've arranged to meet everyone at 7 o'clock!

Jill continued ....

....

6 **Ben** Well, you'll have to go on your own.

Ben answered ....

....

7 **Jill** Last week you wanted to see me every night.

Jill said ....

....

8 **Ben** I'm just too busy this week, Jill.

Ben said ....

....

9 **Jill** When can I see you then?

Jill asked ....

....

10 **Ben** I don't know.

Ben replied ....

....

Jill Goodbye!

10

Relative clauses

3 Join these pairs of sentences with a suitable relative pronoun.

1 My father worked for a telephone company. He retired last year.

....

2 The company is the biggest in Britain. They gave him a lot of money when he left.

....

3 His colleagues gave him a watch. It cost over $1000.

....

4 The Managing Director of the company knew my father well. He chose the watch.

....

5 My father always keeps the watch in a safe cupboard. It is always locked.

....

6 He gave the key to my mother. She never loses things.

....

6

Vocabulary

Phrasal verbs

4 Match a verb and a particle, then complete the text with the phrasal verb in the appropriate form.

Verbs	get	pick	hold	cut	ring	put
Particles	on	off (x2)	through (x2)			up

I was trying to .... [1] to the President last week but I had a few problems. First of all, the person who .... [2] the phone told me he couldn't .... me .... [3] directly to the President but that I could speak to his secretary. So I .... [4] for ten minutes and before I could speak to anyone I was .... [5]. When I tried to ring again, nobody answered the phone so I just .... [6] and forgot about it.

`[ ] 6`

Extreme adjectives

5 Match the base adjective with its extreme form.

A		B	
1	[ ] hot	a	freezing
2	[ ] angry	b	unique
3	[ ] surprising	c	boiling
4	[ ] hungry	d	astonishing
5	[ ] cold	e	terrified
6	[ ] frightened	f	brilliant
7	[ ] rare	g	furious
8	[ ] clever	h	starving

`[ ] 8`

speak, say or tell

6 Complete the expressions with *speak*, *say* or *tell*.

1 .... goodbye to someone

2 .... a joke

3 .... a lie

4 .... someone a secret

5 .... someone a story

6 .... thank you

7 .... the truth

8 .... a foreign language

`[ ] 8`

Language in action

Suggestions; telephoning

7 Complete the dialogues. Use one word in each space.

1 A .... [1] going to the cinema this evening?

  B That's not a .... [2] idea. I'd like that.

  C I'm not so keen. .... [3] have a barbecue?

  A Yeah, that'd be good.

2 (On the phone)

  A Hello. .... [4] someone about courses, please?

  B .... [5]?

  A My name's Webb.

  B OK, Ms Webb. I'll .... you .... [6] to our courses organizer.

  C Clare Humphreys .... [7].

  A Oh, hello. Could you send me some information on your management courses, please?

`[ ] 7`

`TOTAL [ ] 50`

Test 5 (Units 9–10)

Grammar

Conditionals

1 Match the two halves of the sentences.

A	B
1 ☐ I'd buy a house	a if I had enough money.
2 ☐ If I see Jim,	b if I didn't eat so much.
3 ☐ My English would be better	c I'd give half of my money away.
4 ☐ I wouldn't be so fat	d I'll tell him you called.
5 ☐ If you lose your passport,	e if I studied more.
6 ☐ If I were the richest person in the world,	f you have to tell the police.

☐ **6**

2 Complete the sentences with the appropriate conditional form, zero, first or second.

1 If I .... (have) time, I .... (write) to Jim this weekend.

2 Normally if you .... (eat) lots of cake and biscuits, you .... (get) fat.

3 If I .... (be) rich, I .... (not work).

4 If you .... (treat) children with respect, they .... (grow up) respecting you.

5 If my job .... (be) more interesting, I .... (not leave).

6 If someone .... (steal) my new car, I .... (be) very angry.

7 If my son .... (speak) Spanish he .... (study) in Madrid.

8 If her children .... (not watch) so much television, they .... (study) more.

☐ **8**

Passives

3 Re-write these sentences in the passive.

1 The police have arrested two bank robbers.

....

....

2 They found the robbers late last night.

....

....

3 They are also investigating another robbery in the area.

....

....

4 Thieves have stolen two paintings from the local art gallery.

....

....

5 They took the paintings during the night.

....

....

6 The police have found one of the stolen pictures.

....

....

7 They are organizing a national search for the other.

....

....

8 The art gallery usually keeps the most important paintings in a safe room.

....

....

9 During April you can see the paintings in a special exhibition.

....

....

10 The police are watching the art gallery day and night to prevent further robberies.

....

....

☐ **10**

Relative clauses

4 Complete the text. Use *when*, *where*, *why* or *whose*.

My parents still live in the village .... **1** they were born. They bought their house forty years ago .... **2** they were young and have lived there ever since. They say the reason .... **3** they like it so much is because of the pure, fresh air they breathe. My father's parents, ... **4** farm provides the milk and eggs for the village, work hard all day looking after the animals. My mother's parents live in the house next door, ... **5** they have always lived, and are now retired. We always go and stay during the summer .... **6** the children are home from school to have a break from the noisy city we live in.

☐ **6**

Vocabulary

Crime words

5 Choose the correct word.

1 Young people who *break / commit* a crime are not usually sent to prison.
2 The *judge / solicitor* is the person who decides on the punishment for the crime.
3 The suspect is being *questioned / sentenced* by the police.
4 The family whose shop was destroyed by the fire are asking for *compensation / evidence* from the arsonist who started the fire.
5 Two men are being *prosecuted / arrested* for the kidnapping of businessman Martin Shaw last month.
6 Incorrect parking is not a very serious *offence / law*.
7 The police *enforce / commit* the law.
8 The murderer of a local postwoman was *sentenced / prosecuted* to life imprisonment yesterday afternoon.

☐ **8**

Architectural features

6 Find the odd word out in each line.

Example
steel   gutter   iron   copper   .*gutter*.

1 bricks   concrete   balcony   stone   ....
2 rectangular   shutters   round   oval   ....
3 tiles   aerial   chimney   basement   ....
4 basement   attic   ground floor   steps   ....
5 flat   glass   wood   metal   ....

☐ **5**

Language in action

Reasons; checking and correcting

7 Complete the dialogues. Use one word in each space.

1 A Why .... **1** aren't you ready yet? We have to be there in half an hour.

 B Because I can't find my shoes, ... **2**.

2 A Perhaps .... tell me .... **3** you didn't phone yesterday?

 B .... simple .... **4** that I lost your phone number.

3 A Let me see. Your name's Shaun Edwards, ... **5**?

 B No, ... **6**. It's Sian.

 A And let me just check your address. It's Silver Street, isn't it?

 B I'm .... completely .... **7**. It's Golden Road.

☐ **7**

TOTAL ☐ 50

Test 6 (Units 11–12)

Grammar

have or get

1 Complete the sentences with *have* or *get* in the appropriate form.

1 I'm on a diet so I only .... a salad for lunch.

2 Personal computers .... cheaper every year. Soon everyone will own one.

3 Mr Sanderson .... lunch at the moment. He'll be back at 3 o'clock.

4 'Can you .... some bread on your way home?'

5 He .... a lot of problems with his car last week.

☐ **5**

have something done

2 Use the verb in brackets to say what these people are going to have done.

Example
The paint is coming off the walls of my neighbours' house. (paint)
They are going to have their house painted.

1 My hair is too long. (cut)

I ....

2 David's car has broken down. (repair)

He ....

3 My niece wants to wear earrings. (pierce)

She ....

4 My neighbours took lots of photos on holiday. (develop)

They ....

5 I can't carry all this shopping home. (deliver)

I ....

6 Sandra has seen a design for beautiful wedding dress. (make)

She ....

☐ **6**

so and such

3 Complete the text using *so*, *such* or *such a*.

I went to a party last night and I've never had .... **1** good time in my life! I spent most of the evening people-watching and I was amazed that people could be .... **2** strange. First of all there was this model who was wearing .... **3** long dress that she kept on tripping over it! Then there was an actress with .... **4** short hair that she looked like she was going bald. There were .... **5** many people that I can hardly remember them all.

☐ **5**

Third conditional

4 Join these sentences to make third conditional sentences.

1 I went to bed very late. I didn't arrive at work on time.

....

2 Richard drove too fast. He crashed his car.

....

3 Judith started aerobics classes. She hurt her back.

....

4 My parents didn't have enough money. They didn't buy the house.

....

5 I lost the ticket. I didn't go to the concert.

....

6 My brother ate too much last night. He was ill.

....

7 They offered me the job. I took it.

....

8 I didn't have the money. I didn't pay the bill.

....

☐ **8**

all, both, none, neither, either

5 Use the information in the chart to complete the sentences about the people in the class.

Exam results				
	History	Maths	English	Chemistry
Judy	A	C	A	D
Philip	B	C	A	A
Michael	B	A	A	C
Rebecca	C	A	A	C
Pass mark C				

1 .... of them got an A in English.

2 .... of them got a B in chemistry.

3 .... Judy nor Philip got an A in maths.

4 Judy didn't get an A in chemistry and Michael didn't

....

5 .... Michael and Philip got a B in history.

6 .... of them passed their maths exam.

7 .... of them failed their history exam.

7

Vocabulary

The arts

6 Match the words in the list to the definitions.

album   cast   plot   lyrics   portrait   screen
novelist   script

1 The words of a song. ....

2 The story of a book or film. ....

3 The person who writes a novel. ....

4 A film is shown on this. ....

5 The group of people who act in a film. ....

6 The words of a film or a play. ....

7 A record containing a number of songs. ....

8 A painting showing a person's head. ....

8

Money

7 Each of these sentences has a vocabulary mistake. Correct it.

1 My father is 65 so he gets an inheritance.

....

2 'How would you like to pay – in money or by credit card?'

....

3 I'm a bit worried because my bank account is in the black.

....

4 'Can you borrow me some money? I've left my purse at home and I need a drink.'

....

5 I'm going to buy a new car if I can get a mortgage from the bank.

....

6 I put all my values in the hotel safe.

....

6

Language in action

Apologizing

8 Complete the dialogues. Use one word in each space.

1 A Barbara. You .... [1] book you lent me.

B Yes.

A Well, ... [2] I spilt coffee on it. I'm really sorry.

B It doesn't .... [3]. It's not the end of the world.

2 A John. There's .... [4] to tell you. I'm ever so sorry but I can't find your record.

B Don't .... [5] about it. It might turn up.

5

TOTAL **50**

Test 1

1
1 Jim never goes sunbathing.
2 Jim's father washes the car every weekend.
3 Jim's mother visits a museum twice a month.
4 Jim's friends are often late for school.
5 Jim's parents sometimes have dinner in a restaurant.

2
1,2 I've just arrived
3,4 So far I haven't had
5,6 I still haven't seen
7,8 I've already eaten
9,10 I haven't tried … yet

3
1 Rowing is more tiring than sailing.
2 Motor-racing is the fastest sport.
3 Volleyball is more interesting than cricket.
4 Most football players are shorter than most basketball players.
5 A boxer is bigger than a cyclist.

4
1 used to be
2 changed
3 used to spend
4 made
5 sold

5
1 a large rectangular wooden table
2 an expensive gold Swiss watch
3 a small red leather suitcase
4 a beautiful blue and white china vase
5 four big fat Persian cats

6
1 has lived
2 went
3 was
4 has had
5 left

7
1 sunbathing
2 sightseeing
3 surfing
4 snorkelling
5 sailing

8
1 peel
2 add
3 boil
4 drain
5 decorate

9
1 long … worked
2 much
3 rather … mind
4 fancy
5 love to

Test 2

1
1 I've won
2 I've been having
3 I've been looking
4 I've seen
5 I've found
6 I haven't given up
7 I've bought
8 I haven't told

2
1 was regretting
2 had been
3 was
4 was thinking
5 opened
6 walked
7 looked
8 said
9 was
10 added
11 left
12 picked up
13 started
14 wasn't working
15 had locked
16 was beginning/began
17 had heard

3
1 My uncle has worked in the cinema for over forty years.
2 At the moment he is directing a new film in Australia. / He is directing a new film in Australia at the moment.
3 He works in Sydney during the week and at weekends he goes back to Alice Springs to see his family. / During the week he works in Sydney, and he goes back to Alice Springs at weekends.
4 On weekdays he works from 9.00 a.m. to midnight. / He works from 9.00 a.m. to midnight on weekdays.
5 Next summer we're going to visit him at his house in Alice. / We're going to visit him at his house in Alice next summer.

4
1 earn
2 apply for
3 get promotion
4 salary
5 resigned from

5
1 They walk up and down the AISLE.
2 You go to the CHECK-IN DESK.
3 Correct.
4 They sit in the CABIN.
5 You have to fasten your SEATBELT.
6 You find it in the BAGGAGE RECLAIM AREA.
7 Correct.
8 You board it at the GATE.

6
1 Excuse
2 Would … mind
3 Not at all
4 Neither am
5 disagree
6 wonder … could
7 afraid not

Test 3

1
1 I'm going to study / I'm studying
2 I'll get
3 I'm going to travel / I'm travelling
4 will be
5 we'll visit
6 we're meeting

2
1 He's going to drop
2 I'll have
3 I'll carry
4 I'll phone
5 I'm meeting
6 I'm not coming

3
1 0
2 a
3 the
4 the
5 the
6 a
7 0
8 the

4
1 I can stay
2 you have to drive
3 you mustn't smoke
4 Laura can't get married
5 Young people can drink
6 You must carry

5
1 b
2 c
3 d
4 f
5 a
6 e

6
1 e
2 b
3 f
4 a
5 c
6 d

7
1 fiancée
2 groom
3 widow
4 bride
5 father-in-law

8
1 your opinion of
2 Any chance of
3 Go ahead
4 it OK if I
5 Of course / Go ahead
6 Do you think I
7 No way

Test 4

1
1. could
2. might
3. Could
4. could
5. can't

2
1. Jill asked Ben what time he could meet her that night.
2. Ben replied that he wasn't going out that night.
3. Jill said (that) there was an important concert on in the Town Hall.
4. Ben said (that) he couldn't go.
5. Jill continued that she had arranged to meet everyone at 7 o'clock.
6. Ben answered (that) she would have to go on her own.
7. Jill said (that) the previous week he had wanted to see her every night.
8. Ben said (that) he was just too busy that week.
9. Jill asked Ben when she could see him.
10. Ben replied that he didn't know.

3
1. My father, who retired last year, worked for a telephone company.
2. The company, which is the biggest in Britain, gave him a lot of money when he left.
3. His colleagues gave him a watch, which cost over $1000.
4. The Managing Director of the company, who knew my father well, chose the watch.
5. My father always keeps the watch in a safe cupboard, which is always locked.
6. He gave the key to my mother, who never loses things.

4
1. get through
2. picked up
3. put ... through
4. held on
5. cut off
6. rang off

5
1. c 3. d 5. a 7. b
2. g 4. h 6. e 8. f

6
1. say
2. tell
3. tell
4. tell
5. tell
6. say
7. tell
8. speak

7
1. How about
2. bad
3. Why not
4. Can I speak to
5. Who's calling
6. put ... through
7. speaking

Test 5

1
1. a
2. d
3. e
4. b
5. f
6. c

2
1. have ... will write
2. eat ... get / will get
3. were ... wouldn't work
4. treat ... grow up
5. were ... wouldn't leave
6. steals ... will be / stole ... would be
7. spoke ... would study
8. didn't watch ... would study

3
1. Two bank robbers have been arrested by the police.
2. The robbers were found late last night.
3. Another robbery in the area is also being investigated.
4. Two paintings have been stolen from the local art gallery.
5. The paintings were taken during the night.
6. One of the stolen pictures has been found.
7. A national search is being organized for the other.
8. The most important paintings are usually kept in a safe room.
9. During April the paintings can be seen in a special exhibition.
10. The art gallery is being watched day and night to prevent further robberies.

4
1. where
2. when
3. why
4. whose
5. where
6. when

5
1. commit
2. judge
3. questioned
4. compensation
5. prosecuted
6. offence
7. enforce
8. sentenced

6
1. balcony
2. shutters
3. basement
4. steps
5. flat

7
1. on earth
2. that's why
3. you could ... why
4. For the ... reason
5. is that right
6. it isn't actually
7. afraid that's ... wrong

Test 6

1
1. have
2. are getting
3. is having
4. get
5. had

2
1. I'm going to have it cut.
2. He's going to have it repaired.
3. She's going to have her ears pierced.
4. They're going to have their photos developed.
5. I'm going to have it delivered.
6. She's going to have it made.

3
1. such a
2. so
3. such a
4. such
5. so

4
1. If I hadn't gone to bed so late, I would have arrived on time.
2. If he hadn't driven so fast, he wouldn't have crashed his car.
3. If she hadn't started aerobics classes, she wouldn't have hurt her back.
4. If they had had enough money, they would have bought the house.
5. If I hadn't lost the ticket, I would have gone to the concert.
6. If my brother hadn't eaten so much, he wouldn't have been ill.
7. If they hadn't offered me the job, I wouldn't have taken it.
8. If I had had the money, I would have paid the bill.

5
1. All   5. Both
2. None   6. All
3. Neither 7. None
4. either

6
1. lyrics
2. plot
3. novelist
4. screen
5. cast
6. script
7. album
8. portrait

7
1. a pension
2. in cash
3. in the red
4. lend
5. loan
6. valuables

8
1. know that
2. I'm afraid
3. matter
4. something I've got
5. worry

Photocopiable materials

Photocopiable materials
Teacher's notes

1 Who do you think …   p.152
- Copy a sheet for each student in the class.
- Hand out a sheet to each student. They complete each space with the name of a student in the class.
- They then mingle to check their guesses, asking the question *How often do you …?* to the person whose name they wrote in the space. They put a tick if they guessed correctly and a cross if their guess was incorrect.
- Brief whole class feedback.

2 Comparatives game   p.153
- Divide students into groups of three or four. Copy as many sets of cards as there are groups. Cut up the adjective cards and keep in one set, and the country cards and keep in another set. Hand out one set of each to each group.
- Put both sets of cards face down in the centre of the group, and turn over the top country card to start the game.
- The first student turns over the top adjective card and the top country card and makes a sentence comparing the country on the card to the one already on the table using the adjective. They can use a comparative or *as … as* to do this. They then put their country card on top of the country card already on the table. The adjective card is discarded.
- The other students award a maximum of two points for the sentence: one for correct grammar and the other if they consider the sentence to be true.
- The next student now takes the next adjective card and the next country card and makes a comparison with the country card already on the table.
- Play continues until there are no more country cards.
- The student with the most points wins.

3 What's my life?   p.155
- Divide the students into pairs. Copy and cut up one set of the cards (or more for a larger class). Hand out one 'Old Life' card (1990) to each pair. **They must not let the others see this card.**
- Tell students that this was a friend of theirs ten years ago. Elicit *used to* to talk about past habits.
- Ask students if their 'friend' is male or female, and hand out a 'New Life' card (NOW) to each pair. **Again, they must not let the others see this card.** Elicit Present simple to talk about present habits.
- Pairs write six sentences about the two lives to show how different they are, for example, *He used to laugh a lot but now he's very serious.* (clown/politician). Note that there

are specific 'matches' in the cards, but this is not necessary for this activity.
- Pairs read out their sentences and the other pairs guess the two lives.

4 Have you ever …?   p.156
- Pin up a list of irregular verbs on the wall of your classroom. Refer students to this if they have doubts about the past participle form of any of the verbs.
- Copy and cut up one set of the cards. Hand out one card to each student, leaving the remaining cards in a pile face down on the table in front of the teacher. (For a large class, make copies of two or more sets.)
- Using the prompt on the card, students form a *Have you ever …?* question and mingle, asking the other students their question.
- As soon as a positive reply is given, they go back to their place and write a sentence about that person, for example, *Juan has ridden a horse.* If none of the students gives a positive reply then the sentence must begin with *nobody,* for example, *Nobody has seen a ghost.* They then take another card from the pile and start again.
- Play continues until there are no more cards. The winner is the student with the most sentences.
- Feedback can be carried out by focusing on each student and asking the class what they have discovered about them.

5 Present perfect snap   p.157
- Divide students into groups of three or four. Copy and cut up a set of cards for each group.
- Hand out a set of cards to each group. They shuffle and deal them out.
- They pick up their cards and sort them into finished actions ✔ and unfinished actions ✗. If they have any pairs they must discard them.
- The first student lays down a ✗ card and makes a Present perfect continuous sentence, for example, *I've been washing the car.*
- The student with the corresponding finished action lays down their card and makes a Present perfect simple sentence, for example, *I've washed the car.*
- Play continues with this student laying a ✗ card and making the appropriate sentence.
- If a student has no ✔ card, play moves to the person on their left.
- The winner is the first person to play all their cards.

6 Job Swap   p.159
- Copy and cut up one set of cards. Hand out one card to each student.
- They write down at least three positive points of the job on their card.
- Students then mingle to find a job which they think is better than the one on their card. At the same time they have to make out that their job is the best, in order to be able to swap it for a different job.

- Students can only swap jobs if both agree to do so.
- Give students a time limit of ten minutes to mingle and swap.
- Have brief feedback on which jobs students prefer and why.

7 Writing a story   p.160
- Copy a sheet for each student in the class.
- Hand out a sheet to each student.
- Ask them to read the first box and complete the spaces. They can use the picture prompts to help them if they want to.
- Ask students to pass their sheets to the person on their left. They then complete the next box on their new sheet.
- Continue completing the spaces and passing the sheets round until the story is finished.
- Finally, students can read out the stories and vote on the best one.

8 Airport dialogues   p.161
- Divide students into pairs. Copy and cut up as many sheets as there are pairs. Write the numbers 1, 3, 8, 9, 11, 14, 18, 24 on pieces of paper (you will need to write some numbers twice if you have more than eight pairs in the class).
- Hand out a set of strips to each pair. They put the strips in the order that things would happen to them during a journey.
- Have brief feedback and agree on a final order. They number their strips.
- Hand out one number to each pair. Do not let the other pairs know which number they have. Give students time to prepare a brief role play to illustrate the situation in the part of the journey with this number.
- In pairs, students act out their situation and the others guess what it is.

9 Future questionnaire   p.162
- Divide students into pairs. Copy a questionnaire for each pair.
- Hand out a questionnaire for each pair. They have to invent one question for each section with three possible answers, as in the example.
- Tell students that they must give each possible answer a score from 0 to 2, depending how far it indicates that someone is ready for 2050. For example, for question 1 the scores are a2, b1, c0. They write the scores for all their questions on the back of the questionnaire.
- They now exchange questionnaires with another pair, who have to agree on an answer for each question. They circle the answer they agree on.
- When they have finished, pairs turn over the questionnaire and add up their score.
- Meanwhile write these results on the blackboard:
  0–4 The future seems to frighten you. You need to learn to adapt to new situations if you want to continue enjoying life.

5–8 You don't really take the future seriously enough. If you start preparing yourself now, you will be certain to enjoy it when it arrives.
9–12 You seem to be looking forward to the future – carry on and enjoy it.
- Have brief feedback on results.

10 Future ludo   p.163
- Copy the board and put it in the middle of the table. Copy and cut up one set of cards and put them face down in a pile next to the board. You will need a dice and a coloured counter for each group.
- Divide the class into two or four teams. Each team places a coloured counter on the START square nearest them.
- The first team throws the dice and moves the appropriate number of squares. If they land on a black space they must take a card, and complete the sentence on it with a suitable future form.
- If the team answers correctly, they move forward one space. If they are wrong, they move back one space.
- Play continues with the next team.
- If at any stage one team's counter lands on a square already occupied, the first counter is sent back to the start. This team has to start again.
- When students have completed the board they move up their finishing path.
- The winning team is the first team to reach the finish. This can only be achieved by throwing the exact number on the dice.

11 Modals situations   p.165
- Divide students into groups of three or four. Copy and cut up a set of cards for each group.
- Hand out a set of cards to each group. They shuffle and then place the cards face down in a pile.
- The first student takes a card, and makes a sentence containing two modal verbs about the situation, for example, dentist's – *You must open your mouth but you can't speak.* They must not show their card to the others in the group.
- The first student to guess the situation wins the card.
- Play continues with the next student.
- The winner is the student with the most cards at the end of the game.

12 Somebody's match   p.166
- Divide the students into pairs. Copy and cut up a set of cards for each pair.
- Hand out a set of cards to each pair. They match the two halves of the sentence.
- Have brief feedback. One pair reads out one half of a sentence and the other pairs finish it off.

13 Call my bluff   p.167
- Divide students into four groups. Make a copy of the sheet and cut it into four cards.
- Give a card and a dictionary to each group. Tell students to check which of the two definitions for each word is correct. They then invent another incorrect definition for each word and write it on their card.
- The first group writes their word on the blackboard and gives their three possible definitions. Ask the other groups to guess which definition they think is correct. Award one point for a correct answer.
- Play continues with the second group who write their word on the blackboard and proceed to define it as before.
- The group with the most points wins.

14 Extreme adjective dominoes   p.168
- Divide students into pairs. Copy a sheet for each pair, but DO NOT cut out the dominoes yet.
- Hand out a sheet of dominoes to each pair. They complete the dominoes by writing the extreme form of the adjective in the square to the right of the base form. They can use the box at the bottom of the page to help them.
- Check that the dominoes have been correctly completed. Cut them up.
- Ask each pair to shuffle and deal out five dominoes each. They put the remaining dominoes in a pile.
- The first student lays a domino face up on the table. The second student tries to play a domino to match. If they cannot, they pick up a domino from the pile, which they can play if it matches one on the table.
- Play continues with the second student and so on until all the dominoes have been played.
- The winner is the first person in the pair to play all their dominoes.

15 What did you say?   p.169
Stage one
- Divide students into groups of three or four. Copy and cut up a set of cards for each group.
- Hand out a set of cards to each group. They put them in a pile face down on the table.
- The first student takes a card and answers the question on the card with a complete sentence. They then put it face down on the table in front of them.
- Play continues with the second student taking a card and so on until all the cards have finished.

Stage two
- Students focus on the first student.
- The other students have three minutes to remember the information given by the first student by making a sentence in reported speech, for example, *You told us your father's name was Bill.* As they say the sentences, the first student lays the corresponding card on the table face up. If they cannot remember the information the first student can prompt by showing his cards.

- Next, students focus on the second student and so on until all the students have been dealt with.
- The winning group is the one which has remembered the most information about its members.

16 Radio programme   p.170
- Divide the class in half. One half will be presenters, the other half guests.
- Divide each half into pairs to prepare their roles. Give out a role card to each pair.
- The presenters write questions to ask their guests. The guests decide what they want to say about their given topic and rehearse this with their partner.
- Re-group students into pairs of presenter–guest, and ask students to act out their role play.
- If you have access to recording equipment, you could record the students doing their interviews.

17 In the courtroom   p.171
- Divide students into pairs. Copy and cut up enough sheets for each pair to have one role card.
- Hand out a role card to each pair. Give students five minutes to invent a reason for committing their crime, which would leave them free from punishment.
- Re-group students in groups of four to six. Each person in the group should have a different role.
- The first student announces to the 'court' (the other students in the group) why they are there, for example, *My crime is shoplifting.*
- The other students ask as many questions about the crime as possible in three minutes.
- At the end of the allocated time the court discuss their verdict and give their sentence.
- The next student then takes over and so on, until all the students have been sentenced.
- Finally, compare the verdicts of the different groups with the whole class.

18 Passives noughts and crosses   p.172
- Draw a noughts and crosses board on the blackboard. Divide the class into two teams, the noughts and the crosses.
- Copy and cut up one set of cards and put them face down in the middle of the table.
- Pre-teach vocabulary for asking for a square: *top right, top centre, top left, centre right, centre, centre left, bottom right, bottom middle* and *bottom left.*
- Ask the crosses team which square they would like.
- The noughts team then take a card and make a passive sentence from the prompts.
- The crosses team have to say if this sentence is True or False.
- If they are correct, draw a cross in the square they asked for. If they are wrong, the turn passes to the noughts team.
- The noughts team then choose a square and play continues until one team has three squares in a row (in

which case they are the winners) or the board is complete (in which case the game is a draw).

- As a follow up activity, students could make their own cards as a warmer for the next class.

19 What's your problem? p.173

- Divide students into groups of three or four. Copy and cut up a set of cards for each group.
- Hand out a set of cards to each group. They deal out all the cards face down, and then look at their cards individually. They should discard any pairs.
- The first student lays a problem card ☹ face up on the table and states their problem, for example, *My hair is too long.*
- The student with the corresponding solution card ☺ puts this card on the table and gives a solution to the problem, for example, *You need to have it cut.* The cards are then discarded.
- This player then takes a new problem card, and lays it on the table, stating the problem.
- The student who loses all their cards first is the winner of the game.
- After the game students could feedback on the pairs of cards saying what has happened, for example, *He's had his hair cut.*

20 Music trivia quiz p.174

- Divide students into three or four groups of at least two students. Copy and cut up a set of cards for each group.
- Hand out a set of cards to each group. They complete the cards and fill in the answer as quickly as possible. Give them a time limit of ten minutes to do this. They then place their cards in a pile face down in front of them.
- Ask students to think of a name for their team, and write the names on the blackboard to form a scoreboard.
- The first team asks one of their questions. The first team to answer correctly wins a point. If no answer is given, the point goes to the team asking the question.
- The next team then asks a question and this continues until all the questions have been asked.
- The team with the most points wins.

21 Third conditional dominoes p.175

- Divide students into groups of three or four. Copy and cut up a set of dominoes for each group.
- Hand out a set of dominoes to each group. They deal them all out.
- The first student lays a domino on the table and reads out the *If …* clause.
- The student who has the matching second clause lays down their domino, and uses the prompts to make the complete third conditional sentence. (They can use the numbers on the dominoes to help them match.)
- This student then reads out the next *If …* clause. This continues until all the dominoes have been played.
- The first student to use all their dominoes wins the game.

22 Money matters crossword p.176

- Copy and cut up enough crosswords for each student.
- Divide the class into two groups. Hand out a copy of crossword A to each student in the first group, and a copy of crossword B to each student in the other group.
- They work in pairs to check they understand the words in their crossword by taking turns to define the words. Supply a dictionary if necessary.
- Re-group students so that each A student is working with a B student.
- They complete their crossword by asking their partner for definitions of the missing answers. Student A asks B for the definition of an answer of their choice, for example, *What's seven across?* B defines this answer until A guesses it and writes it in their crossword.
- Student B asks A for the next definition and so on.
- Finally, they check their crosswords by comparing them and correcting any mistakes.

1 Who do you think …?

Look at the sentences and think about the other students in your class. Guess which person fits the sentence best and write their name in the space. Ask your classmates *How often …?* to see if you were right.

1 ☐ .... often sings in the shower.

2 ☐ .... never drinks alcohol.

3 ☐ .... usually eats cakes at the weekend.

4 ☐ .... hardly ever smokes.

5 ☐ .... often reads a good book in bed.

6 ☐ .... doesn´t often talk on the telephone.

7 ☐ .... occasionally goes to the theatre.

8 ☐ .... always listens to music in the car.

9 ☐ .... plays cards twice a week.

10 ☐ .... hardly ever walks to work.

11 ☐ .... never goes to bed before midnight.

12 ☐ .... sometimes buys expensive clothes.

2 Comparatives game

Adjective cards

beautiful	clean	sunny	far
ugly	dirty	interesting	noisy
big	cold	boring	quiet
small	hot	modern	polluted
busy	crowded	snowy	wet
cheap	exciting	old	dry
expensive	friendly	near	dangerous

Country cards

England	Poland	Israel	Australia
Greece	Russia	Morocco	New Zealand
Germany	Japan	Kenya	Indonesia
France	China	Chile	Cuba
Italy	Thailand	Brazil	Canada
Portugal	India	Argentina	The USA
Spain	Egypt	Peru	Mexico

Landmark Intermediate © Oxford University Press PHOTOCOPIABLE

4 Have you ever ...?

go to Paris	get stuck in a lift	swim in a river	find some money
lose your wallet	buy a house	drive a Mercedes	cut down a tree
drink champagne	eat caviar	have a fight	make a cake
send an e-mail	write a letter in English	read the Times	go to Britain
see a famous person	blow up a balloon	break a leg	stay up all night
wear a uniform	catch a cold	win a competition	send flowers
sing in public	catch a fish	play golf	fall down the stairs
grow tomatoes	miss a train	see a ghost	fly in a helicopter
cut your own hair	drive a tractor	feed the animals at the zoo	feel nervous
fight with a friend	forget your name	ride a horse	sing in the shower

Landmark Intermediate © Oxford University Press **PHOTOCOPIABLE**

5 Present perfect snap

Landmark Intermediate © Oxford University Press PHOTOCOPIABLE

6 Job swap

Policeman • • •	**Gardener** • • •
Secretary • • •	**Travel guide** • • •
Taxi driver • • •	**Butler** • • •
Lawyer • • •	**Farmer** • • •
Shop owner • • •	**Teacher** • • •
Mechanic • • •	**Doctor** • • •
Computer programmer • • •	**Dentist** • • •
Engineer • • •	**Waiter** • • •

7 Writing a story

Once upon a time there was a _____ called _____
who _____ .

One day he _____
when _____ .

Suddenly _____ and so he
decided to _____ .

Then he _____ his friend, _____ , who
_____ .

Together they _____ but
unfortunately _____ .

When they got home _____
_____ .

The two of them _____
and then _____

At the end of the day they were _____ but happy
to be alive. They _____ to celebrate
and both of them lived happily ever after.

Landmark Intermediate © Oxford University Press

8 Airport dialogues

☐ A friend drops you off at the airport.

☐ You go to the check-in desk.

☐ You show your ticket.

☐ You look at the information screen to find out your Gate number.

☐ You pass through the Security Check but there is a problem with your hand luggage.

☐ You buy some cigarettes in the Duty Free Shop.

☐ Your flight is called.

☐ You find your seat.

☐ The plane takes off.

☐ The plane lands.

☐ You go to the Baggage Reclaim Area.

☐ You go to the Arrivals Hall.

☐ You find a trolley.

☐ You put your suitcase on the conveyor belt.

☐ You get a boarding card.

☐ You go through Passport Control.

☐ You go to the Departure Lounge.

☐ You go to your Gate.

☐ You board the plane and show your boarding card to the flight attendant.

☐ You fasten your seatbelt.

☐ You have something to eat and drink.

☐ You get off the plane.

☐ You collect your suitcase and go through Customs.

☐ You get a taxi to your destination.

9 Future questionnaire

Are you ready for life in 2050? This questionnaire will help you find out the truth!

1 Food and drink

How will you feel about eating genetically produced meat instead of lamb and beef?

a   It will be no problem for you.

b   It will bother you slightly.

c   You will become a vegetarian.

2 Science and technology

3 Schools and education

4 Health and medicine

5 Life expectancy

6 Space

10 Future ludo

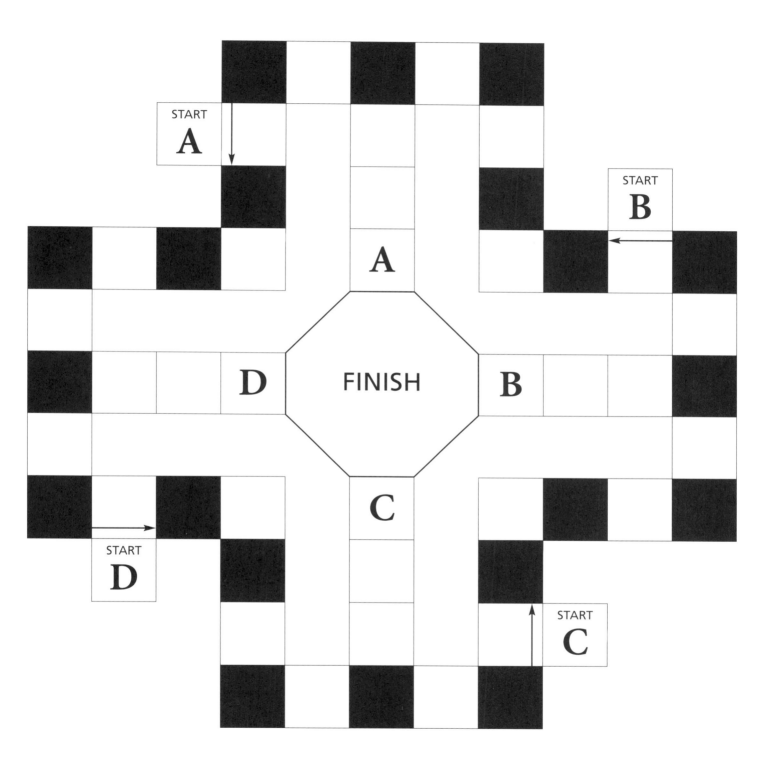

10 Future ludo

I'm sure I (finish) the book by Monday.	This year we (stay) at home in August because we've just bought a new house.	We (drive) to my parent's house instead of taking the train.	I expect the weather (be) better next month.
My nephew (leave) school next year to get a job.	I can't see you tonight. I (go) to the cinema with my brother.	I don't think we (have) enough money to go on holiday this year.	I've decided that I (not get) married.
Don't worry. Your son (phone) if there's a problem.	I (buy) my boyfriend a shirt for his birthday.	My sister says she (give up) smoking next year.	We're going out for dinner on Saturday so we (not be) in.
(In a restaurant:) I (have) the steak please.	My Grandmother (be) 100 next birthday.	The next election (be) in March.	In one hour from now it (be) exactly 10 o'clock.
My best friend (buy) a new car next month.	Our teacher (tell) us about the exam in the next class.	Let me help you with your bags. I (take) the heaviest one.	I'm really tired. I (have) an early night.
Can't you start your car? Don't worry, I (have) a look for you.	Go on! Tell me! I promise I (not tell) anyone.	I'm sure it (not rain) at the weekend.	I (work) late on Thursday so I can't go to the party.
My sister (meet) me at eight so we can go to the theatre.	I'm really nervous because I (go) to the dentist.	Jim (not come) to the meeting because he has a football match.	We (go) away for the weekend as the weather is so beautiful.
My brother (study) medicine at University next year.	'Why are you running?' 'Because I (be) late.'	Look at that boy! He (fall) off that wall!	Look at those black clouds! It (rain).

12 Somebody's match

She's looked for her keys everywhere but she can't find them	anywhere.
I'd like to go on holiday	somewhere hot.
My Grandfather can remember	everywhere he's been in his life.
My brother's depressed. He thinks his life is going	nowhere.
We need more people to play the game. Isn't	anybody else coming?
The place is empty. There's	nobody here.
What's so funny? Why is	everybody laughing?
Oh no!	Somebody has stolen our car!
I'm going shopping. Is there	anything you need?
Listen carefully. I've got	something important to tell you.
My sister's thinking of leaving the country but if she does, she'll have to sell	everything she possesses.
The children are bored. It's raining and they've got	nothing to do.

13 Call my bluff

VEGAN A person who doesn't eat any animal products. A person that grows vegetables. A person	**PLUMBER** A person that likes eating plums. A person who repairs the water system of your house. A person
UNDERTAKER A person A person that organizes funerals. A person who works under the ground.	**NANNY** A person that lives with animals. A person A person who works looking after children.
BULB A thing that grows on your nose. A thing A thing which produces the light in a lamp.	**ROLL** A thing which you eat with your soup. A thing that you use for making cakes. A thing
MUG A thing that you drink tea out of. A thing which you hang on the wall. A thing	**LAWNMOWER** A thing which you use to make bread. A thing that you use to cut the grass in your garden. A thing

GAMBLER A person who plays games to try to win a lot of money. A person that goes walking in the countryside. A person	**DUSTMAN** A person A person who takes away your rubbish for you. A person that sells cleaning products.
BROWSER A person who goes into a shop only to look at things. A person A person that is always complaining.	**TRAMP** A poor person who has nowhere to live. A person A person that rides a motorbike too fast.
WIG A thing A thing that grows on a tree. A thing which you put on your head if you have no hair.	**LIGHTHOUSE** A thing that you put on the table at lunchtime. A thing which stops boats crashing on the rocks. A thing
SLIPPER A thing A thing which you wear on your feet at home. A thing that makes you fall over.	**CORKSCREW** A thing that grows in the countryside in summer. A thing A thing which you use to open a bottle of wine.

14 Extreme adjective dominoes

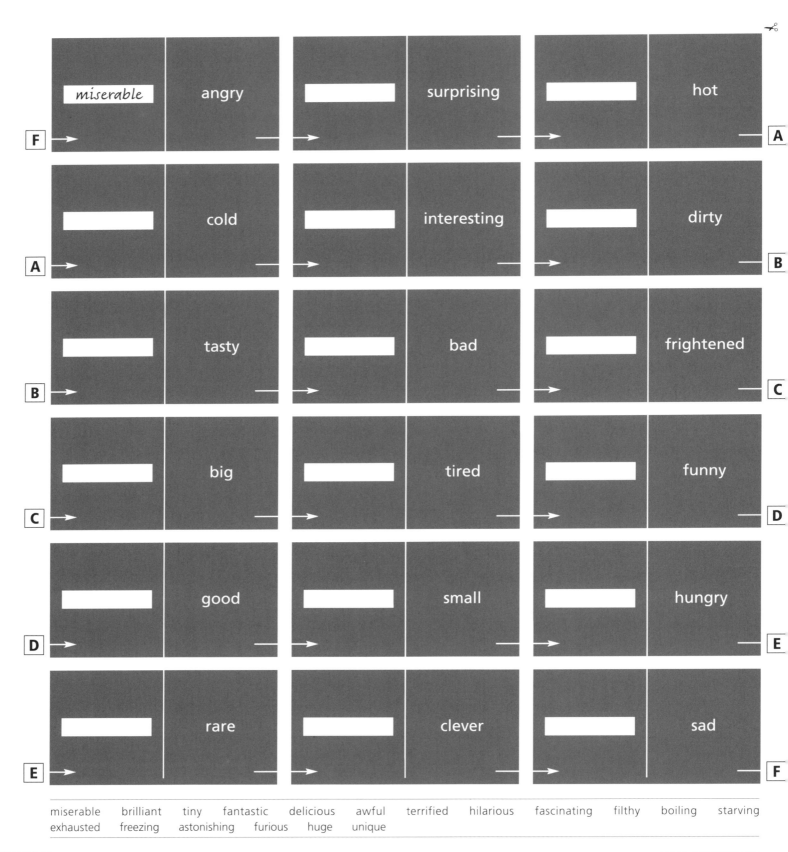

F → | miserable | angry →
→ | | surprising →
→ | | hot → **A**

A → | | cold →
→ | | interesting →
→ | | dirty → **B**

B → | | tasty →
→ | | bad →
→ | | frightened → **C**

C → | | big →
→ | | tired →
→ | | funny → **D**

D → | | good →
→ | | small →
→ | | hungry → **E**

E → | | rare →
→ | | clever →
→ | | sad → **F**

miserable   brilliant   tiny   fantastic   delicious   awful   terrified   hilarious   fascinating   filthy   boiling   starving
exhausted   freezing   astonishing   furious   huge   unique

Landmark Intermediate © Oxford University Press **PHOTOCOPIABLE**

15 What did you say?

What's your father's name?	What's your phone number?	What's your favourite food?	What's your mother's name?
Who do you live with?	How many languages do you speak?	Where do you live?	What sort of car do you drive?
Where did you go on holiday last year?	What was the last film you saw at the cinema?	What did you buy last week?	How much coffee did you drink yesterday?
How long have you been studying English?	Which countries have you visited?	What is the best meal you have ever eaten?	Who is the most interesting person you have ever met?

16 Radio programme

Presenter 1

You are the presenter of a radio programme and today you are going to interview a guest about their past experience of learning English / another language. Write down ten questions you would like to ask your guest.

Guest 1

You are a student of English and you have been invited to appear on a radio programme to talk about your past experiences of learning a language. Practise what you want to say with a partner. The interview will last about five minutes so you might have to think of some extra information.

Presenter 2

You are the presenter of a radio programme and today you are going to interview a guest about their English classes now. Write down ten questions you would like to ask your guest.

Guest 2

You are a student of English and you have been invited to appear on a radio programme to talk about your English class. Practise what you want to say with a partner. The interview will last about five minutes so you might have to think of some extra information.

Presenter 3

You are the presenter of a radio programme and today you are going to interview a guest about the differences between their language and English. Write down ten questions you would like to ask your guest.

Guest 3

You have been invited to a radio programme to speak about the differences between English and your language. Practise what you want to say with your partner. The interview will last about five minutes so you might have to think of some extra information.

17 In the courtroom

A

You have been caught shoplifting.

Think of a story to explain your actions so that the judge will not send you to prison.

Use these questions to help you:

1 What did you steal?
2 Why did you steal it?
3 Have you ever stolen anything before?

B

You have accidentally murdered your boss.

Think of a story to explain your actions so that the judge will not send you to prison.

Use these questions to help you:

1 Why did you murder your boss?
2 How did you murder him?
3 Have you ever done anything violent before?

C

Last night you stole some money from an old lady outside her house.

Think of a story to explain your actions so that the judge will not send you to prison.

Use these questions to help you:

1 Why did you steal the money?
2 How much did you steal?
3 Have you ever robbed anybody before?

D

You have been blackmailing your neighbour for ten years but suddenly they have gone to the police and told them everything.

Think of a story to explain your actions so that the judge will not send you to prison.

Use these questions to help you:

1 Why were you blackmailing your neighbour?
2 How much money did they give you?
3 Have you ever blackmailed anybody else?

E

Last week you set fire to the local school and it burnt to the ground. You are being charged with arson.

Think of a story to explain your actions so that the judge will not send you to prison.

Use these questions to help you:

1 Why did you set fire to the school?
2 How did you do it?
3 Have you ever done anything like this before?

F

Last summer you took part in a bank robbery and the police have just tracked you down.

Think of a story to explain your actions so that the judge will not send you to prison.

Use these questions to help you:

1 Why did you rob the bank?
2 How much money did you take?
3 Is this the first time you have been involved in a bank robbery?

18 Passives noughts and crosses

Ouzo / drink / Greece TRUE	Schnapps / drink / Brazil FALSE – GERMANY
Orujo / drink / Spain TRUE	Haggis / eat / Turkey FALSE – SCOTLAND
Sushi / eat / Japan TRUE	Nan / eat / Thailand FALSE – INDIA
The telephone / invent / Bell TRUE	Penicillin / discover / Marie Curie FALSE – ALEXANDER FLEMING
The aeroplane / invent / the Wright brothers TRUE	Imagine / sing / Paul McCartney FALSE – JOHN LENNON
Carmen / write / Bizet TRUE	The 1812 Overture / write / Beethoven FALSE – TCHAIKOVSKY
Indiana Jones / play / Harrison Ford TRUE	Superman play / Arnold Schwarzenegger FALSE – CHRISTOPHER REEVE
Macbeth / kill / Macduff TRUE	Picasso / play / Marlon Brando FALSE – ANTHONY HOPKINS
Cleopatra / kill / Mark Anthony FALSE – A SNAKE	Cain / kill / Abel FALSE – ABEL WAS KILLED BY CAIN
Saris / wear / India TRUE	Kilts / wear / Australia FALSE – SCOTLAND
Italian / speak / Switzerland TRUE	Spanish / speak / Brazil FALSE – PORTUGUESE

20 Music trivia quiz

Who sang _____?

ANSWER

Who sang _____?

ANSWER

Who composed _____?

ANSWER

Who composed _____?

ANSWER

Name two songs by _____ .

ANSWER

Name two songs by _____ .

ANSWER

Where is / are _____ from?

ANSWER

Where is / are _____ from?

ANSWER

What type of music do / does _____
play?

ANSWER

What type of music do / does _____
play?

ANSWER

What's the name of _____'s most successful
record?

ANSWER

What's the name of _____'s most successful
record?

ANSWER

21 Third conditional dominoes

1 we / not / leave the cinema.	**2** If I hadn't forgotten my umbrella,
2 I / not / get wet.	**3** If you'd paid the phone bill,
3 the phone / not / get cut off.	**4** If I'd run to the bus stop,
4 I / not / miss the bus.	**5** If he'd known about the match,
5 he / turn the television on.	**6** If the post office had been open,
6 we / buy some stamps.	**7** If my boyfriend hadn't gone out with my best friend,
7 I / not / finish with him.	**8** If the plane had crashed,
8 many people / die.	**9** If I'd passed my exams,
9 I / go to University.	**10** If the car hadn't broken down,
10 we / not / be late.	**11** If the restaurant hadn't been so full,
11 we / eat there.	**12** If my brother hadn't fallen off the wall,
12 he / not / break his leg.	**13** If you'd been driving more carefully,
13 you / not / crash.	**14** If I'd remembered to set my alarm clock,
14 I / not / oversleep.	**15** If Sarah hadn't gone out last night,
15 she / get up earlier today.	**16** If the television hadn't been on,
16 we / hear / the telephone.	**17** If the coat had been cheaper,
17 she / buy it.	**18** If it hadn't been so late,
18 they /not/ go home.	**1** If the film hadn't been so boring,

Landmark Intermediate © Oxford University Press PHOTOCOPIABLE